DISPATCHES FROM
THE ABORTION WARS

DISPATCHES FROM THE ABORTION WARS

The Costs of Fanaticism to Doctors,
Patients, and the Rest of Us

CAROLE JOFFE

Beacon Press
Boston

BEACON PRESS
Boston, Massachusetts
www.beacon.org

Beacon Press books
are published under the auspices of
the Unitarian Universalist Association of Congregations.

21 20 19 18   8 7 6 5 4 3 2

This book is printed on acid-free paper that meets the uncoated paper
ANSI/NISO specifications for permanence as revised in 1992.

Library of Congress Cataloging-in-Publication Data
Joffe, Carole E.
Dispatches from the abortion wars : the costs of fanaticism to
doctors, patients, and the rest of us / Carole Joffe.
p. ; cm.
Includes bibliographical references and index.
ISBN 978-0-8070-0128-8 (paperback : alk. paper)
1. Abortion—United States. 2. Pro-life movement—United States.
3. Abortion services—United States. I. Title.
[DNLM: 1. Abortion, Induced—psychology—United States. 2. Health Policy—
United States. 3. Health Services Accessibility—United States. 4. Politics—United
States. 5. Public Opinion—United States. HQ 767.5.U5 J64d 2009]
HQ767.5.U5J64 2009
362.198'8800973—dc22   2009016538

Text design and composition by Wilsted & Taylor Publishing Services

IN LOVING MEMORY OF
FELICIA HANCE STEWART (1943–2006),
ANNE VYGOTSKY JOFFE (1915–2006),
AND GEORGE RICHARD TILLER (1941–2009)

AUTHOR'S NOTE

In this book I use the real names of those whose activities are a matter of public record, who are heads of organizations, and whose written work I cite. However, I have used pseudonyms to protect the confidentiality of many of the abortion providers I cite. A list of those pseudonyms is as follows:

Jeannette James	Abby Trudeau
Justine Gordon	Linda Johnson
Rachel Gould	George Majors
Ruth Childs	Margaret Riley
Rebecca Jacobs	Ethel Bloom
Natalie Diamond	Gary McPherson
Alex Wolff	Sylvia Shore
Christopher Franklin	Iris Foyle
Deborah Fox	Annie Moses
Tim Shawn	Christina Hernandez
Susan Golden	David Bennett
Michelle Lawrence	Julia Miller
Linda Perillo	Renee Bancroft

CONTENTS

PREFACE
xi

I
The Stigma of Abortion
1

II
"You Need a Community with You":
Becoming an Abortion Provider
21

III
The Clinics: Ground Zero in the Abortion Wars
46

IV
Regulating Abortion
62

V
Hospital-Based Abortions:
Chaos, Cruelty, and Some Accommodation
83

VI
Abortion Patients and the "Two Americas"
of Reproductive Health
99

VII

"Every Woman Is Different":
What Good Abortion Care Looks Like

119

VIII

What Kind of America Do We Want?

140

AFTERWORD

"Abortion Is a Perfectly Proper Noun"

160

POSTSCRIPT

The Legacy of George Tiller

162

ACKNOWLEDGMENTS

165

NOTES

168

INDEX

185

PREFACE

Cliché though it may be, there really are abortion wars raging in the United States, wars fought on numerous fronts. The front that most resembles conventional warfare involves attacks on those who provide abortions. Since the 1973 *Roe v. Wade* decision legalizing abortion, eight members of the abortion-providing community have been murdered, and numerous others have been stalked at their homes and churches as well as at their workplaces. Children of some providers are harassed at their schools. Antiabortion fanatics continue to this day to firebomb and vandalize clinics. Staff and patients at these clinics are subjected to constant picketing and often ear-splitting verbal harassment delivered through megaphones. As in other wars, opponents of abortion engage in intelligence-gathering by videotaping those who enter abortion-providing facilities and photographing the license plates in the clinics' parking lots.

But there are many other important fronts in the abortion wars. To an extraordinary degree, abortion dominates our national politics, often serving as the decisive issue in parties' choice of candidates, in the nomination of judges at all levels of the judiciary, in the selection of political appointees to serve in federal agencies. Most strikingly, during the two presidential terms of George W. Bush, an individual's stance on abortion was typically used to determine his or her fitness to serve in positions that had absolutely nothing to do with that issue—for example, a position on a drug advisory panel. The abortion wars have also had an impact on U.S. foreign policy, determining in some instances how much foreign aid a particular country will receive. At recent United Nations conferences, the U.S. delegation's fanatical opposition not only to abortion but to contraception drew scorn from other nations and often left the United States isolated.

State legislatures have also been extremely consequential terrains in the abortion wars, as hundreds of regulations attempting to restrict abortion care in various ways are introduced each year. At the local level, the abortion wars are reflected in how a particular community responds to the presence, or potential presence, of an abortion-providing facility. Whether a landlord will rent or sell a suitable building, whether contractors agree to work on it, whether vendors such as cleaning services will agree to do business with a clinic—all these factors, which typically are not issues in other areas of health care, can determine whether abortion care can survive in a particular place.

The abortion wars have had a dramatic impact on popular culture as well. Several television shows in the 1970s portrayed women choosing abortions in a sympathetic light, which unleashed a flood of complaints to the networks and advertisers by irate opponents of abortion. Ever since, both television and Hollywood have notably avoided a repetition of that mistake.

Finally, American medical culture is an often overlooked but extremely important front in the abortion wars. For various reasons, which I elaborate further in the following chapters, American medicine has supported the concept of legal abortion but has been much more ambivalent about those who actually perform the procedure. This ambivalence has resulted in a chronic shortage of providers. Abortion politics has also led to policies at some hospitals that put women's health at unacceptable risk.

In writing this book about the abortion wars, I am not claiming to provide a balanced account, as do many other social scientists and journalists who address the abortion issue. Rather, I see myself as a war correspondent, embedded with troops on one side of the conflict (the troops in this instance being the abortion-providing community). I also do not aspire to change the minds of those who are convinced that abortion is immoral. My goal instead is to show the costs of these wars. They are costly, obviously, for those seeking abortions and those providing them. But I believe these wars have also proved costly for American society as a whole, causing a degradation of our political culture. The abortion wars have not only brought an unprecedented level of violence and terrorism to health-care institutions; they have also led to a culture of lies about science and medicine at the highest levels of government. I have come to understand the abortion wars as a brilliant distraction that drains energies and resources away from other social needs, including the adequate provision of services that would allow people to have the intimate and family lives they wish for.

In both the subtitle of this book and several times thus far in this preface, I have used the words *fanaticism, fanatics,* and *fanatical.* I do not use such provocative words lightly. People who kill and terrorize those they disagree with on abortion, I believe, merit the designation fanatics, because they view ending abortion as justifying any means. I believe that charges of fanaticism are also fairly applied to those figures in political and religious circles who legitimate such violence (for example, a sitting U.S. senator who has called for the death penalty for abortion providers, or a priest who has called the murder of providers "justifiable homicide"). I see fanaticism at work in the numerous efforts to equate the value of a woman's life with that of an embryo: for example, the official Republican Party platform, which does not permit abortion even in cases of a threat to a woman's life. I similarly view as fanatics those who have taken it upon themselves to redefine many forms of contraception as abortion and who are now seeking to withhold birth control from the vast majority of Americans, who do not share their views.

However, I do *not* believe that most of the individuals who oppose abortion should be considered fanatics. There is no question that most Americans who consider themselves "pro-life" disavow the terrorist acts of the most violent wing of the antiabortion movement. Many of those opposed to abortion, moreover, favor exceptions in cases of threats to the life of the woman and pregnancies that result from rape or incest. Given that at least occasional use of birth control is nearly universal among heterosexually active Americans, we can safely assume that a strong majority of abortion opponents do not embrace the more recent campaign against contraception.

In numerical terms, therefore, those who can reasonably be labeled fanatics make up a very small portion of the universe of abortion opponents. My argument is that the violent actions and extremist political positions of the most fanatical sector of the antiabortion movement, however, have had significant consequences. In a country where systematic political violence is rare (and never before aimed at a particular group of health-care professionals), the attacks on abortion providers have inevitably had a searing impact on Americans' consciousness. For medical institutions, the legacy of this violence (which, after a period of quiescence, reemerged in 2009 with the brutal assassination of Dr. George Tiller) contributes to a reluctance by administrators to incorporate abortion care and a reluctance on the part of some clinicians otherwise drawn to this work to perform abortions. For American society more generally, the violence and endless protesting at clinics have marked abortion as something highly controversial and have therefore added to its stigmatization.

Similarly, the absolutism that would ban all abortions sometimes leads centrist politicians to make costly compromises on how abortion is regulated. Many restrictions that appear reasonable impose cruel barriers for many of the most vulnerable women. Others, such as the requirement that doctors lie to their patients about disproved links between abortion and breast cancer or suicide, may not appear reasonable to the public once people learn of them, but these regulations serve to reinforce the idea that abortion is always embroiled in contentiousness.

In short, the most fanatical elements of the antiabortion movement have established the contours of the abortion wars. These true believers have sought to eliminate from public conversation about abortion what I believe the issue most cries out for: a recognition of nuance. But with the black-and-white view of the world that is characteristic of fanaticism, they have refused to acknowledge the shades of gray that are inevitably present in matters pertaining to sexuality, reproduction, and abortion. Ironically, the wars against abortion waged by fanatics are counterproductive, leading to more unintended pregnancies and therefore more abortions.

What are my credentials as an abortion war correspondent? I am a sociologist with broad interests in reproductive health and reproductive politics. In particular, I have focused on those who make up the workforce in abortion facilities and other reproductive health settings. For the past thirty years or so I have interviewed and observed at clinics where abortions (and usually other reproductive health services) are offered. I have watched young doctors and other clinicians being trained to perform these procedures. I have attended numerous conferences where providers gather to discuss their work lives. Conveniently, the development of a number of Listservs within the abortion-providing community in the past decade has enabled me to transcend the limitations of geography and remain engaged in regular conversation with providers throughout the country.

My observations of the abortion issue over such a long period have allowed me to witness an important transformation in both the strategy and the rhetoric of the antiabortion movement. In the period immediately after *Roe,* women getting abortions were a prime focus of the movement's wrath, demonized as "murderers," "sluts," and, interestingly, "lesbians" (I recall a group of protesters taunting abortion patients outside a Philadelphia clinic in the late 1970s with this accusation). But this antiwoman discourse could not last, for the simple reason that too many women, including some within antiabortion circles, were getting abortions. Women who sought abortions became reframed as victims: "Abortion hurts women" is today one of the leading messages of the antiabortion movement. And providers, those doing the "hurting," became the prime villains in the abortion drama of opponents.

I report on this war from the perspective of these embattled providers of abortion. By *provider,* I mean not only the clinicians who perform abortions but also the clinic directors and managers who have the challenging task of administering the freestanding clinics where most abortions in the United States take place. Very often, as we will see, it is they who suffer from physical attacks, who deal with the police when surrounded by aggressive protesters or when suspicious packages arrive, who deal with lawyers when state legislators pass yet another restriction, who plead with the plumber to come fix the frozen pipes even though the plumber's fellow church members have urged him not to provide service to the "baby-killers." As such, clinic directors and staff members are important combatants in the abortion wars.

This book was started during the presidency of George W. Bush, an unusually harsh and dispiriting time for those who work in the field of reproductive health, including abortion care. It is being completed in the first months of the presidency of Barack Obama. Like virtually all the providers and advocates whom you will meet in this book, I am heartened by the election of Barack Obama and eagerly look forward to his presidency. I am hopeful that with this change of administration, some lessening of the abortion wars may be possible. Specifically, I hope that opponents of abortion will come to agree with supporters that the root problem that must be addressed is that nearly half of all pregnancies in the United States are unintended. When the problem is framed this way, then solutions are at least partly found in improved contraceptive access and in factually accurate and in-depth sex education—options that were decisively repudiated by the Bush administration. But even if this hoped-for progress on reducing unwanted pregnancies occurs, some abortions will always be needed, and our new president clearly understands that.

These promising possibilities of the Obama presidency notwithstanding, I have no illusions that the abortion wars will be "over" simply because of the outcome of the 2008 election. Antiabortion forces received a setback in that election, but the movement, including its most violent wing, is hardly going away, as the murder of Dr. Tiller made tragically clear. Most important, the day-to-day events in abortion clinics—the trenches from which most of my dispatches will be sent—are affected as much by local events as by national ones. In places where antiabortion sentiment remains strong, provision will remain very challenging. The stigma that I believe explains so much about the place of abortion in American culture runs deep, and will change only slowly. Nevertheless, I hope the following pages reveal that in the abortion wars, women who seek abortions and the men and women who provide them are themselves resourceful and committed combatants.

THE STIGMA OF ABORTION

Consider the following incidents that occurred in the United States during the first eight years of the twenty-first century.

These events were directly tied to the presidential administration of George W. Bush:

False information on the links between abortion and breast cancer and the purported ineffectiveness of condoms was posted on government Web sites.

After the United States invaded Iraq, Bush's potential appointees to the Coalition Provisional Authority in Baghdad were asked about their positions on *Roe v. Wade*.

Several high-ranking officials within the U.S. Food and Drug Administration (FDA) resigned in protest when the agency disregarded the views of an overwhelming majority of its expert advisory panel and, bowing to Bush administration pressure, refused to make emergency contraception (EC) available over the counter.

Consider as well these incidents from the relatively new world of "fetal politics":

A measure on Colorado's 2008 ballot sought to define fertilized eggs legally as "persons," which would severely restrict access to abortion, contraception, fertility treatments, and scientific research.

A group calling itself the NAAPC (the National Association for the Advancement of Preborn Children) filed suit in California to stop research on stem cells.

And these events occurred in local communities:

In Fargo, North Dakota, a routine confirmation of the appointment of a police chief was temporarily derailed because it emerged that some fifteen years previously, the then twenty-four-year-old officer and his girlfriend had decided upon a (legal) abortion. After the man apologized to local politicians for his "mistake," his appointment went forward.

In Waco, Texas, opponents of abortion urged a boycott of Girl

Scout cookies because local troops had collaborated in a sex education program with Planned Parenthood—a program that did not mention abortion.

An increasing number of pharmacists in locations across the United States, loosely affiliated with a group called Pharmacists for Life, refused to fill prescriptions for both emergency contraception and monthly birth control pills, claiming that these drugs caused abortions.

And consider these legal developments:

In the 2007 Supreme Court case *Gonzales v. Carhart,* a majority of the Court upheld a ban on a method of second-trimester abortion that medical experts felt was the safest in certain situations. In that decision, the Court, for the first time, also held that it was constitutional for an abortion law to have no exception for the health of the pregnant woman. (Notably, an almost identical measure was overturned by the Court two years earlier, but this time the Court had two new Bush appointees, both of whom voted with the majority.)

A South Dakota law that mandates that physicians must inform abortion patients that they are "terminating the life of a whole, separate, unique, living human being" was upheld in several levels of judicial review.

Consider now examples from popular culture:

Three popular movies from 2007, *Knocked Up, Waitress,* and *Juno,* feature young women who experience unplanned pregnancies. In the first two films, abortion is barely mentioned; in the third, the heroine considers the option, then rejects it after a visit to a clinic that was portrayed in lurid, unrealistic terms. These films continue Hollywood's (and television's) traditional aversion to dealing with abortion in a thoughtful manner, because of fears of controversy.

Next consider two recent real-world examples of teenagers whose unintended pregnancies received widespread public attention:

Jamie Lynn Spears, the sister of the pop icon Britney Spears and a television star in her own right, became pregnant at the age of sixteen. Bristol Palin, daughter of Sarah Palin, the Republican vice presidential candidate in fall 2008, became pregnant at seventeen. Both young women were unmarried. Both decided to continue the pregnancy. While premarital sexual activity and out-of-wedlock pregnancy once would have been roundly criticized, especially by conservatives, in both of these cases the young women were commended by leading conservative figures for "doing the responsible thing" by rejecting the option of abortion.

Finally, consider these incidents from the world of medicine:

A young doctor, still in her residency, is afraid to tell her supervisors that she has received off-site training in abortion.

A woman receiving an abortion nervously asks the doctor if her "real doctor" will be able to tell she has had the procedure.

An ob-gyn who performs abortions, among many other medical procedures, is denied membership in a country club. A club member confides to the physician that the denial is because of his abortion activity.

An appreciable number of abortion patients whose insurance covers this procedure prefer to pay out of pocket, for fear there will be a paper trail of the abortion.

These are just some examples taken from the literally hundreds of such incidents I have recorded in my files. These incidents show us, first, how diverse the fronts in the abortion wars are: conflicts over abortion occur in politics, in the legal world, in popular culture, in medical offices and pharmacies, in daily life. Second, many of these examples show the powerful stigma that now attaches to abortion. The late sociologist Erving Goffman, the author of a book titled *Stigma*, has most influenced my understanding of this phenomenon. Goffman defines stigma as "an attribute that is deeply discrediting." Similarly, he describes the stigmatized individual as one who is "disqualified from full social acceptance." In a famous phrase, included in the subtitle of his book, Goffman also refers to the "spoiled identity" of the stigmatized individual.

Goffman's ideas can be readily applied to much of what I have mentioned above. For example, if either Jamie Lynn Spears or Bristol Palin had opted for an abortion, and if that abortion had become known to the public, it would have "discredited" Spears as an acceptable teen entertainer and Palin's mother as an acceptable Republican vice presidential candidate. Of course, celebrities aren't the only ones at risk of being stigmatized because of an abortion; patients who worry that doctors or insurance companies will find out their secret make that very clear. As for those who provide abortions, Goffman's description of stigmatized individuals as those "disqualified from full social acceptance" aptly describes the predicament of some of the health professionals you will meet in this book.

Another illustration of the stigmatizing power of abortion is its capacity to spread into other areas and, in Goffman's term, to "spoil the identity" of those connected with these issues. In the case of the Girl Scout cookie boycott, the criticism of the Scouts' collaboration with Planned Parenthood is a classic example of guilt by association. Though only 3 percent of Planned Parenthood's services involve abortion services (the rest involve other reproductive health services, such as contraception, the diagnosis and treatment of sexually transmitted infections, cancer screenings, and prenatal care), the organization has become demonized in antiabortion circles because of its connection with abortion. The furor over EC reflects an alarming development that I will comment on repeatedly throughout this book: the efforts of elements of the antiabortion movement to redefine contraception itself as abortion. (EC in fact is a higher-than-normal dosage of an ordinary oral contraceptive; if taken within seventy-two hours of unprotected intercourse, it is highly effective in preventing pregnancy.)

Why such controversy over abortion?

Why these wars? Why has abortion emerged as one of the most divisive issues in American society, dominating our politics and culture to such an unprecedented degree? Interestingly, polls on abortion have remained quite stable since *Roe v. Wade* was decided in 1973, and consistently show that a majority of Americans want abortion to remain legal, even while many express ambivalence about the issue. According to Gallup Poll data from 2008, 53 percent of Americans consider themselves "pro-choice" and 42 percent consider themselves "pro-life." Less than 20 percent of the population wants abortion banned in all circumstances.

But opponents of abortion, though numerically in the minority, have in the years since *Roe* gained the upper hand rhetorically. While antiabortion forces have not succeeded in outlawing abortion altogether, they have succeeded in intimidating its supporters, making the public defense of abortion a very challenging task. Think of the messages we hear constantly from the antiabortion movement: "Abortion stops a beating heart," or, more recently, "Abortion hurts women." Whether one agrees with them or not, these are powerful, clear, and easily understandable. In contrast, there is no consensus in the abortion rights movement as to how we speak about abortion. For some, abortion is described as "sad but necessary." An older, more radical tradition within the movement has used the slogan "On demand, without apology." "Safe, legal, and rare" gained currency during the Clinton administration and is still favored by many, though others feel it devalues both those who receive and those who perform abortions. Perhaps the most telling linguistic dodge is that the word itself has been erased by many politicians who support abortion, as in the euphemistic phrase "I support a woman's right to choose." At the same time, use of the word *choice* is criticized by many within the reproductive rights movement, because it suggests that abortion is a consumer item that can be freely chosen by all women, when this is hardly the case.

Most concretely, opponents have succeeded in making it very difficult for some women, especially the most vulnerable—that is, the young, the poor, women of color, the rural—to obtain an abortion. This has been accomplished in part through political pressure that has kept Medicaid (the federal health-care program for the poor) from paying for abortions in most circumstances. But even if they could scrape together the funds to pay for an abortion, many women, especially those without the resources to travel to another state, simply can't find a way to obtain one. The hostile climate facing abortion providers has created a chronic shortage of abortion facilities, especially in nonmetropolitan areas.

Finally, abortion opponents have succeeded in making many abortion recipients, whatever their own feelings about the morality of abortion, ashamed of having one and fearful that others will find out. Not surprisingly, Erving Goffman speaks of the shame that frequently accompanies stigma, especially in situations when the stigmatized individual realizes that she could have chosen another course, as is the case for those having elective (that is, non–medically necessary) abortions.

There is no simple answer to explain why this medical procedure has such an embattled status, especially when, according to the most recent data, one out of three American women will have an abortion by the end of her reproductive years. Obviously, abortion is more than just a medical procedure. I am well aware, and respect, that many Americans fervently oppose abortion on religious or moral grounds. Abortion is officially opposed by the Catholic Church (to which one fourth of Americans belong) and by various other religious denominations as well (though it should be pointed out that Catholic women have abortions at about the same rates as others). The question that has long intrigued me is not why some are opposed to abortion but rather how this issue has come to occupy such a polarizing place in American society. Nowhere in the European democracies, to which the United States is so often compared, is abortion such a central component of domestic politics. Significantly, in Europe, where abortion is far less contested and more easily available, the rates of both unintended pregnancies and abortions are considerably lower.

So what is it about American culture that makes abortion so controversial, so subject to stigma? I think many Americans' discomfort with abortion cannot be separated from the larger discomfort with sexuality that is such a striking feature of American society. I am hardly alone in noting the unhealthy combination of sexual puritanism and sexual saturation that characterizes present-day America. For example, a long history of controversy over the content of sex education programs culminated in the George W. Bush years in restricting federal funding to programs promoting abstinence only until marriage, despite research showing that premarital sex is now nearly universal among Americans. These programs are expressly forbidden to mention anything about birth-control methods (except, as critics have pointed out, misinformation about contraceptives' effectiveness). Though evaluations have repeatedly shown that they don't work in preventing sexual activity among teenagers, abstinence-only programs have received huge infusions of funding. After an evaluation commissioned by Congress confirmed previous findings, Congressman Henry Waxman, for years a leading critic of these programs, said in disgust, "American taxpayers appear to have paid over one billion dollars for programs that have no impact."

At the same time, this is a society in which thongs and other sexually provocative clothing are marketed for seven- to ten-year-olds, five-year-olds have makeover parties, and sexually explicit, often violent media depictions are everywhere, especially on the Internet.

The American Psychological Association recently released a report detailing its concerns about the "oversexualization" of young girls in the contemporary United States. Professionals at the National Sexuality Resource Center in San Francisco convincingly argue that America is a society sorely lacking in "sexual literacy," which the center's director, Gilbert Herdt, defines as "the knowledge and skills needed to promote and protect sexual wellness—having healthy intimate relationships, being able to prevent disease, understanding sexuality beyond just the act." Yet the groundbreaking *Our Bodies, Ourselves*, which has won international acclaim for its ability to educate people about health and sexuality issues in accessible terms, routinely shows up on librarians' lists of the books that conservatives in the United States most wish to ban. The bans, one of the book's editors told me, are mainly a response to the straightforward discussions of such topics as masturbation and same-sex relationships, not to mention abortion.

The relevance of all this for abortion is that in a society deeply conflicted about sexuality, particularly female sexuality, there is some inevitable antagonism toward abortion recipients. I still remember my shock, hearing an antiabortion Pennsylvania politician in the early 1970s, in the period shortly after *Roe*, sneeringly comment about women who sought abortions, "If you play, you pay." In my view, one of the most perceptive (and still highly relevant) observations on the rise of the antiabortion movement and its direct connection to sexuality was made by the late journalist Ellen Willis. In 1973, as a new antiabortion movement quickly emerged in response to the *Roe v. Wade* decision, she wrote:

A lot of people who intellectually abhor everything the anti-abortionists stand for are emotionally intimidated by their argument. The right-to-lifers' most dangerous weapon . . . is their ability to confuse and immobilize potential opponents by tapping the vast store of sexual guilt and anxiety that lies just below this society's veneer of sexual liberalism. Patriarchal culture, with its deeply anti-sexual ideology, has existed for some five thousand years; the radical idea that people have the right to sexual freedom and happiness has been a significant force for little more than a century.

Another factor that has complicated social attitudes toward abortion is fairly recent developments in the field of obstetrics, specifically the spread of ultrasonography and fetal medicine. Ultrasounds began to be introduced into contemporary obstetrics as a routine part of prenatal care in the late 1980s (some fifteen years after *Roe*). They have now spread beyond medical settings: pregnant women can get them at a shopping mall, bypassing a physician's office altogether. Widespread use of ultrasounds has therefore changed many people's relationship to the fetus; it is now very common for expectant parents to proudly display ultrasound printouts as "baby's first pictures." As we will see later, mandated ultrasounds for abortion patients have become a new weapon in the antiabortion arsenal.

Similarly, dramatic advances in fetal medicine have also altered the cultural perception of the fetus. What not so long ago might have been regarded as the stuff of science fiction—removing a fetus from a woman's uterus, performing corrective surgery, and then replacing it in the uterus—is now possible, though fetal surgery still has very uncertain outcomes and carries some risk for women. The fetus, in short, has become a patient in its own right. The sociologist Monica Caspar, in her book *The Making of the Unborn Patient*, notes that this new branch of medicine inevitably influences abortion politics, with women who select fetal surgery being seen by some health professionals and others as more "heroic" and "life-affirming" than women carrying compromised fetuses who choose to abort. Advances in neonatology have also helped to sustain the lives of premature infants who once would not have survived. Some percentage of these premature babies are able to survive at around the same stage of gestation that a small number of later abortions take place.

Most pregnant women and their partners, fortunately, do not have to make use of these new advances in fetal medicine. But the very existence of these medical breakthroughs has heightened cultural awareness of the fetus and has complicated people's feelings about abortion in a way that was not true when *Roe* was decided.

The things I have mentioned here—objections to abortion on moral and religious grounds, ambivalence about sexual activity unconnected with procreation, heightened cultural awareness of the fetus because of ultrasounds and fetal medicine—all help explain why a sizable number of Americans either oppose abortion outright or approve of it only under quite limited conditions. But these reasons do not in themselves explain *how* abortion has come to occupy such a pivotal place in American culture. The bumper sticker one often sees on abortion supporters' cars—"If you don't like abortion, don't have one"—hasn't worked at all. Many of those opposed to abortion don't want anyone to have one, and they have mobilized into a powerful political force.

ABORTION AND THE RELIGIOUS RIGHT

To fully understand the "career" of abortion—how it came to be the most divisive issue in American domestic politics—we need to examine the starring role it has played in the rise of one of the most important social movements in recent time, the religious right. Social conservatives affiliated with the religious right (initially known as the New Right and sometimes still referred to as the Christian Right) are one of the three major pillars of modern conservatism, and indeed of the Republican Party, along with economic conservatives, who favor an economy as free as possible from government regulation, and the so-called neocons, who favor an aggressive U.S. foreign policy. In light of the economic meltdown that occurred in fall 2008 and the Iraq war debacle, the religious right is arguably the most unified and influential component of the conservative movement at present, the loss of the 2008 presidential election notwithstanding. When pundits speak of the base of the party, they are typically referring to the social conservatives who make up the religious right.

The religious right was set in motion in the 1970s, primarily as a reaction to the social movements of the 1960s, especially the women's and gay rights movements of that era. I remember well, as a young sociology student at that time, noting that the significant changes these movements called for—in sexual values and behaviors, relationships between the genders, and social policies—were exhilarating to some, deeply offensive to others, and confusing to still others. Right-wing strategists shrewdly realized how provocative the demands of feminism and gay activists were to many previously apolitical Americans, especially housewives who felt devalued by the high-profile demands of the feminist movement for women to enter the paid labor force on equal terms with men. These strategists organized a countermovement, a multipronged defense of the "traditional" family.

Interestingly, the first campaign of the New Right was not specifically about abortion, or even sexuality, but about child-care programs. As it happens, I was then writing a doctoral dissertation about child-care programs in California and following the issue closely. I was very excited when, in 1971, Congress passed the first federally funded child-care bill, authorizing some $2 billion for new centers. (Previously there had been only temporary funding for this purpose, passed during the Depression and World War II.) This bill was widely seen as one of the first legislative victories of the newly energized feminist movement. Like many others who supported working mothers, I was surprised and disappointed when President Richard Nixon vetoed this bill, denouncing it for its "family-weakening" implications. His veto came about mainly in response to an overwhelming outpouring of letters from alarmed housewives, organized through their churches, who had been stirred to action by New Right operatives with dire warnings that the government was going to take over the care of their children. "The opening shot in the battle over the family" is how a New Right spokeswoman described this successful campaign to defeat child care.

Though clearly this mobilization against the child-care bill had tapped into a potent and until then unrecognized political force, child care was not an ideal target for the new movement. Too many otherwise sympathetic women were entering the labor force and in need of child care themselves. In contrast, the *Roe v. Wade* decision in 1973 provided the New Right with exactly what it needed. Opposition to legal abortion served as a "battering ram," as the political scientist Rosalind Petchesky aptly put it in her classic book on the subject, *Abortion and Woman's Choice*, galvanizing hundreds of thousands (ultimately millions) of people, many of whom were also sympathetic to the other issues the New Right would soon be organizing around: sex education, teenage pregnancy, out-of-wedlock births, homosexuality, and opposition to social welfare and other social programs.

This is not to suggest that all those opposing abortion bought into the whole New Right package. The Catholic Church, though one of the most vigorous and financially important participants in the campaign against legal abortion from the time of *Roe* to the present, has periodically broken with other actors in the antiabortion coalition because of the Church's long-standing support for programs serving the poor and, more recently, its staunch defense of undocumented immigrants. Nor, of course, do I believe that every individual who is opposed to abortion is necessarily "conservative," identifies with the religious right, or is a Republican. My point rather is that social conservatism, an extremely influential force in American politics, was able to come to power largely because of its skillful use of the abortion issue.

This new movement continued to gain steam throughout the 1970s. Some of the first mass membership organizations affiliated with the New Right—Phyllis Schlafly's Eagle Forum, and the Moral Majority, founded by Jerry Falwell—became increasingly visible on the national scene. These organizations, similar to those that followed a bit later, such as Focus on the Family and the Family Research Council, had a broad agenda, but opposition to abortion was always a central issue. Meanwhile, a number of organizations that were specifically devoted to overturning legal abortion sprang up immediately after the *Roe* decision, the National Right to Life Committee being the most significant. In 1976, only three years after *Roe,* the power of antiabortion forces to affect policy at the congressional level became evident with the passage of the Hyde Amendment, which forbids the use of public funds for abortions except in very limited circumstances.

The turning point in the fortunes of the broader religious right—the movement's "coming-out party," as one writer put it—was the election of Ronald Reagan in 1980. Social conservatives worked tirelessly on behalf of Reagan, and after his victory their status as a key constituency of the Republican Party became assured. The payback to the religious right took place with both crucial appointments and favored policies. The Reagan years marked the beginning of abortion "litmus tests" for appointments to the Supreme Court and elsewhere in the judiciary. Nominees' records on abortion also played a key role in filling posts throughout the federal bureaucracy, often previously obscure positions.

One of the most interesting cases of such payback positions that I have followed since the Reagan era—often with fascinated horror—

has been that of the DASPA, deputy assistant secretary for population affairs in the Department of Health and Human Services. The DASPA, despite the obscurity of the position, actually plays a very important role, as she or he is in charge of all federal family planning programs. One of the DASPA's major tasks is to oversee the Title X program, which disperses funds to help low-income women and teenagers obtain contraceptive services as well as breast and pelvic exams, pregnancy diagnosis and counseling, and screenings for sexually transmitted infections. Historically this position was held by a career professional in the federal bureaucracy with a background in women's health. The first person in charge of Title X, for example, was Dr. Louis Hellman, a pioneer in the struggle to make birth control available to poor women.

The criteria for the position changed with the election of Ronald Reagan. His choice for the DASPA was a former home economics teacher with no bureaucratic experience but, as one writer put it, "a superb pro-life résumé." (She had been one of the founders of the National Right to Life Committee.) But it was the DASPA appointee of Reagan's successor, George H. W. Bush, that really drove home how utterly subversive such appointments could be. Bush's selection for this position was William Reynolds "Reyn" Archer III, the son of an influential Texas congressman. He was an obstetrician-gynecologist who publicly and proudly proclaimed himself sexually abstinent at the age of thirty-seven. The man selected to run the nation's family planning program was quoted in the press as saying, "When it became possible for women to buy contraceptives on their own, men lost their manhood." He is also remembered for telling a congressional hearing that he believed women who visited federally funded family planning clinics should not be told of the availability of nearby abortion services, even if their lives were at stake.

In contrast, the DASPA who followed Archer in President Bill Clinton's administration was the late Felicia Stewart, my former colleague, to whom this book is dedicated. Stewart was a highly respected physician whose specialty was reproductive health. Her major achievement in that office was to convince the Food and Drug Administration (FDA) to rule on the safety of EC. This in turn led to the approval of a dedicated product for EC, now known as Plan B. In short, Dr. Stewart did what one would expect someone in this position to do: she determined the safety and efficacy of a contraceptive option and worked to make it more available to the public.

George W. Bush's selection as DASPA was Eric Keroack, a Boston-area doctor who served as the medical director of A Woman's Concern, a fleet of "crisis pregnancy centers" (CPCs) in the Boston area. CPCs, which received millions of dollars in public funding under Bush, are notorious for their misleading advertising to women seeking abortions; once in the center, women are harangued about the evils of abortion and are given blatantly false information about the medical risks of the procedure. (A study by Congress found that 87 percent of CPCs receiving federal funds gave such faulty information—for example, that abortion leads to breast cancer, infertility, and mental illness.) The Web site of Keroack's organization claimed that "crass commercialization and distribution of birth control is demeaning to women, degrading of human sexuality, and adverse to human health and happiness." This, to me, is Orwellian! The individual in charge of helping poorer Americans obtain birth control thinks that the major service his office provides is "demeaning and degrading"? (Shortly after Keroack took office, he abruptly resigned because of allegations of Medicaid abuse stemming from his private practice in Massachusetts and other irregularities in his record.)

Archer and Keroack, with their impeccable antiabortion and anti-birth-control credentials, were selected, as I have said, to please the religious right supporters of the two presidents Bush. Yet to point to an irony that will be revisited throughout this book, while Dr. Stewart was a firm supporter of abortion rights, her work as the DASPA actually led to fewer abortions. Shortly after EC became available as a dedicated product, the Guttmacher Institute, a private organization that studies reproductive health, estimated that this medication averted some 50,000 abortions per year.

Along with appointments, much of the payback to the religious right by Republican presidents since 1980 has been through pushing policies favored by this group. Most of these have had a domestic focus, but opposition to abortion (and contraception) has also been a staple of U.S. foreign policy since the Reagan years. One particularly controversial measure has been the "global gag rule," a policy that the Reagan administration announced at a 1984 United Nations conference on population. The policy stipulates that no U.S. foreign aid will fund family planning services in countries or agencies that use their *own* monies for abortion services or even counseling about abortion. In what has seemed to me like a game of ideological Ping-Pong, Bill Clinton reversed this policy in his first days in office, only to see it quickly reinstated by George W. Bush. Barack Obama, as widely expected, overturned the gag rule early in his presidency. I suspect that when the next Republican president is inaugurated, she or he will reinstate the rule. Advocacy groups such as the International Women's Health Coalition have told numerous heartbreaking stories of the hardships this gag rule has imposed on the world's most impoverished women in developing countries. The loss of this funding has not only led to higher rates of unwanted pregnancy—leading in turn to higher rates of unsafe abortion—but also has left such women vulnerable to HIV and other sexually transmitted infections. Similarly, George W. Bush's otherwise laudable infusion of significant funding for international AIDS work, PEPFAR (the President's Emergency Plan for AIDS Relief), has been marred by the insistence that fully one-third of these funds be devoted to abstinence counseling.

The importance of these national and international policies notwithstanding, the power of the religious right and the centrality of abortion on its agenda are, if anything, even more evident on the state level. Since *Roe v. Wade,* literally hundreds of laws regulating abortion have been passed by state legislatures, typically spearheaded by politicians with ties to the religious right. These regulations (which are explored in more depth in chapter 4) range from waiting periods for an abortion, parental notification and consent laws, and mandated state scripts which must be read to abortion patients, to cumbersome and often expensive requirements involving physical renovations that are imposed on medical facilities offering abortion care.

In states where the religious right is strong, not just laws about abortion but measures that speak to the whole range of issues on the movement's agenda are frequently introduced. For example, some states have passed laws that transfer family-planning funds to CPCs, which do not provide contraceptive services. Some have passed laws that protect pharmacists who do not wish to fill prescriptions for contraceptives. To be sure, some laws and policies promoted by social conservatives are so out of the mainstream that even in the reddest of states, they either are not passed or do not survive judicial scrutiny. For example, some lawmakers affiliated with the religious right in South Dakota proposed legislation that would have led to a year of jail time and a $500 fine for teachers or school counselors who referred students to facilities that provided abortions or family planning services, but the bill was ultimately withdrawn.

In Kansas, the former attorney general, Phill Kline, pushed for a reinterpretation of the state's child abuse laws that would have required teachers, health-care providers, or school counselors who were aware of any sexual contact between teens under sixteen (including kissing) to report such activity to state authorities. Kline's reinterpretation, mockingly dubbed by opponents the "kiss and tell law," was ultimately struck down by a judge. Among the strongest opponents of this policy were health professionals, who testified that such a policy would prevent teenagers from seeking treatment for sexually transmitted diseases. But policies like the "kiss and tell" measure, even when not directly tied to abortion, have a way of circling back to that core issue. It was widely believed that Kline, an ardent opponent of abortion, was pushing this policy as a way to entrap abortion providers in his state, who by this measure's definition were dealing with "abuse victims" when performing abortions on teenagers. By this logic, the failure of providers to report any abortion performed on a teenager under sixteen would have constituted breaking the law.

I believe that extreme measures such as these, and the Colorado "fetal personhood" initiative cited at the beginning of this chapter, have contradictory effects on the public, even when they are defeated (as the Colorado measure soundly was). On the one hand, these initiatives reveal the very radical nature of the religious right's agenda, which goes well beyond opposition to abortion; such an exposé, from my perspective, is a positive development. On the other hand, I believe these kinds of endless ballot measures (in spite of its defeat, organizers of the personhood initiative immediately announced plans to expand to even more state ballots in the future) reinforce the idea that abortion is a contentious and stigmatizing issue.

Finally, the religious right has been widely commended by observers across the political spectrum for its political skills at the local level. The movement has always been committed to building power from the ground up, and has, in the journalist Michelle Goldberg's words, "turned conservative churches into little political machines." Elections for school board and city council positions have been particular targets of the movement, serving the dual functions of grooming leaders for future careers on a larger political stage and affecting local policies. Here too abortion has played an important role. The most prominent recent example of the movement from the local to the national stage of a religious right figure is Sarah Palin, the Republican vice presidential candidate in 2008. Palin began her political career, as she proudly announced at the GOP convention, in her local PTA, and then ran for city council and later for mayor of Wasilla, a town of 7500 in Alaska. Her mayoral race in 1996 was noteworthy because until then mayoral races in that town had focused on nonpartisan issues such as taxes and policing. Palin's candidacy, in contrast, raised "hot button" issues favored by social conservatives, such as abortion and gun rights. Also unusual for Wasilla, she received visible support from Christian groups outside the town.

At every step of her political ascent, Palin made clear her strong opposition to abortion, including in cases of rape and incest. She joined with others in her community in a campaign that successfully pressured a local hospital to stop providing abortion services. When asked on national television whether she thought that those who bombed abortion clinics were "domestic terrorists," she declined to answer.

But whether or not local politicians affiliated with the religious right go on to higher office, their active involvement at the grassroots level has been very effective in "changing the culture," to use a phrase favored by the antiabortion movement. Consider again two of the incidents mentioned at the beginning of this chapter: the police chief in North Dakota who had to apologize for the legal abortion his girlfriend had had many years before, and the call for the boycott of Girl Scout cookies because of the Scouts' collaboration with Planned Parenthood. These events, like the contentious ballot measures I have cited, make it abundantly clear that just about anything to do with abortion will bring controversy and will make some people very angry and judgmental. Therefore, even those who support abortion are reluctant to defend it openly. Some have referred to this difficulty in defending abortion as the "ick factor." Given the repeated finding of pollsters that most Americans prefer abortion to remain legal, it is a fear of controversy, more than actual moral opposition, I am convinced, that mainly accounts for the stigmatized situation of abortion today.

THE STIGMA OF ABORTION IN MEDICAL CULTURE

Physicians in the United States support legal abortion at higher rates than the general population. This is hardly surprising: doctors, more than others, know what can happen if desperate women take matters into their own hands to try to end a pregnancy. But what I have come to see, over and over, is that in a peculiarly medical version of "not in my backyard," American physicians often don't support abortion provision in their own medical institutions.

Why is this? To some degree, political mobilization by antiabortion activists has reached into medicine as well. There is a pro-life caucus within the American College of Obstetricians and Gynecologists (ACOG), and there are groups strongly opposed to abortion within other relevant medical specialties, such as the American Academy of Family Physicians. The Christian Medical and Dental Society is a group which, in its own words, "aim[s] to stand up to the evil aspects of modern culture," and abortion is one of its key concerns. During George W. Bush's two presidential terms, his administration was especially adept at finding physicians affiliated with the religious right who were willing to give scientific legitimacy to some of the administration's more extreme positions on abortion and contraceptive issues, including the alleged ineffectiveness of condoms.

But the current ambivalent relationship between medicine and abortion predates the rise of the religious right. To understand this seemingly strange phenomenon—support of abortion but not of abortion provision—we have to go back to the pre-*Roe* era. During the so-called century of criminalization, from the 1870s, when all states had criminalized abortion, to the 1970s, when some states first legalized the procedure, illegal abortions were very common. Many of these procedures were done by women attempting to self-abort, and some were provided by those whom, in an earlier book, I have called "doctors of conscience," that is, physicians already well established in medical practice who risked imprisonment and loss of their medical license because of their compassion for women with unwanted pregnancies. But some portion of illegal abortions was done by "back-alley butchers," a term often used synonymously with "criminal abortionist." These terms referred to both lay and medical practitioners, who were notorious for their greed, lack of ethics, and often medical ineptitude. Women were frequently injured, sometimes killed, by these people.

The image of the back-alley butcher continues to linger to this day, serving different functions for different groups. For the anti-abortion movement, the butcher becomes a stand-in for all abortion providers, present as well as past. For supporters of abortion, the butcher is a symbol of what could happen again in this country if *Roe* were overturned. For some, though certainly not all, sectors of the medical community, the horrible tales passed down about butchers reinforce the notion that abortion was something undertaken by doctors who could not make it elsewhere in medicine and who represented the worst examples of unethical practitioners.

More recently, acts of violence against and harassment of abortion providers have contributed to medicine's uncomfortable relationship with abortion. Starting with a few scattered incidents shortly after *Roe,* antiabortion violence dramatically escalated in the late 1980s, culminating in the 1990s with the murders of a number of abortion providers and their associates. After the 1998 killing of Dr. Barnett Slepian, a Buffalo, New York, physician, the worst of such antiabortion violence diminished for a period, only to reemerge in May 2009 with the murder of Dr. George Tiller of Wichita, Kansas. Yet even in the eleven-year period between these murders, enough unacceptable events of a violent nature, such as the firebombings of clinics, occurred to remind medical professionals that this branch of medicine has been targeted like no other.

Moreover, I have seen repeatedly that connection of the abortion issue with antiabortion activism has become a barrier to abortion provision for many within the medical community, even when fears of violence do not appear to be a factor. Though things are changing, American medicine has historically been quite a conservative profession, reluctant to engage in controversial issues. Picketing, which remains common at many facilities that provide abortions, is therefore of great concern. As we will see in the next chapter, the gatekeepers to abortion services—administrators in hospitals, senior partners in group medical practices—are very much afraid of protesters and the resulting hassles and unwanted attention such activity might bring in the way of police, television cameras, and so on.

A legacy of "back-alley butchers" that still reverberates in the medical imagination, a history of severe violence (which has not entirely disappeared), the vociferous objections of a minority of physicians, and an aversion to the controversy that the introduction of abortion services would probably provoke—all these combine to make mainstream medicine very reluctant to engage with abortion, in spite of the profession's abstract support. The result of all this, as I will document, is a chronic shortage of abortion-providing facilities and a less than welcoming climate for those doctors and other clinicians who do commit to providing abortions.

THE COSTS OF THE ABORTION WARS

The areas of American life that I have touched on briefly in this chapter—politics, law, popular culture, religion, and medicine—are some of the fronts in the abortion wars that have raged for nearly forty years in the United States. This is not a complete listing. Indeed, I am hard-pressed to think of any basic American institution that has not been touched by the abortion conflict. The cumulative effect of these various battles is to reinforce for Americans, no matter what their personal feelings about the issue are, how stigmatized an issue abortion is. To be publicly supportive of, or even connected to, this issue can be, to quote Erving Goffman again, "deeply discrediting." But though the battles might be waged almost anywhere, ground zero in these wars is wherever actual abortion provision takes place. While in other fronts—for example, in politics—the abortion conflict can be thought of as a war of ideas, in the clinics the war becomes more literal. Yet it is also in the clinics and private offices of providers that some of the most heroic acts of resistance take place.

But before moving on to the stories of these brave providers and their patients, let us consider the costs of this seemingly endless conflict. Those bearing the greatest cost are the women who face an unintended pregnancy and wish to have an abortion. For too many women in this situation, finding an abortion provider and being able to afford the procedure are insurmountably difficult. Because of the obstacles that have been put in their way, a portion of these patients end up not having the abortion at all or having the procedure later in pregnancy than they otherwise would have, which makes the procedure more costly and relatively more dangerous. A smaller number of women, predominantly those with intended pregnancies who become very ill and need a hospital-based abortion, face considerable difficulties in getting the care they need in a timely and dignified manner. Though I have studied this issue for thirty years, I have been astonished to discover the cruelty these women have recently been subjected to by rigid hospital policies that would deny them essential health care.

The costs to abortion providers are quite obvious. Many of them work in conditions with unacceptable levels of harassment and with the potential for serious violence. Even when they do not face such threats, many of these dedicated health professionals have unfairly paid the price of marginalization by colleagues elsewhere in medicine.

Finally, I believe that there have been serious costs to American society as a whole. The climate of intolerance, if not fanaticism, that too often emanates from antiabortion circles has been insufficiently challenged by our leaders, and this silence has helped create conditions for violence. Americans will doubtless always disagree about abortion, but these disagreements can and should take place in a civil manner. The integrity of our scientific and medical institutions has been compromised by the repeated willingness of government officials to let politics trump science: research has been hampered, and the American people have been lied to on important matters relating to reproductive health.

To be sure, the results of the 2008 elections suggest that a growing number of citizens might be ready to recognize the costs that this fanaticism has imposed on society. But if we are to move beyond the abortion wars, we have to face the often ugly reality of what has occurred on the wars' multiple fronts.

II

"YOU NEED A COMMUNITY WITH YOU"

Becoming an Abortion Provider

In reporting from the war zones of contemporary abortion provision, I am not only interested in the question of why young doctors would choose to go into this most embattled part of American medicine. I am equally intrigued by how this field can produce new providers, given the turmoil that erupts within many medical institutions whenever the abortion issue is raised. Training new providers and launching them successfully into practice is of crucial interest for both sides in the abortion wars. As both well know, even if abortion remains legal, it is a hollow victory for the abortion rights side if there are not enough doctors to perform the procedure. The shortage of providers has been an issue ever since *Roe v. Wade* and has only worsened in recent years. Many of the first generation of doctors who performed legal abortions as a result of *Roe* have reached retirement age or shortly will.

A few medical groups want abortion essentially banished from American health care, except in the rarest circumstances. Examples include the Christian Medical and Dental Association and the pro-life caucus of the American College of Obstetricians and Gynecologists. But these groups do not reflect the views of most in medicine today. Those who are most relevant to producing new abortion providers—medical faculty in residency programs, hospital administrators, department heads—are not usually against abortion. However, they are strongly averse to controversy, and they know that controversy is exactly what occurs when medical institutions attempt to deal with this issue.

I want to illuminate some of the barriers to abortion care in this country by exploring how the stigma surrounding abortion is manifest in medical residencies, workplaces, and the communities in which new abortion providers live. But I will also share some of the creative responses of those committed to providing this service as they seek to normalize this exceptional aspect of reproductive health care.

As I reflect on what I've learned about doctors struggling to become abortion providers or trying to help others do so, I keep thinking of a remark by Dr. Suzanne Poppema, who performed abortions for many years on the West Coast. Poppema, recently the chair of an organization called Physicians for Reproductive Choice in Health (PRCH), said to me, "You can't just be a doctor in this field—you have to be a political activist too." She is absolutely right. Whether those involved in abortion embrace the identity of activist enthusiastically or reluctantly, they are forced to act as members of a *social movement* as well as of the medical profession. Far more than in other fields of medicine, abortion providers need to engage in activities that we typically associate with grassroots movement organizers: attracting new recruits, establishing strategic alliances both within medicine and outside it, advocating with politicians and the general public, working on media strategies, and so on. This level of activism rarely occurs among, say, kidney specialists.

Using this social-movement lens, one of the main things I observed in the contemporary abortion scene was hardly a surprise: in difficult situations, people need allies. This point was made to me by Dr. Jeannette James, who was finishing a family medicine residency in a large East Coast city where she had learned to perform abortions. In a beautifully lilting Caribbean accent, James responded to my question: "Will I provide abortions in the future? Certainly I will keep providing here . . . but I can't see being the only one in a place like Arkansas, or something like that. You need a community with you if you are going to provide abortions."

Dr. James, like many others I met, was torn between the gratification of offering a desperately needed service to patients and apprehensions about having a public identity as an abortion provider in a hostile environment, without supportive colleagues. Potential abortion providers are keenly aware of the violence that periodically visits this field, especially when they have young children. Justine Gordon, a primary-care physician whose practice focuses on adolescents, spoke with enthusiasm about the discussions under way to provide early abortions in her large hospital on the East Coast, since many of her patients experience unwanted pregnancies. Her husband dropped by during our interview at an outdoor café as I asked her if she had any security concerns. She seemed fairly confident that no one would cause her trouble in her present setting.

But Gordon is the mother of an adorable three-year-old son, whose picture she proudly showed me. With her husband nodding assent, she expressed her reservations about providing abortion care if the family were to leave this large metropolitan area. "If my family moved to North Dakota or someplace like that, I just don't think I could do it. I can imagine saying to my patients, 'I'm sorry, my son is more important to me than this issue.'"

Rachel Gould, a family physician in a large city, had recently begun to provide early abortions in her clinic. She too is the mother of a toddler. She told me that she had seen media accounts of the harassment at the home of a well-known abortion provider in her area and found them quite disturbing. The doctor was afraid to sit in front of her windows because several abortion providers had been shot in their homes. When Gould read this, she thought to herself, "I'm sitting right in front of a window as I'm reading this! And I think about my son . . . God forbid, if anything should happen to me, I don't want him to think, 'Oh, my mother was trying to help other women, but she wasn't there for me.'" Gould wonders how nervous she should be and acknowledges that she is confused about what precautions are rational and what is excessive. She had casually mentioned to her neighbor that she had started performing abortions but then felt uneasy about the conversation. "Do I need to be quiet about this, or am I making too big a deal about it, and worrying too much?"

It is not just personal safety that these doctors worry about. They are also concerned about the potential taint to their professional identities. For those in family medicine, like Dr. James, who look forward to practicing the full spectrum of medicine that this specialty typically involves, there are concerns that abortion will overwhelm the rest of their practice, given the shortage of abortion providers. These new providers also worry about the reactions of colleagues elsewhere in medicine. When Dr. Ruth Childs returned to her West Coast family medicine residency after training in early abortion on the East Coast, she "didn't know who it was okay to talk to, who it was okay to tell about my experiences. You never know who your allies are on this front." After being questioned further by one of the senior physicians in response to her vague remark about doing a "women's health rotation," Childs decided to come clean. "I was grateful to hear him say it was okay to tell him." Childs's senior colleague went on to explain that he used to perform abortions but no longer does so, having wearied of fighting the many procedural roadblocks put in place by others in his practice. He encouraged Childs to take his place in this long-standing struggle. "He said this is something women need to stand up for now."

Hearing Dr. Childs's concerns was one of many times in the course of researching this book that I was reminded of the disturbing similarity between the present moment and the pre-*Roe* era. In a previous research project, I interviewed concerned physicians who sought to find reliable colleagues who could give their patients safe and dignified abortion care when the procedure was illegal. Now it is stigma and threats to personal safety rather than legality that keeps providers from openly identifying themselves to one another. This exchange recounted by Dr. Childs, it is worth noting, took place on the liberal West Coast.

Similarly, though Dr. Gould had second thoughts about the wisdom of telling her neighbor about her involvement with abortion, she wanted affirmation from medical colleagues and was disappointed when it wasn't forthcoming. Though she feels strongly supported by her medical director, who also provides early abortions, she is disappointed by the reactions of the other clinicians with whom she works and socializes. She describes all her colleagues as pro-choice, but they draw the line at actual provision, and they failed to respond to an e-mail she sent about her recent decision to perform abortions. "I feel a bigger sense of loneliness around [abortion provision] than I do about anything else," she told me.

On an e-mail Listserv, a young physician who was about to leave her family practice residency in the Pacific Northwest to take up a position in the South expressed similar "coming out" concerns. She wrote of her uncertainty about whether it would be appropriate to do abortions in her new practice and confessed that she had not even raised the issue: "It's been a long time since I have had to negotiate in a not necessarily pro-choice environment. . . . I do not wish to offend." Concluding that her best bet to continue providing abortion care would be to do so away from her practice, she ended her e-mail by asking her colleagues, "Does anyone know where abortions are being done in [her new state] and how I can get discreetly in touch with local providers?"

In nearly any other field of medicine, these experiences would be downright bizarre. A resident in gastroenterology, one assumes, would not be afraid to tell a senior faculty member that she had received specialized training on the East Coast; someone starting his career in orthopedics probably would not be torn about telling his neighbor what he does; a new cardiologist in town would not ask for advice on how to find other cardiologists "discreetly," and so on. In no other area of medicine are the personal security issues so overwhelming. The field of abortion has become so thoroughly politicized since the *Roe* decision—both in the larger culture and in medicine itself—that the challenge facing would-be providers is how to establish some sense of normalcy in settings that are often anything but that.

THE CHALLENGES OF ABORTION TRAINING

The shortage of abortion providers is a long-standing problem, and it has been getting worse. According to the Guttmacher Institute, the leading research organization on reproductive health, the number of abortion facilities in the United States fell from 2,380 in 1992 to 1,787 in 2005 (the most recent year for which data are available). As this figure reflects the number of facilities, not of individual providers, it's difficult to get a concrete sense of the number of providers. Concerns about stigma and harassment make some abortion providers reluctant to identify themselves to researchers; their preference is to do this work under the radar.

Abortion services are also poorly distributed—they tend to be clustered in large cities, and nearly absent in rural areas, which leaves about one third of American women in a county without an abortion provider. Not surprisingly, abortion care is more accessible in blue states than in red ones. Some states—for example, Mississippi and the Dakotas—are down to only one known provider as of this writing. Moreover, access is even harder than these figures suggest. Clinics in hostile territories are often dependent on doctors who fly in from the outside, and abortions are scheduled on only one or two days a week. Bad weather that makes it impossible to fly or to drive for a few hours means that abortion services won't take place that day.

The lack of routine training in the most relevant specialty, obstetrics and gynecology, is a main reason for the shortage of abortion providers. Reflecting the history of stigma in this field, routine abortion training wasn't implemented in most ob-gyn programs after *Roe*, even though abortion has been one of the most sought-after procedures by women of reproductive age.

The training situation started to improve in the mid-1990s. One reason was the founding of Medical Students for Choice (MSFC). This group initially mobilized in response to increasing antiabortion activity. Two events were particularly important: the first shooting of an abortion provider, Dr. David Gunn, in Florida in 1993, and a mass mailing to U.S. medical students of a very offensive pamphlet denouncing abortion providers, sent by an antiabortion group. One of MSFC's first activities was to petition the Accreditation Council for Graduate Medical Education (ACGME), the group that sets standards for residency training, to make abortion training a required component of ob-gyn residency programs. MSFC's activities, coupled with renewed efforts among longtime advocates within the physician community, led ACGME to take action—more than twenty years after the *Roe* decision.

In 1995 ACGME issued new requirements that stipulated that ob-gyn residencies seeking accreditation must make routine abortion training available. Those residents who had moral objections to abortion could opt out of such training. This opt-out provision reflected long-standing policy: shortly after *Roe v. Wade*, Congress had passed the Church Amendment, which recognized physicians' rights to refuse to participate in abortion without being sanctioned by their employers. The 1995 ACGME ruling also permitted institutions with such objections (for example, Catholic hospitals) to opt out, as long as they made provisions for residents who requested training to receive it elsewhere.

But in an unprecedented intrusion into medical education, the U.S. Congress acted to effectively nullify ACGME's new requirement. A measure known as the Coats Amendment (named after

Dan Coats, the fervently antiabortion legislator from Indiana who sponsored it) states that residency programs will be deemed accredited—and thus not at risk of losing federal funding—even if they do not comply with the ACGME ruling. Furthermore, a number of states have enacted legislation that prohibits public institutions from providing elective abortion services, making it far more difficult for residency programs in these institutions to comply with the ACGME mandate. (Some institutions manage this situation by arranging for residents to be trained off-site, in freestanding clinics.)

Since the ACGME mandate in 1995, training in ob-gyn residencies has improved, although there is nowhere near full compliance. Knowledgeable people in the field have told me that today more than half of all ob-gyn residencies offer some training, though this may refer to optional rather than routine training. And, as I discuss in more detail at the end of this chapter, in some cases training in ob-gyn has been facilitated by special advocacy efforts from outside the residency programs themselves.

THE POTENTIAL ROLE OF
PRIMARY-CARE CLINICIANS

The medical specialty most associated with abortion care historically has been the field of obstetrics and gynecology, and this is still is the case. But starting around 2000, some physicians in family medicine, internal medicine, and adolescent medicine began making concerted efforts to become abortion providers. Also, in states where it is legally permitted, advanced practice clinicians (APCs)—nurse midwives, physician assistants, and nurse practitioners—have trained in early abortion methods. This interest arose in large part because of changes in abortion technologies that made the participation of those who are not ob-gyns more feasible.

The abortion-providing community was introduced to "medication abortion" when researchers found in the early 1990s that methotrexate, a drug widely used for cancer treatment and other medical conditions, was also effective in terminating a pregnancy within the first nine weeks of gestation. Second, and more important, mifepristone (formerly referred to as RU-486, or the "French abortion pill") was approved in France in 1988. Although domestic abortion politics delayed the drug's final FDA approval until fall 2000, mifepristone underwent clinical trials in the United States starting in the mid-1990s. Medication abortion has the potential to increase the pool of abortion providers because a different level of training is required. Rather than performing a procedure that involves entering the uterus with instruments, the clinician counsels the patient, determines the gestational age of her pregnancy, and gives her some medication.

In the interval between mifepristone's approval in France and its approval in this country, the abortion-providing community began using the manual vacuum aspirator (MVA), a handheld syringe with a soft cannula (tube) and a valve that makes it possible to empty the contents of the uterus safely early in pregnancy. An earlier version of this apparatus was used by some feminist health activists for "menstrual extraction," both as a means of early abortion and to remove menses instantly. Today the MVA is widely used in the developing world because it does not depend on electricity. Moreover, some countries that outlaw abortion allow "menstrual regulation clinics" when there has not been a technical verification of pregnancy.

In the United States in the 1990s there was a resurgence of interest in the MVA because of recent technological advances that permitted very early and reliable pregnancy detection, and also because of a growing popular demand for safe and effective early abortion—a demand that had been stimulated by news accounts of the "abortion pill" in France. Veteran providers established new protocols for the MVA, allowing women to obtain an abortion as soon as they received a positive pregnancy test. In contrast, most facilities using vacuum aspiration machines do not offer abortions until about six weeks after a woman's last menstrual period. MVA abortions can also be performed easily in a physician's office. These two new technologies, medication abortion and the MVA, together have had the positive result of enabling more abortions in the United States to occur earlier in pregnancy. In-office abortion also facilitates continuity of patient care—a core value for primary-care fields. Recent data tell us that nearly one out of three women in this country have an abortion by the age of forty-five. Before these innovations, most patients had to go elsewhere for an important medical and, in the language of these specialties, "psychosocial" event.

I have long been interested in the possibility that these new technologies will bring new providers to the field. Around the time that the FDA approved mifepristone in 2000, I interviewed primary-care physicians and APCs who had sought training in these early abortion methods. When I asked about their motivations to offer abortions, without fail they brought up the theme of continuity of care.

One of those I spoke with was Rebecca Jacobs, an intense young assistant professor of family medicine in the medical school of an East Coast university. She recognizes the controversial nature of abortion; nonetheless, she feels that abortion care is a natural part of her specialty. When she started to offer medication abortions, she said, "I began to feel I was helping them in a way that was very special. And it wasn't about abortions, it was about *them*. And their whole problem. Ultimately I was helping them to have the life that they wanted to have. One of them had three kids, she was thirty and single. . . . She wasn't sure what to do . . . but she knew that this wasn't a good time for another child. And I went through that myself." Here Jacobs paused and recollected her feelings about finding herself, already the mother of two young children and about to undergo a divorce, with an unwanted pregnancy. She continued, "They [patients] are going to go through with this, and if it is something I could be a part of, I should be."

When I asked Jacobs to elaborate on what she meant by "be a part of," she replied, "To be there for my own patients. To help guide them through this, help them understand what to expect, to talk about their feelings. To help them feel like it's difficult but okay, and that their life and what they choose to do with it is extraordinarily important."

In a similar vein, Dr. Natalie Diamond, another young assistant professor on the East Coast, but in an adolescent medicine program, speculated about the logic of bringing early abortion—either medication or MVA—to her specialty: "The attraction is to get to provide truly comprehensive care to a young kid. A kid comes in and she's in trouble. We would have the option of offering her an abortion, if that's what she wants, in a pretty confidential way. She doesn't have to go to another place, meet a brand-new doctor—she can stay connected to her regular doctor."

Actually bringing abortion services to primary care, as I was repeatedly to see, can be quite cumbersome. Expanding early abortion care to new terrain means taking on some opponents who are morally opposed to abortion, and some who are okay with the idea of abortion but not with the problems it brings.

STARTING A RESIDENCY TRAINING PROGRAM

Alex Wolff, an energetic and gregarious man in his forties, is a faculty member in a family medicine program on the East Coast. I had heard that his residency was among the first in this specialty to attempt routine training in medication abortion. When I visited Wolff at his hospital office, he walked me through the unexpected twists this campaign had taken. Talking to him was not unlike hearing a soldier recall an ultimately successful but nonetheless bruising battle.

Wolff himself had received training in both medication abortion and the MVA earlier in his career and had worked briefly at a Planned Parenthood clinic. He described himself as "passionate" about integrating abortion into his field, but admitted to a certain naiveté when planning for this in his own program. He especially conceded the mistake he had made by talking only to faculty at the outset and not to residents. He told me of the "explosion of anger" when a few of the residents who were opposed to abortion on religious grounds heard of these plans. In the first of many indications that Wolff would receive that dealing with abortion was different from other matters in academic medicine, the objections of this minority of residents led some of his colleagues to reconsider this training, even though most of the faculty had already approved it in principle. In other spheres of medical training, it is safe to say, residents' wishes typically do not trump those of faculty. Furthermore, it had already been made clear that no one would be forced to undergo this training because of the legally required opt-out provision.

In light of the unexpected turmoil in his program, Dr. Wolff quickly realized that implementing abortion training needed to be handled differently from other curricular additions. As he put it, "Providing a service as controversial as medical abortion required that the group as a whole come to terms with the decision, or we needed to rethink whether to proceed. We needed to set up a meeting with concerned residents, a more open-ended format than our usual resident-faculty meetings. I was concerned that these folks [strongly antiabortion residents] would go so far as to try to take matters into their own hands . . . even do public disclosure [the plan was to offer abortions to regular patients of the program, not to the public at large], and risk us all being targeted by the antis."

Such fear of being "targeted by the antis" was a major concern of both those who supported the incorporation of abortion care into the residency program and those who did not. In the immediate aftermath of the residents' "explosion," a faculty member who had initially been supportive of this step "became really upset," as Wolff remembered. "He said, 'Look, I've been providing care at this health center for twenty years. My patients . . . know what to expect when they come here. I will not tolerate patients having to walk through a line of protesters when they're bringing in their kids for a checkup or they are coming for their blood pressure check.'"

Wolff scheduled the meeting of residents and faculty in his program, and he encouraged an "open expression of feelings" about the prospect of incorporating abortion. The atmosphere ultimately got very tense among the residents at the meeting. "So now we have a shouting match, with the pro-choice people talking about how we felt it was our obligation to serve women and people had the right to choose, and the anti-choice folks are saying, 'You can't talk about a right to choose when what you are choosing is murder.' It got very unpleasant . . . and when we left, everyone felt unsettled."

Things calmed down the next day, with conciliatory e-mails passing back and forth. Eventually Wolff and his colleagues were able to work out an arrangement that involved several compromises. Rather than routine training of all residents, with those who objected to abortion being able to opt out, this particular program decided to post a sign-up sheet that put the burden on interested residents to opt in. In another unusual step, those faculty members most committed to abortion service and training agreed to have a dedicated beeper just for abortion-related calls. (In most hospital-based training programs, residents typically take night duty and are the first called for any problems patients are experiencing.)

The faculty at this residency program also took the quite unusual step of offering this new service secretly. As Wolff explained to me, "We decided we were going to take our patients into our confidence and we were going to say to them, 'We are providing this service to you because of our feeling that you wanted our help and you were an existing patient of ours. We ask you not to discuss this with your friends because we don't want people who are not our patients calling us up, and we don't want to get the word out that abortions are taking place in Urban Family Health Center.' So far there's been a very positive reaction."

If outsiders do call, they are referred to a local Planned Parenthood facility. This requirement for secrecy for a legal service is quite unique in contemporary medical settings. Once again I had an eerie flashback to my earlier study of doctors operating in a pre-*Roe* environment, when patients had to be sworn to secrecy. This time, however, the fear is not of the police but of protesters. Just as the faculty member quoted above did not want his patients subjected to protesters, Wolff and his allies knew that the hospital administrators, wary about the idea of abortion within family medicine from the start, would "freak" if antiabortionists came to the hospital. "Our feeling was that the minute we had protesters outside our door, the administration would be telling us to close up shop."

Numerous other negotiations are necessary for the Alex Wolffs of this world in order to make abortion training a reality in family practice residencies. Often one of the stickiest issues is that of backup: in a small percentage of cases (anywhere from 1 percent to 5 percent), mifepristone does not completely work and the patient needs a more conventional vacuum aspiration abortion. Sometimes this can be provided by faculty members within family practice who have this training, and sometimes it involves arranging backup services with the departments of ob-gyn and emergency medicine, as sometimes that is where these patients show up. Similarly, the protocols used in most institutions that offer medication abortions require the patient to have an ultrasound to determine the stage of her pregnancy. While training in ultrasonography is part of the overall training for some family medicine residents, in other cases the department of radiology or ob-gyn needs to be willing to perform the abortion patients' ultrasounds.

Each of the negotiations with these other departments—which, in conventional medical terms, are higher in the hierarchy than family medicine—can evoke both turf issues and antiabortion sentiments. While individual ob-gyns, for example, might be supportive, departments as a whole often balk at providing such backup. This resistance can stem from clear-cut opposition to abortion; it can also result from wariness about "cleaning up other people's messes," as one ob-gyn told me.

Abortion advocates deal with this by diplomacy and by scouting out possible allies. "The thing I've done to minimize [turf issues] is to avoid conflict whenever possible," Philip Austen told me. Austen is an assistant professor in a family practice residency who worked tirelessly to bring medical abortion training to his program over a period of several years. In words that illustrate how the struggle to establish training is usefully understood as a social movement enterprise, he went on to say, "I mean we've got to find the right people, in the right departments, who are going to be on our side."

Yet another challenge to establishing abortion training within residency programs is the reluctance, if not downright refusal, of many of the necessary support staff, especially nurses, to take part in abortion care. That problem is discussed in chapter 5.

CHAMPIONS

Clearly abortion training at Alex Wolff's residency program simply would not have happened if he had not been willing to expend such an enormous amount of time and energy. Wolff's program is not unique in that sense. In virtually every family practice residency I know of that has successfully incorporated abortion training, there has been someone willing to take on the role of champion—someone who undertakes all the politicking and negotiations that this project entails. Obviously, a deep commitment to abortion care as part of women's reproductive health is what drives such a person. But there are costs as well as gratifications to being an abortion champion.

Being a champion takes time, and time is in short supply among doctors. Another cost is the potential of frayed, sometimes explosive relations with colleagues. I have heard numerous accounts of champions who were shunned by some of their peers, sometimes even screamed at, and occasionally subjected to petty acts of vindictiveness.

But even if collegial relations remain on an even keel, being a champion often overwhelms the rest of one's professional identity.

"My colleagues see me as a fanatic," the coalition-building Dr. Austen told me with a sigh. Austen's commitment to this issue indeed ran deep. Earlier in his life, while a college student, he had experienced an unwanted pregnancy with a girlfriend—"I didn't want to marry her, I didn't want to have children with her"—and both he and the woman involved were very grateful that the option of a legal abortion existed. But abortion was not *all* he was interested in. He had very strong research interests in other fields, particularly in the link between poverty and obesity, and he was concerned that the enormous amount of time he spent on abortion would sabotage this research agenda. He was also concerned about how his engagement with abortion would affect his professional standing:

> It [abortion involvement] is a bit of a tricky issue with me, because right now my obesity stuff, which is what I think of as who I truly am going to be as a doctor, that's starting to take off. . . . I feel a little bit like I have a split personality, and I have not talked about my obesity stuff to everyone in the abortion world, and I don't talk about the abortion stuff with obesity colleagues. But we're starting to publish about our abortion experience and someone did a Google search, and our names popped right up . . . and some of the community people involved with obesity, I'm not sure how happy they'll be with that, if they find out.

POST-TRAINING ISSUES

What becomes of residents who have been trained in abortion? Actually, an inadequate training opportunity no longer appears to me to be the major problem contributing to the shortage of abortion providers. In spite of the problems outlined here—political interference from an antiabortion Congress and the delicate negotiations that champions within primary care have to undertake—training has actually gradually increased since about 2000, owing to the arrival of new early abortion methods and to renewed efforts by national pro-choice medical organizations. The more severe problem occurs when trainees confront the barriers to putting their training into practice.

It is impossible to say with precision how many clinicians who have been trained in abortion procedures go on to provide this service. In one of the most substantial studies to date, Dr. Jody Steinauer, a physician researcher at the University of California at San Francisco (UCSF), and her colleagues surveyed over 5,000 ob-gyns who had become board-certified between 1998 and 2001 about their current practice. Of the 2,149 who responded to the survey, only 22 percent had provided elective abortions in the past year. (Some ob-gyns perform medically necessary abortions, as when the patient's life or health is threatened, but do not provide elective abortions, which form the vast majority of abortions sought in the United States.)

In a smaller, qualitative study done recently, Lori Freedman, a young sociologist also at UCSF, interviewed thirty-five ob-gyns who had recently completed residency and had received some abortion training. She found that only a tiny number were providing elective abortions, even though most expressed strong support for legal abortion. The major stumbling blocks were the policies of the hospitals where her respondents had privileges and the restrictions imposed by the group practices they had joined. Some of these hospitals were Catholic institutions, which forbid abortion and several other reproductive services in their facilities. Some were secular hospitals that had merged with Catholic facilities, an increasingly common situation that subjects them to Catholic directives on reproductive health care.

But the group practices in which these young physicians sought employment were also opposed to abortion, to a startling degree. Here the issue was not church affiliation but quite plainly fear of controversy. In numerous cases Freedman found that those joining a practice were asked to sign a contract stipulating that they would not provide abortions to patients of the practice. In some cases these contracts called for the physicians to sign away their right to provide abortions *off-site*, such as at a Planned Parenthood facility. One doctor interviewed by Freedman recalled being asked by the senior partner in a group practice in the Midwest if he had ever performed an abortion. When the interviewee replied that he had, the older physician replied, "Well, from now on I'm going to take that as a 'no.' And if I ever find out that you perform an abortion, I'll see to it that you never practice medicine in [this state] again!"

In my own interviews, I found similar obstacles to trainees' abilities to provide abortions, especially when individuals moved from the urban areas of their residencies. I think particularly of the case of Dr. Christopher Franklin, an exceptionally outgoing resident in a family medicine program, whom everyone affectionately called Ace. I watched Ace perform abortions one afternoon in a West Coast clinic under the watchful eye of Deborah Fox, a veteran abortion provider and trainer. Dr. Fox later told me that Ace was one of the most technically proficient and empathetic trainees she had ever worked with.

I observed Ace's warmth toward his patients, his unhurried manner, his willingness to answer all questions, his conversation with the patient throughout the process, as he told her exactly what he was doing and what to expect next. Between patients, as Ace sat in the tiny clinic kitchen grabbing a snack, he told me how meaningful he found this part of his practice. "I wouldn't want to do just this—I like delivering babies, I like working with elderly patients—but it's very gratifying to be able to help someone at a problem point in her life."

A few months later I followed up with Ace as he was completing his training and looking for a job. He told me that he was being strongly recruited by a group practice in a rural midwestern state. I asked him if this job would permit him to do abortions. He replied that he had raised this with his potential employers. "They said everyone in the practice was pro-choice but didn't want to get involved. They didn't want 'the hassles.'" This left Ace in a bind. Even if he were permitted to do abortions, he would be on his own. That is, he couldn't count on his partners to offer the backup essential in all fields of medical practice.

Any doctor who wants or needs to leave town—for a conference, for a vacation, for a family emergency—of course needs colleagues who will look after his or her patients. But with abortion the situation gets more complex, because of the small number of doctors who are providers. In some cases, a non-abortion-providing physician can offer perfectly adequate backup if necessary. But in too many other cases, such backup can be very problematic. For example, doctors not familiar with the working of mifepristone might not know how much bleeding is normal and order a transfusion when it is not warranted, adding anxiety and cost to the procedure for the patient. Similarly, uterine perforations occasionally occur in aspiration abor-

tion, leading abortion providers to worry about the "punitive hyster-
ectomy" that an antiabortion ER doctor might order. In short, given
the politicization that accompanies abortion care, those providing
this service desire backup from those who share both their skill set
and their commitment to this field. Echoing the point made by Dr.
James at the beginning of this chapter, about the abortion providers' need for community, Ace wistfully acknowledged to me that he
probably would not be performing abortions in his new job, because,
as he put it, "I can't go solo."

Tim Shawn also completed a residency in a family medicine program where he learned to do early abortion procedures. That Shawn
even sought this training was somewhat of a surprise to him (he
could, after all, have opted out). He told me he came from a very
Catholic family and would not think of telling his parents and other
relatives what he was doing. Nevertheless, as he went through medical school, and particularly when he met his fiancée, also a physician,
he became convinced that abortion was part of what a responsible
family medicine doctor should do.

Shawn's first job after his residency was as director of a small
clinic offering primary care to low-income people in a rural area in
the Pacific Northwest. At the time of his interview he did not bring
up the issue of abortion. "I guess I just sort of figured I'd be doing
them. . . . [I]t didn't occur to me that I had to bring it up then."

But the politics of abortion soon became a central issue for Shawn
at his new post. No one had ever offered abortions at his clinic, and
Shawn was in no rush to do so, but while ordering supplies early
in his tenure, he decided to order some of what he would eventually need. "So I figured I'd start with some cervical dilators, because
there's lots of times you need them for other gyn procedures, not just
abortions . . . and when I mentioned to the nurse that at some point
I might be doing abortions, she sort of freaked out, and she said, 'I
hope we never do these here—I don't want to be part of it.' "

The story took a more disturbing twist when Shawn needed to
use the dilators he had ordered, not for an abortion but for another
procedure. "I ordered the dilators and I *saw* them come in, and then
they just mysteriously disappeared! I was doing an endometrial bi-
opsy on somebody and I needed a dilator, and they were nowhere to
be found. No one could find them. I'm almost positive [that nurse]

threw them away." Shawn, whose relationship with the nurse was already very rocky, did not confront her about his suspicion. The nurse was fired shortly thereafter for unrelated reasons.

In the end Shawn was not able to provide abortions at his clinic. One major stumbling block was ambiguity about whether this was permissible, because the clinic received federal funding. Some cautious administrators have interpreted the rules to mean that no abortions can take place in facilities that receive such funds. Another impediment was that the malpractice policies of the clinic did not appear to cover abortions. Indeed, lack of malpractice insurance has been a major obstacle in the spread of abortion care, especially among medical practitioners who are not ob-gyns.

Even assuming that these obstacles could be overcome, the deal-breaker for Shawn was the realization of how little support he would have at the clinic. While the two other doctors on the staff were not vocally against abortion, they were not interested in doing them. Shawn's boss, the executive director of the fleet of clinics that Shawn's facility was a part of, was discouraging, especially over the ambiguity of the malpractice policies. "He wasn't mean about it, but it certainly wasn't one of those things that he was going to bend over backwards to somehow let me do," Shawn said. Shawn himself was too junior to be a champion, and without a director willing to take on that role, it just wasn't going to happen.

Shawn next investigated whether he could offer abortions at a site other than his clinic. His training had taken place at a Planned Parenthood clinic, and he had very positive memories of that experience. But the Planned Parenthood facility in the nearest big city did not need him. Reflecting the uneven distribution of abortion providers I have already spoken of, this liberal city appeared actually to have an oversupply of doctors trained to perform abortions. It was precisely in Shawn's rural area that the need was greatest.

One option did present itself in the first year of his new job: to moonlight on weekends at another rural clinic, where he would just perform abortions. Tempted though he was, Shawn did not pursue this. As we have seen with other young doctors, Shawn simply could not imagine performing abortions in isolation. Reminiscent of Ace and his hesitation to "go solo," Shawn was "nervous about going into the middle of nowhere and basically turning them out by myself."

Like Ace, Tim Shawn was concerned about what would occur if one of his patients had a complication. And here we see one of the key paradoxes of abortion, especially early abortion. Medically speaking, this procedure is so safe—more than ten times safer than childbirth, according to the American Medical Association—that novices don't necessarily experience a complication during their training. In his residency, for example, Shawn completed around fifty abortion procedures without incident, and observed others. But as Dr. Maureen Paul, a veteran trainer and the editor of a leading textbook on abortion, told me, it might take hundreds of procedures before a provider experiences a perforation or retained tissue in the uterus. What Shawn, with his limited experience, most wanted was a situation similar to his training environment, "a place like Ocean View clinic, where you are doing them right next to somebody who has been doing them for years, and if you have a question or an issue, you just ask." All health professionals at the start of their careers presumably worry about inadvertently harming patients and want to have trusted senior colleagues whom they can call on for advice. But with abortion, I came to understand, this fear of working in isolation has a special intensity. Given abortion's deeply contested status, Ace and Tim Shawn had good reason to fear the potential legal consequences if a complication arose.

When I last spoke to Shawn, about eighteen months after he left his residency, he still had not found a setting in which he felt comfortable doing abortions, and he worried that his skills in that field would get rusty.

INTEGRATING ABORTION INTO
A FAMILY MEDICINE PRACTICE

Not every family practice doctor who wants to provide abortions is prevented from doing so, even in rural areas. The story of Susan Golden is in some ways one of the most successful I have encountered. She was able to overcome the various obstacles that prevented Ace and Shawn from acting on their desire to provide abortion. Golden, in her mid-forties at the time of our contact, had a deep political commitment to reproductive rights, dating back to her college days. But it never occurred to her that she could actually be an abortion provider as a family practice doctor until she went to a meeting of her state chapter of the American Medical Women's Association (AMWA). There she heard a guest speaker, an ob-gyn named Michelle Lawrence, give a talk on mifepristone, shortly after that drug had been approved by the FDA. Hearing Lawrence's talk convinced Golden that integrating medication abortion into her practice was feasible. The clincher, as Golden remembered it, came when she chatted privately with Lawrence after her presentation and the experienced doctor offered to be available to consult by phone if any problems arose.

Susan Golden's motivation to start giving her patients mifepristone stemmed not just from an abstract belief in reproductive rights. She practiced in a rural section of a large midwestern state that was a three-and-a-half-hour drive to the nearest freestanding abortion clinic. The ability to offer this medication to her patients with unwanted pregnancies seemed a reasonable way to help them avoid seven hours of travel (not to mention provide an essential service for those without cars).

Around the time Golden met Dr. Lawrence, she was in the midst of setting up a new office practice in her town. Unlike Ace and Tim Shawn, she did not face the problem of operating in isolation. She had a partner, Linda Perillo, who was supportive of the plan to offer abortion. That solved the problem of having someone trustworthy to take calls if Golden was unavailable. Moreover, though none of the ob-gyns in her town openly offered abortion, they were quietly supportive of Golden. On the rare occasions when she needed backup aspiration services to complete a mifepristone abortion, these physicians were there for her.

This is not to suggest that starting abortion care was all that simple. The two partners had to purchase an ultrasound machine, which cost them over $10,000. They had to negotiate a new malpractice insurance policy, and several companies turned them down as soon as they heard of the plan to offer abortions. Finally they found a company, but their rates were raised by several thousand dollars, even though, as Golden told me, "These abortions are among the safest things I do." Golden and Perillo also knew that they had to hire office staff very carefully; they needed "people who were going to be comfortable with abortion . . . a tough bunch who could handle whatever might happen."

For about two years I periodically spoke by phone or communicated by e-mail with Susan Golden, starting shortly after she began providing abortions. At each of our contacts, she confirmed that medically speaking, her abortion work was going very well. After about a year of this activity, she told me, "It's worked great! Very smoothly. No problems at all in the time we have been doing this. We've been doing about four or so per week. Only one person had to be resuctioned by one of the local ob-gyns." She also told me that she had never had to call Dr. Lawrence with any questions, though she appreciated the security of knowing she was there.

Socially, however, things were considerably more complicated. "Shortly after we started, one of my patients—a very conservative Christian—came into my office, all in a dither, and said, 'Dr. Golden, do you know that they are talking about you on Christian radio? They are saying you do abortions here and they are calling you and Dr. Perillo 'Sisters of Satan'! And a little while after that, this prayer group started coming to our office every day, Monday through Friday—they'd come right at noon, say prayers for about twenty minutes, then leave."

Golden called the police and had them explain to the prayer group exactly how close to the clinic they were allowed to be. Though not thrilled with the group's presence, Golden considered its members to be harmless. More worrisome to her was a lone protester who seemed more menacing: "We have one very strange guy who stands out on the highway median all day. He must be wearing a leg bag or something, because he doesn't go anywhere to pee, he doesn't eat, he doesn't drink, he just stands out there with his signs, very graphic pictures, and he's a little more scary because he's obviously more of a zealot, he's creepier. So far, though, nothing has happened. We are in touch with the police about the situation."

One late afternoon in winter, when it had already become dark, one of Golden's staff members noticed two men in a pickup truck "lurking" in the office's private parking lot. Golden rushed out, confronted the men, and had a tense exchange with them, questioning why they were there. She then returned to the building and called the police. Acknowledging later that she had acted rashly by attempting to deal with the situation herself, she said, "The idea that these two guys might be out there when one of my staff was going to be the last leaving the building just infuriated me." Hearing this story reinforced for me that for many in Golden's situation, abortion-related violence always hovers as a possibility. It is difficult in situations like this to distinguish between "normal" worrisome behavior and what might be a threat from the violent wing of the antiabortion movement (which was periodically an active presence in Golden's state).

Golden was not entirely surprised at the various security issues that emerged after she and Dr. Perillo became publicly associated with abortion. Earlier in her life she had done volunteer clinic escort work at an urban abortion clinic, which involves accompanying arriving patients through lines of hostile protesters. Her parents live near one of the cities where an abortion provider was shot. Nevertheless, when Golden decided to apply for membership in the National Abortion Federation, the major professional association of abortion providers in North America, she was taken aback by the "security assessment" she received from a NAF staff person who visited her clinic. "She was talking to me about altering my driving routes to and from work, and whether or not I should be wearing a bulletproof vest, and all these kinds of things, and I'm like, 'Oh my God, whoa!'"

In spite of these sobering reminders of the threat of violence, Golden continued with her abortion provision for several years, until illness forced her early retirement. Providing this service did not lead to an overall loss of patients. For example, the patient who had first heard of Golden's abortion work on Christian radio showed a touching loyalty. "She thought about it for a couple of weeks and she consulted her priest and a number of other individuals and she actually became more angry with the protesters and the radio station for misinformation than upset that we were providing that service," Golden said. Especially moving to Golden was the statement of one patient, an evangelical Christian, who told her, "What someone else does is not my business. And if someone is going to deal with an unplanned or unwanted pregnancy, you are exactly the kind of person I would want to be there and help them make the right decision." All told, Golden estimates she lost about five or six patients because of the abortion issue, but she believes she gained more because of it.

Perhaps the most demoralizing incident of her several years as a family practice doctor who provided abortion did not involve violence. Rather, the incident brought home the social ostracism that is the fate of many such doctors. Golden and Perillo had been invited to participate in a community health fair. They were asked to speak about options for new parents regarding infant care. However, when word of these doctors' participation in the program got out, the owner of the building where the health fair was scheduled to take place withdrew his offer, owing to pressure by an antiabortion group. The health fair was abruptly canceled, as there was not enough time to find an alternate site. In the uproar that followed the cancellation, many in the community, including the local newspaper, expressed outrage that the mere participation of these physicians had caused the loss of the site. The two doctors were gratified to see this support but were still shaken by the incident. Recalling this event several months later, Dr. Golden said, with evident frustration, "We weren't even going to *mention* abortion. This was supposed to be about helping parents of newborns!"

What conclusions might we draw from Susan Golden's several years of providing medication abortion? Most fundamentally, her experience shows that the integration of abortion into a primary-care practice can be done safely and smoothly. Of the patients in her practice who were opposed to abortion, most did not leave, and some, as we have seen, voiced surprising and moving support. Yet in spite of the tiny role that abortion played in their overall medical practice, Golden and her partner could not escape the attention of antiabortion forces, and this brought some worrisome security issues as well as community-wide controversy. In terms of what these two doctors' experience might suggest about the potential of others' providing early abortion care in underserved rural areas, the simplest answer, I think, is that some will be passionate enough about this issue to put up with the negative aspects, and some, quite understandably, will not.

Another lesson I draw from my conversations with Susan Golden is, once again, how important community is for abortion providers.

Golden's support system was both local and national. Locally she had the support of her medical partner, her office staff, and some physicians in the community willing to provide backup services. When the health fair crisis occurred, she received an unexpected endorsement from her town's newspaper. Nationally, it was through her membership in AMWA that she first met Dr. Lawrence and became aware of the possibility of becoming an abortion provider. Golden went on to join NAF, trusting that she would find, at its various conferences, like-minded colleagues with whom to discuss the unique challenges of this work.

ABORTION PROVIDERS AS ACTIVISTS

Thinking about Golden's contacts with AMWA and NAF reinforced for me the central role that a number of national abortion rights organizations play in the abortion wars. Though I have painted an admittedly bleak picture of the obstacles that face would-be abortion providers, I have also witnessed again and again the determined "push-back" of the medical wing of the abortion rights movement. Groups I have mentioned in this chapter—Planned Parenthood, PRCH, NAF, AMWA—as well as others have organized special abortion-related lectures and training sessions for clinicians unable to receive them in the context of their residencies. Medical Students for Choice organizes an "externship" program that allows its members to spend a month or two with a veteran abortion provider. Family medicine and other primary-care clinicians have worked tirelessly, often against vehement opposition, to include abortion-related sessions at professional meetings and articles on abortion care in professional journals.

The most significant efforts to effect changes within mainstream medical institutions come from two recently established programs, both based at UCSF: the Kenneth J. Ryan Residency Training Program in Abortion and Family Planning and the Fellowship in Family Planning. Both of these programs are funded by a private donor. The Ryan program offers technical and financial assistance to ob-gyn residencies that seek to comply with the ACGME mandate. It also works with these residencies to devise appropriate opt-out rotations for residents opposed to abortion training. As of 2009, the Ryan program had worked with forty-nine ob-gyn residencies in twenty-six states and two programs in Canada. The Fellowship in Family Planning currently has sites at seventeen ob-gyn programs and one family medicine program and provides postgraduate training in research and clinical skills in contraception and abortion. Additionally, the fellows typically spend several months working on reproductive health issues in an international setting. As of 2009, there are 170 current and former fellows, many of whom now serve as faculty members in leading medical schools. Their presence in these institutions and the impressive body of research they have published in the most prestigious medical journals have done much to counter the stigmatized image of the "abortionist" that haunted much of mainstream medicine in the period after *Roe*.

In the course of my travels, I have met many of the fellows in this program. In some ways they resemble postgraduate fellows in other medical specialties: ambitious young doctors who work extremely hard and who will be the next generation of intellectual leaders in their fields. But in other ways the fellows in family planning are different. As an ironic consequence of the seemingly endless war that characterizes their field, these fellows are imbued with a palpable sense of mission and a feeling of solidarity with other abortion providers that is rarely found elsewhere in contemporary medicine. This political as well as professional identification with abortion work is hardly confined to those holding fellowships in academic medicine. I have witnessed it among providers on the front lines, like Susan Golden and the brave clinic administrators we will meet in the next chapter, at gatherings of Medical Students for Choice, and indeed everywhere that abortion provision takes place. That social movements create other social movements in reaction is a sociological truism. Just as *Roe v. Wade* led to the emergence of the modern antiabortion movement, so has the extreme wing of that movement created a powerful abortion rights movement within American medicine.

THE CLINICS

Ground Zero in the Abortion Wars

In my encounters with the unique world that is abortion provision, I quite often find myself muttering to no one in particular, "You can't make this stuff up." This story, told to me by Liz Scott, a veteran clinic administrator in the Midwest, prompted that comment yet again.

> I had a waiting room full of patients that morning in January. The doctor scheduled for that day, Dr. Burns, had never let me down. He drives in from about seventy-five miles away, and over the years, no matter what the weather, he always made it. But that day, a horribly cold day, he called in early in the morning, and said, "Liz, I feel awful about this, but my car wheels just spin on the ice. I can't even get out of the driveway." So there I was, stuck with a waiting room full of patients and no doctors! I felt terrible—some of these patients had come from far away, in very difficult travel conditions, had paid for babysitters and motels . . . and we weren't scheduled to have another abortion clinic until the next week. I was just desperate.
>
> Right then, one of my staff came in. Before starting work she had been at the health club up the street from our clinic. She said, quite casually, "Hey, guess who I just saw at the club? Alice!" Alice is a wonderful young family doc whose family lives in our town. Last year, while she was still a resident, she spent time with us at the clinic, training under one of our docs, and we knew her as a great abortion provider and a good person besides. She apparently was back home, visiting her family for the holidays.
>
> So as soon as I heard that she was in the health club, I

ran out of the clinic, not even stopping to put on my coat. I stormed in, ran right past the person at the desk. I ran around like a crazy person, from room to room! I couldn't find her! Finally I spotted her through the window of the sauna. I banged on the window till she heard me and came to the door. I breathlessly explained the situation. She ran to the shower, got dressed, and came over. So in the end we *did* have an abortion clinic that day. . . . [W]e started a little late, but all our patients did fine.

Liz, now pushing sixty, is noted for her droll sense of humor. Without it, her job would be impossible. Finding a doctor in a sauna was unusual even for her, but just about every day in her clinic brings new challenges. In fact, the day of the sauna episode, the pipes in her facility froze. She then had to plead with an antiabortion plumber to come to the clinic.

Why does Liz have to depend on doctors who either drive considerable distances or fly into the regional airport, even though her clinic is in a midsized town with about twenty-five ob-gyns? Because none of the local doctors are willing to work in her clinic. In most cases, we can reasonably assume, this is not because of their antiabortion views. The reluctance to work there is a result of the intense pressure brought by a small but vociferous group of antiabortion physicians and activists. Any local physician who worked at the clinic, it has become amply clear over the years, would risk having referrals dry up and picketing at his or her office.

Those who contemplate working in Liz's clinic also have reason to fear that their children will be harassed at school and pickets will show up at the churches where they worship. I recall hearing an abortion provider from the Midwest describe at a professional meeting his shock when he went to his church and saw antiabortion militants handing out leaflets to his fellow congregants that denounced him as a "baby-killer." Similarly, I remember the wife of an abortion provider, also from the Midwest, telling how she and her husband had to be helicoptered out of their home to attend a child's wedding because protesters had blocked their driveway.

Freestanding abortion clinics—facilities that are either solely devoted to abortion care or offer the procedure as one of several women's reproductive health services—are ground zero in the abortion wars. These clinics are where most of the violence and harassment perpetrated by abortion opponents take place. The workforce of the clinics, including physicians, administrators, and other staff members, are the most likely to be stalked by extremists at their homes, churches, and other public places. Clinics have become such targets, quite simply, because they are where most abortions in the United States take place. According to the most recent data, 94 percent of the approximately 1.2. million abortions performed each year in this country take place in these facilities, with the rest being divided between hospitals and private doctors. (In most European countries, in contrast, more abortions take place in hospitals that are part of national health-care systems, resulting in much lower levels of harassment.)

Freestanding clinics began in the early 1970s, shortly before the *Roe v. Wade* decision, when New York State and Washington, D.C., had already liberalized their abortion laws. Women from all over the country began to fly to these places in large numbers for abortions, and hospitals were unable to meet this demand. Technological advances had made it feasible to offer high-quality abortion care in a freestanding facility on an outpatient basis. The vacuum suction machine, introduced to American physicians in 1968, facilitated abortions with a much lower complication rate than the previous method, D&C (dilation and curettage), and new methods of local anesthesia meant that a hospital surgery suite was no longer necessary. Furthermore, the costs were far lower than in a hospital, and clinic directors were (and still are today) free to hire staff members, such as nurses, counselors, and receptionists, supportive of abortion and abortion patients. In contrast, hospitals back then did not have the flexibility to assign only supportive staff members to abortion work, a situation that continues in many hospitals today.

The freestanding model has had a "good news/bad news" impact on abortion in the United States. On the positive side, the clinics have an outstanding safety record. Studies done shortly after *Roe* showed that abortions done in clinics had a lower complication rate than those done in hospitals. In the 1980s, the American Medical Association (AMA) found that "legal abortion was more than ten times safer than childbirth," and most of these abortions were performed in clinics.

Clinics today have kept abortions as affordable as possible. The average price of a first-trimester abortion in a clinic remains extraordinarily low: $415, according to the most recent data, in comparison to as much as several thousand dollars for an in-hospital procedure. Compared to the escalating price of health care in other fields, it is quite astonishing to see how little the price of an abortion has changed since the procedure was legalized.

But this concentration of abortions in freestanding clinics has had major drawbacks as well. First, it has allowed abortion care to become marginalized from the rest of medicine. Liz Scott's experience is typical; local doctors feel no commitment to these facilities beyond using them as a referral source for their patients who need abortions. It can be argued that the existence of the clinics since the early 1970s has enabled ob-gyns and other doctors who support legal abortion to avoid the complexities of providing abortions themselves. Second, the freestanding nature of these facilities has made them a highly visible and attractive target for their enemies.

How much violence and harassment actually occurs at the clinics? The National Abortion Federation has tracked incidents of violence and disruption directed at abortion providers since 1977. According to the organization's statistics, since that time there have been 8 murders, 17 attempted murders, 41 bombings, 100 butyric acid attacks (butyric acid is a very foul-smelling agent), 175 arsons, and 656 alleged anthrax threats. In addition there has been constant picketing, which can be very aggressive, involving intimidation and verbal abuse directed at both patients and staff. Nearly 80 percent of larger abortion facilities (those that provide more than 400 abortions per year) report being picketed. Patients and (more often) staff members are subject to harassment outside the clinic as well. There have been numerous disturbing cases of stalking that have sometimes necessitated restraining orders against certain protesters.

Generally speaking, conservative states are more likely to experience serious incidents of violence and intimidation than liberal ones, though there are some dramatic exceptions. Incidents also vary over time, with larger political factors often playing a role. Starting in 1992, when Bill Clinton became president, there was a considerable reduction in blockades and sieges at clinics because of new legislation, FACE (Freedom of Access to Clinic Entrances), which for the first time made impeding access to clinics a federal crime and resulted in jail sentences for offenders—something local judges had often refused to impose. (When I lived in Philadelphia in the 1970s and 1980s and served on the board of a clinic, a certain judge would typically praise the protesters who were brought before him "for their good work" and let them off with symbolic fines of $25.) Yet it was also during Clinton's presidency that the most horrible of all antiabortion violence began, with the murders of seven members of the abortion-providing community.

The first killing of an abortion provider occurred in Pensacola, Florida, in 1993, when Dr. David Gunn was shot by an antiabortion extremist. A year later another doctor and a clinic escort were killed, also in Florida. This was followed by the shooting of two receptionists at two different clinics in Boston, also in 1994. In 1998 a security guard was killed and a nurse was severely maimed by a bomb planted at an Alabama clinic by the same individual who had bombed the Atlanta Olympics and a gay nightclub. Emily Lyons, the nurse, has partially recovered from her injuries and has become a spokeswoman for the human costs of such terrorism. She minces no words when describing what the bombing did to her: "I lost my left eye, it damaged my right eye, broke the right side of my face, first-, second-, and third-degree burns on the front of my body, broke my left leg . . . tore the muscle and skin off the front of my leg, hole in my abdomen—my intestines were hanging out."

Later in 1998 the abortion-providing community suffered another tragedy when Dr. Barnett Slepian, an ob-gyn who provided abortions at a clinic in Buffalo, New York, was shot through a window as he stood in his kitchen on a Friday evening. The man convicted of this murder was implicated in a prior string of shootings of abortion providers in both Canada and the United States.

During the two presidential terms of George W. Bush, the most egregious acts of violence actually decreased. What this contrast suggests, not surprisingly, is that when the most extreme sectors of the antiabortion movement experience a presidential administration that supports abortion rights, violent acts increase, and during the tenure of a highly visible pro-life president, these acts decline.

This pattern continued with the election of Barack Obama in November 2008. Shortly after the election, a fire of "suspicious origin" broke out at a clinic in Nebraska, and in Minnesota an anti-abortion zealot crashed his SUV into a clinic. Most tragically, the following spring, Dr. George Tiller, who for years had been a target of antiabortion extremists, was murdered as he was serving as an usher in his church. Dr. Tiller's unique role in the abortion-providing community will be discussed further in chapter 7.

Virtually every clinic that provides abortion today is preoccupied with issues of security. One of the sadder aspects of the abortion wars is the degree to which these clinics, which want to provide a warm and welcoming place for their patients, have had to turn themselves into armed fortresses, with bullet-proof glass windows, security cameras everywhere, and ID checks.

What is it like to be working in a clinic when violent events occur? In what follows, I relate some of the war stories that clinic administrators in different parts of the country have told me. My aim, however, is not simply to show the fear and disruption that such violence can cause. I also want to document the determination shown by clinic workers to push back against this domestic terrorism.

ANTHRAX IN THE MIDWEST: JO AND PATTY'S STORY

Just days after the murder of Dr. Barnett Slepian in October 1998, about a dozen abortion clinics in the United States began to receive letters claiming that the powdery white substance enclosed in the envelope was anthrax and that anyone who opened such a letter would die. Notably, about eighty of these letters were received by clinics *before* the anthrax attacks that occurred right after the events of September 11, 2001. All of the anthrax letters sent to abortion clinics ultimately proved to be hoaxes, but the costs—in disruption to clinic operations, in resources expended by law enforcement, in the psychological toll on staff, patients, and others (such as mail carriers)—was enormous. Over 500 (of the total of about 650) of these incidents have been attributed to one antiabortion extremist, Clayton Waagner, now in jail, while the others remain unsolved.

One of the first clinics that received an anthrax threat was a small center that was part of a Planned Parenthood affiliate in the Midwest. Some years after this incident, I spoke with Jo, still the executive director of that affiliate, and Patty, then the manager of the center that received the threat. I was astonished to learn that this particular center did not even perform abortions. Adding to the irony, the anthrax threat occurred on a day when the clinic was providing prenatal services! As Patty reminisced, "We had started our prenatal care just a few months earlier. . . . We were the only one [of that affiliate's sites] to be doing prenatal, and we were so excited about that, so jazzed."

The anthrax incident occurred early on that fateful day. As Patty continued,

> We'd get the mail around nine. . . . And we're always cautious if something looked suspicious, but that letter looked okay. Allegra, one of the clinic assistants, opened the mail that morning, and all of a sudden, I hear her crying out, "Oh God, oh God!" So I rushed over and there was this letter with this powder-like substance in it, and it had a skull and crossbones on it, and it said something like "You have been anthraxed."
>
> So our adrenaline starts flowing, I immediately get on the phone with PP headquarters and talk with our security director, Dan. Very soon, hazmat people [government officials who deal with hazardous materials] were there, cops are everywhere, no one had ever really been around that type of situation before.

Once Patty had alerted the main office of Planned Parenthood of this crisis, immediate efforts were made to contact Jo, the executive director. In the surreal mixture of the extreme and the mundane that seems to occur often in this world, Jo learned of this incident from a call to her cell phone while she was at a hair salon. "So there I was, sitting under the dryer, unable to move," she said, "knowing that I needed to be there!"

Back at the center there was some confusion among authorities as to how to deal with Allegra. She had been immediately isolated from others, but the next steps were not clear. Some of the officials wanted her to strip down and be sprayed and decontaminated right there, while others thought it would be sufficient to take her to a hospital emergency room for such decontamination, which is what ultimately occurred. Jo and Patty remember that it was not only an extremely terrifying experience but it was also very humiliating for Allegra.

Fortunately, there were only a few patients in the clinic at the time, and they were rescheduled and sent home. Later that day, when lab results confirmed that the anthrax attack was indeed a hoax, the clinic reopened, and staff members saw the afternoon patients as planned.

Reflecting on this event with me, Patty recalled the predictable shock and fear that she and her colleagues felt at the time. "Well, of course we had talked about the possibility of something happening at the clinic, but it's like being in a car accident—you don't really think it could happen to you . . . until it does." And unlike a random car accident, this incident was one of targeted terror. As Patty put it, with a considerable understatement that I was to hear often from clinic staff members who had experienced extreme incidents, "Someone did not like us, obviously, and did not want us to be here."

But Patty's recollection of the event also included no small measure of pride at how well she and her coworkers had managed the anthrax threat. "We were a well-oiled machine. We were right on it. No one panicked. The drills we had gone through [in the event of a bomb threat] paid off. And yeah, it was very scary . . . but we knew exactly what to do."

In the aftermath of the incident, no one resigned, not even Allegra, who had been subjected to the grueling decontamination procedures. Both Jo and Patty acknowledged that they could not remember for certain whether any patients stopped coming to the clinic. They did remember, however, the outpouring of support from patients and others in the community. As one of them said, "Some of our patients went out of their way to tell us, 'We're sorry this happened to you, we want you to be here, we're going to keep coming here.'"

A FIRE IN THE SOUTH:
THE STAFF OF MAGNOLIA STREET CLINIC

"I've been here twelve years. . . . There have been bomb threats where we had to evacuate. . . . We've had anthrax threats, we've had glue put in our doors so we couldn't get into the clinic. . . . [S]o we've had a lot of things going on over the years, and because we got through them, we thought we were invincible. So when the call about the fire came, it was like we were shot in the heart." So said Vicki, a nurse at a clinic in a southern state that was devastated by fire not long ago. On a conference call with Vicki and her fellow staff members, I heard similar accounts of others' shock and horror when they first were alerted about the nighttime fire.

Carla, a counselor at the Magnolia Street Clinic, regularly tracked the various extremist antiabortion Web sites because of the threats directed at Deb, the owner of the clinic, and the clinic itself. Like Jo and Patty, Carla said, "As much preparation as we've had, the drills and stuff like that, and as involved as I've been with the Web sites, I was just completely floored by the phone call, and in utter disbelief. As prepared as you think you are for this kind of thing, you never really are."

As both Vicki's and Carla's comments make clear, Magnolia Street was no stranger to troubles of various kinds. The clinic had sustained unsuccessful arson attempts over the years. Deb was in near-constant litigation with protesters because of her attempts to limit their very aggressive "sidewalk counseling" of patients, which often involved screaming epithets at staff and patients through a bullhorn. But this fire was of a different order entirely. The damage to the clinic was so severe it was impossible to conduct daily operations there. The staff's reaction was summed up by Sue, the clinic bookkeeper, when she recalled the brief period when the firefighters allowed the staff to enter the building to reclaim what was salvageable: "Stepping over the broken glass and seeing the smoke damage, and slipping on the wet floors—and seeing the building you love just trashed . . . I felt I was in the middle of a war zone."

But the story I heard from the seven or eight staff members of Magnolia Street about the fire is not only one of heartbreak and anger. It is also a story of quite extraordinary resolve among a group of women to triumph over their unknown enemy and keep doing the job they loved. They were able to start up the clinic again, thanks to effective leadership, a history of goodwill built up over the years in key sectors of the surrounding community, and unusually intense bonds among a staff ("sisters," as one put it) with a shared sense of mission.

Deb was out of town when the fire occurred. The morning after the fire, Barb, the clinic receptionist, picked her up at the airport, "dreading" having to take her to the burned-out building. As Barb and other staff members told it, Deb wept for a bit and then swung into action. Fortunately, she and others were able to salvage the appointment book and most patient files. The staff set up a card table outside the clinic—"We got a lot of sunburn"—greeted patients who showed up for their appointments, referred them to another facility, and called other patients to reschedule. A local doctor, a long-standing ally of the clinic, agreed to see patients who were scheduled for follow-up care at his private office. Various people in the surrounding community came by with baskets of food for the staff and expressions of support. In the midst of all this, Deb arranged for several sessions of group therapy with a mental health professional to process feelings about the fire.

The quite astonishing speed at which the Magnolia Street Clinic was able to reopen was due both to Deb's can-do personality and the cooperation she received from the various agencies with which she was dealing. To expedite insurance claims, the fire chief worked overtime to produce a report for her the first day after the fire. The local police chief expressed his deep personal sympathy to Deb and other staff and pledged to do all he could, along with federal agents of the Bureau of Alcohol, Tobacco, and Firearms, to find the perpetrator. Workers from a cleaning company that the clinic had done business with for years came immediately to start cleaning soot from carpets and walls, and "worked miracles," according to the staff. An office-supply company that also had a longtime relationship with the clinic donated new furniture to replace what had been burned beyond reclamation.

But perhaps the most generous and crucial response was that of the contractor in charge of reopening the clinic. The original builder of the clinic, he too had a long and cordial relationship with Deb and many of the staff. As Sue put it, "I think he was as upset as we were. . . . He and his men were here working seven days a week, from sunup to sundown, just to get us to the point where we could see patients in the building again." When one of the clinic staff members thanked a worker for the long hours that he was putting in, he replied, "Well, you were here for my wife when she needed you." Within six weeks of the fire, the staff was back in the beautifully restored offices, without the loss of a single team member.

Such responses reminded me of the famous saying by the late Massachusetts congressman Tip O'Neill: "All politics is local." The extraordinary degree of cooperation that Magnolia Street received from the community is not unique in the world of abortion provision, but it can hardly be taken for granted. The response of Magnolia's contractor contrasts sharply with a recent major development in the abortion wars: the efforts of antiabortion contractors in a number of states to organize boycotts of new facilities being built by Planned Parenthood. This has led to lengthy and costly delays in the opening of these new centers. Similarly, hearing of the local police chief's immediate expressions of sympathy to the Magnolia staff and his resolve to find the perpetrators, I recalled the tepid response of law enforcement officers when protesters laid siege to the Philadelphia clinic where I was a board member in the 1980s. "They [the protesters] can close us at will, and the cops won't do a damn thing," the clinic director said in disgust.

The supportive response that the Magnolia Street Clinic received undeniably speaks to O'Neill's emphasis on the local. This clinic had been a fixture in the community for almost thirty years. Deb, who was part of the clinic from the start, had very deliberately set out to cultivate positive relationships with the various agencies that she was now so dependent on. Another part of the explanation, I believe, is that while many Americans may be ambivalent about abortion, they are unequivocally opposed to terrorism, particularly since 9/11. The abortion-providing community had insisted for years to law officials and to the media that clinics were subject to acts that could only be construed as terrorism—murders, kidnappings, fire bombings, and so on—but such arguments were often ignored. However, the events surrounding 9/11 made it easier for many, including those in Magnolia's community, to comprehend the violent attacks on the clinics as authentic domestic terrorism.

Despite the various acts of support, however, the staff, predictably, acknowledged feeling traumatized by the fire. Kate, a medical assistant, spoke of "bursting into tears" as she waited at a car repair place shortly after the event. Barb told of the disorientation she felt at losing her workplace: "Your family life can be screwed up, your relationships, whatever is going on in your personal life, those might be screwed up too, but you *know* you've got the security of your job—'Okay, it's eight-thirty, I'm going to go to work, I can focus on the patients'—and suddenly it's gone! I felt violated."

Understandably, some husbands, parents, partners, and others raised the question of whether it was wise to continue working at Magnolia—which the staff, to a woman, did not want to hear. As in other extreme situations, survivors felt understood only by others who had been there. "They [family members] were sympathetic but missed the depth of it," as Sue said.

For the Magnolia staff, being together in the days after the fire was their salvation. "I just felt this tremendous need to be around my coworkers. . . . Pulling together is what really saved all of us," said Carla. Kate agreed and went on to say, "The only people who knew what I was feeling were my sisters here at the clinic." She then told of the emotional turning point for the staff, when they spent a weekend preparing for the clinic to reopen. "I have never been more proud of the people that I work with than on that weekend. . . . We had boxes coming in, and everyone was assigned a room, and we were singing and laughing. It was just . . . amazing."

DOUBLE TROUBLE IN THE NORTHEAST: ABBY'S STORY

Abby Trudeau, who directs a clinic in a northeastern city that offers both abortions and gynecological services, has for the past several years been picketed regularly at her home by antiabortion protesters. One of the people who show up at her house is a well-known militant within the antiabortion movement who has been ordered by a judge to remove material from his Web site that urges violent actions against abortion providers. The doctor who works in Abby's clinic is also picketed on a regular basis at his home.

When protesters distributed letters asking "Do you know your neighbor kills babies?" to Abby's neighbors, they were repulsed and expressed sympathy for Abby. As she put it, "Whatever the neighbors felt about abortion, they knew they didn't want crazy people in their neighborhood." At one point her neighbors even got together and wrote a letter to the main protester, telling him that he was not welcome in their neighborhood. While touched by the gesture, Abby told the group that such a letter was actually counterproductive, given that in her view, this individual craved attention more than anything.

Abby, needless to say, is upset about the picketing at her house. When it first started, she was, by her admission, "hysterical." After several years she has more or less gotten used to it but finds it extremely annoying, although no longer very frightening. "Actually, the people I am most scared of are the ones who *don't* picket regularly at my house or clinic," she explains. "It's the loners who read the extremist Web sites that I'm most afraid of—it's them I think about at night, or if I'm home alone."

But Abby's problems go beyond this very uncomfortable intrusion into her neighborhood. Although it is in the "liberal" Northeast, her clinic exists in a local political environment that is particularly challenging. Since the clinic's opening in a narrow downtown alleyway without sidewalks, there has been protesting and "sidewalk counseling" at the entrance. The staff has called the police because of numerous incidents of harassment of patients and employees. The police required the protesters to get permits, but the city refused to issue any, saying that the street in question was too small for such protests. The protesters continued their activities without a permit, and the police continued to issue citations.

Ultimately the antiabortion activists sued the city in federal court, claiming civil rights violations because of the city's failure to issue permits for their protest activities. A judge ruled that the permit requirement was unconstitutional, because the protesters were acting as individuals, not as a group. More lawsuits and countersuits were filed. A mayor who had been quite supportive of the clinic decided not to run for reelection and was replaced by someone far less sympathetic. In an act that Abby and her colleagues found deeply demoralizing, the city agreed to pay the protesters a large cash settlement. The new mayor suggested in a recent meeting with Abby that the whole mess, which has now dragged on for about four years, is the clinic's fault and that the clinic should pay the city's legal expenses.

Adding insult to injury, the protesters taunt clinic staff members by calling out their full names, and in some cases their addresses, hinting that this information was obtained by a private investigator who was paid for with the settlement money. The last time I spoke with Abby, in the summer of 2008, protesters were still a constant presence.

A BUTYRIC ACID ATTACK IN THE SOUTH: LINDA'S STORY

Butyric acid is a clear, colorless liquid with an extremely unpleasant odor reminiscent of vomit. Starting in the early 1990s, antiabortion activists began to stealthily introduce this acid into abortion clinics, forcing offices to close temporarily and costing thousands of dollars in cleanup costs. As mentioned earlier, the NAF estimates that there had been about one hundred such attacks on clinics in the United States and Canada by the end of the 1990s, costing in excess of $1 million in damages.

Linda Johnson is the director of a clinic in a midsized southern city that experienced such an attack. Now in her sixties, she has vivid memories of a close friend who died after an illegal abortion before *Roe,* and this experience, more than anything else, brought her to work in this field. Each time we speak, I am struck by her humanity, and by her stubborn optimism in the face of very challenging circumstances.

Linda's clinic had also experienced an anthrax threat, bomb threats, and various blockades, but hands down, the butyric acid attack was the most difficult challenge in her thirty-odd years of abortion care: "It was just horrible! The smell was unbearable; it took us forever to clean up. It cost us $23,000 . . . and even today, *ten years later,* sometimes you can still get a whiff of it." What haunts Linda the most about the incident is that on the day of the attack, her clinic was offering prenatal services. "One woman who was there, she was early in pregnancy, she kept asking us, 'Will this damage the fetus?' . . . We had to say that we honestly didn't know. She was so scared, she ended up terminating. I still think about her."

When I asked Linda how the other tenants in the building that houses her clinic responded, I was surprised to hear her say that they had all been supportive, even though they too were affected by the smell. "They saved their anger for the crazies, not for us," Linda said. Our conversation then turned to similar instances in which others had been caught in the crossfire of the war against her clinic: the postman who had to undergo precautionary medical procedures after he delivered the anthrax threat; the FedEx delivery workers who were subjected to verbal abuse by protesters; the building tenants, inconvenienced yet again when they had to evacuate because of a phoned-in bomb threat. In each case, according to Linda, these individuals acted gracefully and professionally. As the postman who delivered the purported anthrax letter said to her, "I'm just doing my job."

Reflecting on these stories, I realized that an underreported aspect of the abortion wars in America is the millions of supportive "civilians" who quietly aid the community of providers, some with a history of deep gratitude for the abortion they or a loved one once had. For example, a veteran East Coast clinic director told me that when her clinic was subject to one of the first "invasions" by the group Operation Rescue, a gruff waitress in a coffee shop across the street, who until then had never voiced support for the clinic, quickly emptied the place and invited the director to bring in the terrified patients to wait till the police had cleared the clinic of protesters.

To be sure, not all clinics have been recipients of such acts of kindness and solidarity. And even those that have received such support still have plenty to worry about. Many of the women I have mentioned in this chapter have one or more personal nemeses—protesters who seem particularly fixated on them. Almost as a casual afterthought during our conversation, Jo mentioned that an FBI agent had recently informed her that someone against whom she had once had a restraining order had just been released from prison. Linda told me about her longtime stalker, a "screamer" who lives in the same town and denounces her whenever their paths cross, whether it's in a grocery store or, in one particularly upsetting incident, in the nursing home where Linda's mother was convalescing. But I remain convinced that the antiabortion movement would be much further along in its goal of stopping abortion care if not for the largely overlooked determination of many decent everyday Americans to stand with the provider community against its foes.

STAYING THE COURSE

One of the questions that has intrigued me for years is, how do those who have experienced such unacceptable violence and threatening behavior at their workplaces and elsewhere manage to remain in this field? One way is by finding great strength in one another. They have deep bonds not only with immediate coworkers but also with their colleagues all over the country. The members of the abortion-providing community, sustained by periodic national gatherings and participation in various lively Listservs, have stronger and more emotional ties than other medical groups precisely, I believe, because of their shared history of confronting intimidation.

On a day-to-day basis, humor also helps. To give an example: One administrator recounted to a group of her colleagues how she left her clinic one day just as a protester on her steps was intoning, "Holy Mother of God." Without missing a beat, she said, "It's okay— you can call me Ginny." The dedication of the many volunteers who help out at the clinics, particularly as escorts to help guide patients past demonstrators, is also very moving to the staff.

But I have learned that the main thing that keeps people in this uniquely challenging field is, hardly surprisingly, a profound belief in what they do. When I asked Abby, arguably the most beleaguered of all those mentioned in this chapter, how she remained in this job year after year, she seemed genuinely puzzled by my question. "I don't think anything could stop me from what I am doing," she said. "It's the patients that keep me going. Just knowing what a positive impact we have on their lives, and how appreciative they are. Not even once has it crossed my mind to stop doing this work."

IV

REGULATING ABORTION

"Some will rob you with a six-gun, some with a fountain pen." I think about these words from a Woody Guthrie song of the Depression frequently while contemplating the challenges faced by abortion providers. While nothing is worse than violent attacks against providers and their patients, these incidents, thankfully, happen only occasionally. Yet clinic directors deal *every day* with a host of cumbersome regulations that make offering abortion care seem like running an endless obstacle course.

I am not suggesting that regulation is a bad thing, in abortion or elsewhere in the health-care system. I believe very strongly that all health-care facilities should be overseen by public agencies to assure patient safety and well-being. But much of the regulation to which abortion care is subject is unreasonable by any standard. It is impossible to escape the conclusion that much of the regulatory apparatus—court rulings, state laws (of which there are more than four hundred), local ordinances, and so on—that governs abortion is simply intended to make the provision of this service unfeasible from the provider's standpoint and undesirable from the pregnant woman's standpoint.

The intent of some of those who seek to regulate abortion was revealed several years ago in a shocking statement from Bill Napoli, a legislator in South Dakota. Napoli was a leader of that state's effort to put on the ballot a measure that would have limited abortion to cases in which a woman's life was in danger, with no exception for pregnancies resulting from rape or incest. When a journalist asked Napoli how he could justify the lack of exceptions, the legislator insisted that some exceptions could be possible. Here are the circumstances under which he found abortion permissible: "[She] would be a rape victim, brutally raped, savaged. The girl was a virgin. She was religious. She planned on saving her virginity until she was married.

She was . . . sodomized as bad as you can possibly make it, and is impregnated. I mean, that girl could be so messed up, physically and psychologically, that carrying that child could very well threaten her life." Napoli's statement is so bizarre and coldhearted—what about a woman who was *not* a virgin who was similarly brutalized? or who was a virgin but not a religious one? or who was raped but not "savaged" to the degree he deemed necessary?—that it no doubt contributed to voters' repudiation of the measure in 2006. (Voters rejected a slightly different version of the ban in 2008.)

I am not suggesting that most of those who seek to limit abortion would go as far as Napoli in deciding who is abortion-worthy. But the thicket of regulations that face would-be abortion providers in many states makes it difficult for many trained doctors to incorporate abortion care into their regular practices. Compliance with complex regulations is easier for a network of clinics, such as the Planned Parenthood operation, or individual clinics with a higher volume of patients and the resources to hire an attorney to help monitor state and local regulations. But for a small clinic or a lone practitioner, dealing with regulations can be overwhelming. In the pages that follow, I offer a glimpse into the different kinds of regulations and legal rulings that govern this field, and that contribute to the shortage of abortion providers in many areas.

TRAP LAWS

One expert on these regulations is an insightful and witty woman whose day job is running an abortion clinic in a southern state. She also blogs, under the name Moiv, on various progressive Web sites about the unique challenges facing abortion providers.

Moiv's comments about clinic "regs" (as providers refer to them) are reminiscent of Guthrie's lyrics: "The TRAP [Targeted Regulation of Abortion Providers] is what providers of abortion care worry about even more than the threat of bombs and bullets. . . . While the possible loss of *Roe* certainly looms on the horizon, it's not at the top of the list for me. . . . Just about anyone in America's abortion-providing community will tell you that the most imminent and potent threat to the continued existence of safe and legal abortion care in most parts of the United States is the TRAP—and that's just what it says it is."

What are these TRAP laws to which Moiv refers? The Center for Reproductive Rights, which, along with the American Civil Liberties Union, provides major pro bono legal defense for abortion providers, offers this explanation: "TRAP laws target the medical practices of doctors who provide abortions, and impose on them burdensome requirements which are different and more stringent than the legal requirements imposed on other medical practices. These excessive and unnecessary government regulations increase the cost and scarcity of abortion services, harming women's health and inhibiting their reproductive choices."

Whenever I hear colleagues in the abortion-providing community discuss the TRAP laws, I am astonished that they are able to provide any abortions at all. Besides the significant rise in costs, these laws threaten patient privacy by authorizing unannounced inspections when patients are present and impose onerous administrative policies that are not applied to other health-care facilities, such as requiring facilities to hire registered nurses to do tasks for which they are overqualified. The demand that abortion clinics performing second-trimester procedures meet the requirements of an ambulatory surgery center (ASC) is a common TRAP law, imposed currently in about ten states. ASCs are health-care facilities that are considerably more sophisticated than outpatient clinics and physicians' offices. They are used for surgical procedures that do not require an overnight stay but that are quite invasive, such as removal of lymph nodes and bladder tumors.

As Tracy Weitz and Bonnie Scott Jones point out in an article in the *American Journal of Public Health*, TRAP laws requiring abortion clinics to be licensed as ASCs do not require such licensing for other medical procedures of "comparable complexity and risk," such as surgical completion of miscarriage, sigmoidoscopy, and minor neck and throat surgeries. They offer a case study of Texas, where the ASC requirement was imposed on clinics offering abortions after sixteen weeks of gestation. In 2003 more than twenty providers in the state offered abortions beyond sixteen weeks, and 3,066 such abortions were performed in the state that year. When the 2004 law requiring certification as an ASC went into effect, almost none of these clinics were able to comply with the necessary physical renovations. One clinic director told Weitz and Scott Jones that it would have cost three quarters of a million dollars to make the required upgrades. The number of post-sixteen-week abortions in Texas in 2004 fell to 403, an 85 percent decrease from the year before.

I spoke with a clinic director in Texas whose facility was not able to afford to upgrade to ASC status. Before the 2004 law went into effect, this clinic could perform abortions up to twenty weeks' gestation, though the vast majority of its patients were seen earlier. Deeply frustrated, the director told me, "Every week we still have to turn away women who are too far along for the present limit. Throughout 2004 I kept demographic stats on our turn-aways, and as you would probably suppose, they were overwhelmingly young, unmarried, and members of racial and ethnic minorities." Referring these women to the handful of clinics in the state that ultimately managed to receive ASC status was not really an option, she said. "These women can't afford to pay several thousand dollars for an abortion that used to cost a fraction of that here."

There is a particularly cruel irony with these TRAP laws. On the one hand, rules such as the ASC requirement have worked to create a serious shortage in the number of facilities that provide second-trimester procedures. On the other hand, various other common abortion regulations have worked to create a higher demand for these later procedures. Everyone—the public, patients, providers themselves—agrees that earlier abortions are preferable to later ones. Such abortions are safer, cheaper, and for many people more morally acceptable. Yet 150,000 women each year still require abortions in the second trimester. For some in especially heartbreaking cases, it is not until the second trimester, or even later, that certain fetal anomalies become known or the pregnancy becomes a threat to the woman's health. The other major recipients of second-trimester procedures—teens and low-income women—often have difficulties getting the necessary money and, depending on what state they are in, complying with waiting periods and parental notification and consent laws. By the time the money has been found and the restrictions complied with, many of these women are in their second trimester. Studies by social scientists on the impact of these kinds of regulations show they can lead to fewer abortions *and* to an increase in those occurring later in pregnancy.

STATE MANDATES ON "INFORMED CONSENT"

Another area in which antiabortion legislators have been very active is the imposition of mandated "informed consent" scripts—information that providers must make available to patients verbally and/or through written materials. Moiv, commenting on the *sixty-nine* printed pages of regulations covering abortion care (and abortion care only) in Texas, offers this example of what can befall an abortion provider in a hostile environment.

> Yesterday morning your patient called the clinic to arrange an appointment, and received the requisite state-mandated information "orally by telephone," meaning that she heard a message you recorded for that purpose. She came in for her appointment today as scheduled, and you performed her abortion procedure. The patient is relieved and grateful, and thanks you repeatedly before she goes home. Everything's fine, right? Wrong. According to your own surgical notes, you began her procedure at 10:37 AM, but the documentation in her chart says she heard the recorded information yesterday morning at 10:38. The law says the waiting period has to be a full twenty-four hours.
>
> Whether you overlooked the documented time, misread someone else's bad handwriting, or simply forgot to check your watch doesn't matter; none of those excuses is a defense under the statute.

Moiv then offers another example.

> Thank goodness, this next patient looks like a safer proposition. Her chart says she received her required information way last week. The only thing is, she and her counselor hit it off and got started talking during their session, and somehow it slipped the counselor's mind to have the patient initial

every single blank on the state's certification form and sign it—you know, the form that says you told her every single item of misinformation on the government's lengthy list.

What is this "misinformation" that Moiv refers to? In thirty-three states, specific laws govern the informed-consent information that abortion providers must offer their patients. Authentic informed consent is not the problem. In 1982 the President's Commission for the Study of Ethical Problems in Medicine and Biomedical and Behavioral Research released an authoritative review of the principles of informed consent, stating that this practice should include three related elements: patients must possess the capacity to make decisions about their care; their participation in these decisions must be voluntary; and they must be given adequate, appropriate information to make the decision before them. The abortion-providing community has no quarrel with this understanding of informed consent. From the earliest days of legal abortion provision in the United States—nearly ten years before the commission's 1982 report—providers were implementing such informed consent as part of the new field of abortion counseling.

As abortion became more and more politicized in the years after *Roe*, some state legislatures began to impose heavily ideological requirements on informed consent. These requirements truly make a mockery of the principles set out by the commission, especially the one that stipulates that patients must be given "adequate, appropriate information." In a rigorous review conducted by the Guttmacher Institute in 2007, researchers found that twenty-three of the thirty-three states that had specific requirements for informed consent in abortion included "information not in keeping with the fundamental tenets of informed consent."

One of the major areas of misinformation noted by the Guttmacher study is that of the alleged health risks of abortion, including breast cancer, reduction of future fertility, and mental illness. All of these supposed "findings" are misleading, if not simply untrue. The alleged link between abortion and breast cancer has been a favorite antiabortion talking point for some time. Early in George W. Bush's presidency, this allegation was displayed on the Web site of the prestigious National Cancer Institute (NCI). In response to many complaints from within the scientific community about the NCI's capitulation to ideologues within the Bush administration, the institute convened the world's leading experts to examine all available evidence on the topic, and in early 2003 issued a statement acknowledging that "induced abortion is not associated with an increase in breast cancer risk." Nevertheless, more than five years after that statement, the written materials given to abortion patients in six states still include inaccurate information about the risk of breast cancer after an abortion.

The situation is similar with respect to infertility and abortion. The overwhelming consensus in the medical community is that this is not a concern. A leading medical textbook in this field, *A Clinician's Guide to Medical and Surgical Abortion*, states flatly that "vacuum aspiration during the first trimester, the most commonly performed procedure, poses virtually no risk to future reproductive health. Specifically, there are . . . no measurable risks for secondary infertility." Nevertheless, women in South Dakota are informed, without any qualification, that "infertility is a risk of abortion." Similarly, the Texas materials claim—again without any contextualization—that abortion-related complications "may make it difficult or impossible to become pregnant in the future or carry a pregnancy to term." Given that studies show that about half of all abortion recipients plan to have children (or additional children) in the future, these women are being unnecessarily and irresponsibly frightened.

A number of states require the abortion provider to inform the patient of the pain allegedly felt by the fetus (or "unborn child," according to South Dakota's required script) at any stage of the abortion, though medical experts say that pain receptors are not developed until between the twenty-third and thirtieth weeks of gestation. Similarly, though 90 percent of abortions occur in the first trimester, women in a number of states are given detailed descriptions of fetal development throughout pregnancy, including, in the Guttmacher study's words, "loaded language in an apparently deliberate attempt to 'personify' the fetus."

But to me, the most offensive aspect of such state-mandated counseling is the distorted information that women are given about the psychological impact of abortion. Since the 1980s, the antiabortion movement has relentlessly pushed the idea of a "post-abortion syndrome" (PAS), claiming that recipients of abortion will suffer long-term mental health effects from having the procedure. I remember well the surprising turn of events when this issue first attracted national attention. When Ronald Reagan took office in 1981, part of his payback to his antiabortion constituency was the appointment of individuals who passed the abortion litmus test. For surgeon general, the nation's leading spokesperson on health matters, he selected C. Everett Koop, a distinguished pediatric surgeon who had no public health experience. Dr. Koop did have, however, a long track record as an outspoken opponent of abortion.

Shortly after taking office, Koop was essentially ordered by the White House to produce a report "proving" the negative mental health effects of abortion. He enraged his fellow conservatives in the White House (and pleasantly surprised liberals, including me) when he failed to produce such a report. His commitment to scientific integrity overrode his loyalty to the president. As he said in a letter to Reagan, "I have concluded in my review of this issue that, at this time, the available scientific evidence about the psychological sequelae of abortion cannot support either the preconceived beliefs of those pro-life or those pro-choice."

Since the Koop incident, several major studies by researchers have refuted the notion of post-abortion syndrome. A task force of the American Psychological Association has several times found that the major psychological effect of an abortion is a feeling of relief. Dr. Nada Stottland, who in 2008 served as president of the American Psychiatric Association and whose specialty is reproductive health issues, has repeatedly discredited the PAS notion; as she told the *New York Times*, PAS "is a made-up disease" that exists nowhere in psychiatric literature. This is not to deny that a small number of women do have some psychological difficulties after an abortion, and for them follow-up care is warranted and recommended by providers. Perhaps the most sensible statement on the subject is a study published in the *Archives of General Psychiatry* in 2000; it concluded that the best indicator for a woman's health after an abortion is her mental health before the abortion.

In spite of mental health experts' rejection of the notion of the negative mental health effects of abortion, the antiabortion movement has continued to push this idea and has been successful in making it part of some states' mandated counseling. In these states, women are informed that abortion can lead to suicidal thoughts or to PAS. In other words, women who may be at an especially vulnerable moment in their lives are being told by authority figures that they may become suicidal or mentally disturbed. As I will discuss, mental health professionals were especially dismayed when a recent Supreme Court decision legitimized the notion of PAS.

Why do I find the content of these state mandates on "abortion counseling" so offensive? It's not only because giving patients (or anyone else, for that matter) incorrect medical information is profoundly unethical. I also find these mandates disturbing because I have seen authentic abortion counseling at its best. Early in my career as a researcher in this field, I was fortunate to encounter Terry Beresford, one of the pioneers in the field of abortion counseling. Beresford had been the director of counseling at the Preterm Clinic in Washington, D.C., one of the first freestanding clinics in the country. When I met her some years later, she was considered a leading trainer in the field, and she generously allowed me to observe some of the training sessions she held for counselors from clinics all over the Northeast.

The abortion counseling promoted by Beresford and her colleagues is, to put it mildly, light-years away from the kind of state-mandated misinformation that goes on today. It involves factual informed consent that tells the patient what her forthcoming procedure will involve, including a medically accurate discussion of the risks as well as instructions for post-abortion care. But this form of counseling aspires to much more than that. I learned two especially important points from Beresford about abortion counseling. First, the decision to have an abortion absolutely has to be that of the pregnant woman, made freely, without coercion from others. Second, all women are not alike, and a "one size fits all" approach to counseling is not appropriate. As Beresford and several colleagues have written, in a chapter in *A Clinician's Guide to Medical and Surgical Abortion*, "Appropriate, sensitive communication *that focuses on the needs of each patient* is fundamental to quality abortion care. . . . The key to achieving effective clinician-patient communication is empathy— the ability to give the clear, comforting message that one is not superior to the patient but shares with her a common bond of humanity."

The chapter includes recommendations as to how to deal with special situations, such as counseling patients who have been sexually abused and counseling women from culturally diverse backgrounds who may be facing a particular conflict between the values of their families or country of origins and the values of their country of residence.

Unfortunately, this kind of quality counseling is becoming increasingly hard to deliver in many abortion facilities. In part this is due to costs. So much money must be expended on security issues, such as twenty-four-hour video cameras, especially thick bullet-resistant glass, and so on, that budgets for training and hiring good counselors have become imperiled. But this form of counseling has also become scarcer because in so many places the time that can be reasonably devoted to patient counseling is consumed by compliance with state-imposed guidelines.

Abortion providers in the twenty-three states that require them to give some misinformation to patients are in a difficult bind. On the one hand, if they don't comply, they will be breaking the law and putting themselves and their facilities at legal risk. On the other hand, by imparting information that they know to be untrue, these doctors are violating one of the core tenets of medical ethics. Some get around this by openly making it clear to the patient that they disagree with what they are bound by law to say. Others add disclaimers to the mandated message. One provider in the South shared with colleagues on a Listserv how he gave the breast cancer message required by his state: "By law I am required to tell you that there is a 'possibility' of an increased risk of breast cancer later in life for women who have had an abortion. However, there is no medical evidence to support this idea. In fact, this has been taken very seriously and proven by medical research not to be so." This same doctor also added, after enumerating the list of other possible risks from abortion he was obliged by law to impart, "To put the risk of abortion in perspective, let me say this: Be sure to buckle your seatbelt and drive carefully on the way to the clinic and back home. Your trip to and from the clinic in your car will probably be the most dangerous part of your abortion." Interestingly, in four of the states that mandate content to be distributed to patients, doctors are specifically permitted to dissociate themselves from that material.

The providers who arguably face the greatest ethical challenges are those in South Dakota. A recent regulation has made an already very hostile climate worse. As I write this, there is one clinic left in the state, and it flies in doctors from out of state because local doctors fear working there. In the summer of 2008, the courts upheld a 2005 law that stipulated that a woman getting an abortion in South Dakota must be told by her doctor that the procedure "will terminate the life of a whole, separate, unique, living human being." Quite astonishingly to me, the Eighth Circuit Court held that Planned Parenthood had failed to show that the required statement is "ideological, untruthful, [or] misleading." Doctors providing abortions in South Dakota also have to inform patients in writing of the litany of antiabortion talking points we have already discussed, including the alleged connection of abortion to suicide, infertility, and so on. The woman receiving the document must sign it and the doctor must certify in writing that she received this information and understood it, "as far as the physician could ascertain." The failure of a doctor to comply with all these steps can result in license suspension or revocation and a class 2 misdemeanor. Commenting on this alarming measure, Zita Lazzarini, a health policy lawyer, correctly noted that it has relevance well beyond the physicians serving the seven hundred or so women who receive abortions in South Dakota each year: "These provisions mark a substantial inroad into the physician-patient relationship that ought to worry any practicing physician."

REGULATING TEENAGERS

Teenagers seeking abortions have long been the particular object of regulations by state legislatures. Thirteen states have laws requiring parental notification before an abortion, and twenty-four states have laws requiring parental consent (a handful of states allow a grandparent to substitute for a parent). A majority of Americans, including those who consider themselves to be pro-choice, support these laws. But the reality is that most teenagers, especially younger ones, do tell at least one parent of their intention to abort. It is very common at clinics to see mothers, and sometimes fathers, accompanying their daughters for this procedure. As I have seen repeatedly over the years, when teens are counseled in clinics, they are typically asked if they have discussed their pregnancy with their parents. If the answer is no, often the counselors will offer to help the teenager role-play the way she might inform her parents or propose to convene a joint session with her and her parents.

If clinic staff members appear to agree with legislators and the public at large about the desirability of parental involvement, why is the provider community so strongly against these reasonable-sounding parental notification and consent laws? The answer, like so much else in the abortion-providing world, is the realization that "one size fits all" policies just don't make sense. In a small number of cases, informing the parents of a teenager's pregnancy and intent to abort can lead to physical abuse or rejection from the house. Sometimes worse tragedies can result. In the past few years, providers in different parts of the country have discussed with each other a perceptible rise in the number of women—mainly, though not exclusively, teenagers—who are taking matters into their own hands because abortion has become inaccessible to them. In some of these cases, the main reason behind the desperate acts is the fear of telling parents.

Linda, the director of a southern clinic whom we met in the last chapter, wrote on an e-mail list that her local hospital sees between twelve and twenty patients per year who have attempted to self-abort or who have been subjected to inept illegal abortions. In a follow-up interview, she told me of several young women who swallowed whole bottles of quinine pills, believed by some to have abortifacient properties, with castor oil. Most disturbingly, she told me about a teenaged patient who came to her clinic after a failed attempt at self-abortion: "She had burned herself so badly with bleach that we couldn't even examine her [because] her vaginal tissue was so painful."

To be sure, this rise in extralegal attempts at abortion stems from several sources. Some women, especially younger ones, are just too poor to afford an abortion, even a first-trimester one. Others stay away from clinics because of shame and stigma or misinformation about what occurs there. But some teenagers stay away because they cannot surmount the obstacles that have been put in their way by regulations.

Two recent tragedies involving teenaged couples give a sobering reminder of the price paid because of the laws surrounding abortion for teens. In each case, one in Michigan, the other in Texas, the young couples at some point sought an abortion, which in both states requires parental consent. Each of the couples apparently was given inadequate and misleading information, one by a CPC, the other by a private ob-gyn's office.

What these young people *should* have been informed of was the option of a judicial bypass: a measure set up precisely for teenagers who feel they would be at risk if they told their parents about their pregnancy and intended abortion. Additionally, Erica Basoria, the young Texan woman, apparently was misinformed as to how late in her pregnancy she could legally obtain an abortion.

Instead, feeling that they had no other recourse, each couple attempted to end the pregnancy themselves. In the Michigan case, the young man, with his girlfriend's consent, hit her abdomen repeatedly with a small baseball bat until she miscarried. In Texas, again with his girlfriend's consent, the young man stomped on her belly, producing a stillbirth of twins. Both young men were arrested. In Michigan, the male in question was sentenced to community service—ironically, at a CPC, the kind of institution that had misled him in the first place! Most shocking, however, Geraldo Flores, the Texan, was convicted under the recently passed Texas Fetal Protection Law, and he is now serving a life sentence in a Texas prison for homicide. As of this writing, his case is under appeal.

Flores's life is most likely ruined, and needlessly so. His girlfriend, Erica Basoria, according to court reports, was initially ambivalent about abortion, though as events would show, in the end she was determined to end the pregnancy. But consider how different the outcome would have been if her ambivalence had been dealt with in a clinic, with a supportive counselor. This counselor probably would have sought, with her permission, to involve the two families in the decision-making. Also, the counselor no doubt would have raised the possibility of adoption. Whatever Basoria's ultimate decision, to continue the pregnancy or not, the result would have been far preferable to having a young man spend his life in jail.

I have thought a lot about this preventable tragedy. It is not simply that this couple was misinformed by Basoria's ob-gyn, or that their state had parental consent requirements, or that there were very

few abortion clinics in their immediate area. We can only speculate about the level of shame and ignorance about abortion and
contraception—indeed, about sexuality itself—these young people
experienced, raised as they were in a state that prides itself on its
abstinence-only sex education policies. Not surprisingly, Texas has
the second-highest rate of unplanned teen pregnancy in the United
States. It remains to be seen whether these two stories and similar
news accounts of other teenagers' attempts at self-abortion are just
rare tragic events that happened to capture the attention of ever-
hungry-for-sensation cable news stations or are cautionary tales of
what will be more common as abortion grows more inaccessible.

States with parental notification and consent regulations must
include a judicial bypass option, and this can be very helpful to teenagers with an unwanted pregnancy. A young woman goes before a
judge, essentially explains why informing her parents would be det-
rimental to her, and asks the court for a waiver of either consent or
notification. However, every lawyer I know who has helped teenagers
negotiate this system has commented on how intimidating, if not
terrifying, this process can be. As one lawyer told me, "Imagine being a scared fifteen-year-old, having to go before a judge and talk
about your sex life and other intimate details." Moreover, the judicial
bypass system is not immune to the intense politicization of abortion
that exists everywhere else in the United States. The sociologist Helena Silverstein has given in her book *Girls on the Stand* a very infor-
mative and alarming account of how courts treat pregnant minors.
In her exhaustive review of two hundred courts in three different
states (Alabama, Pennsylvania, and Tennessee), she found extraordinary disregard of both the letter and the spirit of the judicial bypass
option. In place of the impartiality that one would expect from legal proceedings, Silverstein found instances of judges who ordered
that minors receive counseling from pro-life ministries and who ap-
pointed attorneys for the "unborn child" at bypass hearings. In some
places it was so hard to find a judge willing to hear such cases that the
girl's pregnancy advanced too far for her to receive a legal abortion.

Let's look at how one court handled a minor's request for a
waiver. This case, not discussed by Silverstein, is one that the Colorado Court of Appeals heard in the summer of 2007. The sixteen-

year-old in question, "Jane Doe," asked a lower court for such a waiver and was denied. The appeals court affirmed this denial. In doing so, the court agreed with the trial court's finding of "clear and convincing evidence that the petitioner was not sufficiently mature to decide whether to have an abortion." This is quite baffling to me: two courts found an adolescent too immature to decide on an abortion but mature enough to have a child? To have a child, moreover, in a family context in which the girl apparently felt so estranged from her mother that she was willing to go through two court hearings in order to avoid having her mother find out about her pregnancy? This difficult relationship hardly promises that Jane Doe will receive support from her mother throughout the pregnancy and after the birth of her child.

How did the appeals court decide that Jane Doe was too immature to decide on an abortion? One factor it cited was that "petitioner exhibited only minimal understanding of the risks of the abortion procedure" and that "she had not considered any mental or emotional ramifications of abortion other than that it might lead to her 'becoming depressed or something like that.'" The hearing transcript notes that "petitioner knew that abortion carried risks and that 'you could die from having it, but it's rare.'"

Looking at this transcript, I came to the conclusion that the sixteen-year-old Jane Doe was more knowledgeable about the actual medical evidence of risks of abortion than the judges who decided her fate. At the time of her appearance before these two courts, she was ten weeks pregnant. The risk of death in the first trimester is 0.6 deaths per 100,000 abortions. The teenager was absolutely correct in saying that the possibility of death is "rare." With respect to her qualified statement that an abortion "might lead to depression," as we have already seen, she was also correct to suggest that this is only a slight possibility.

Another factor cited by the court in its determination of her "immaturity" was "her focus on her own needs." But sixteen-year-olds are *supposed* to be focused on their own needs! That is one of the major markers of adolescence. It appears therefore that Jane Doe wanted an abortion for the reason that many young women want an abortion: she recognized that she was not ready to be a parent. The judges in this instance were clearly substituting ideological judgments for

legal ones. If this Jane Doe had spouted the misinformation dissemi-
nated by the antiabortion movement about the physical and mental
risks of abortion, would these judges have deemed her sufficiently
mature for the procedure?

REGULATING MEDICAL PROCEDURES: THE SUPREME COURT DECISION IN *GONZALES V. CARHART*

"We've got to keep our patients safe and our doctors out of jail."
These are the words of a speaker I heard in the spring of 2007 at a national gathering of abortion providers. The meeting, by coincidence,
happened just a few days after the Supreme Court announced its decision in *Gonzales v. Carhart,* upholding a ban passed by Congress on
the procedure that doctors call "intact dilation and extraction" (or
intact D&E), which opponents have sensationalized as "partial birth
abortion." The ban provides for a two-year jail term and a fine of
$250,000 for those convicted of performing this procedure.

Normally I would be startled to hear a nationally known and
respected physician at a professional conference strategizing about
how to keep herself and her colleagues out of jail. Normally, moreover, I would not expect to see Congress or the Supreme Court place
its own judgments about appropriate medical practice over that of
the most relevant professional associations of doctors involved in a
particular branch of medicine. Indeed, the only doctor in the Senate
at the time this ban was passed was Tom Coburn of Oklahoma, an
antiabortion zealot who is on record as favoring the death penalty
for "abortionists and other people who take life." To no avail, the
American College of Obstetricians and Gynecologists, the Planned
Parenthood Federation of America, and the National Abortion Federation spoke out forcefully against this ban.

But of course nothing in American politics or jurisprudence is
"normal" when it comes to abortion. This decision arguably represents the first time in history that the Court has held that physicians
can be prohibited from using a specific medical procedure that they
deem necessary to benefit their patient's health. As Justice Anthony
Kennedy said in the majority's decision, "The law need not give abortion doctors unfettered choice in the course of their medical practice, nor should it elevate their status above other physicians in the

medical community." When I first read this statement, I was struck by how different in tone this was from the language used in the 1973 *Roe v. Wade* decision. Compare it to the following, from *Roe:* "The decision vindicates the right of the physician to administer medical treatment according to his professional judgment up to the points where important state interests provide compelling justifications for interventions. Up to this point, the abortion decision in all its aspects is inherently and primarily a medical decision, and basic responsibility for it must rest with the physician." Indeed, I remember at the time that *Roe* was handed down, many feminist health activists were upset that the Court was giving too much deference to the physician and not enough to the pregnant woman who was presumably making this decision.

From my vantage point as one who has studied the abortion-provider shortage for many years, I was also struck by the irony in Kennedy's statement that "abortion doctors" should not be given "unfettered choice in . . . their medical practice." Why not? Very few doctors in the United States perform abortions, and of those who do, only some perform second-trimester procedures. The intact D&E procedure was rarely performed. The complexities of this technique and the circumstances in which it is best used are known to a relatively small number of doctors. At the several trials that preceded the Supreme Court hearing, the government's "expert" witnesses did not include one physician who had ever performed the disputed procedure. One of the government's witnesses had never performed any kind of abortion.

One of the abortion doctors who should not be given "unfettered choice," according to Justice Kennedy, is George Majors, an African American ob-gyn I met at the conference. Over coffee, Majors, fit-looking and appearing to be in his sixties, told me that for years he has practiced in a very disadvantaged neighborhood in a large East Coast city. His decision to serve such a community was made from a deep political commitment; with his elite Ivy League medical training he could easily have chosen a more comfortable life in the suburbs. His patient load today consists mainly of low-income African Americans who are longtime residents of the city and recent African immigrants. Though trained as an ob-gyn, Majors provides a wide range of services, ranging from primary care to abortion. He is among the small number of abortion providers who provide second-trimester procedures. When I asked him whether he uses the intact D&E method, he sighed and told me, "Well, I *used* to do them. Sometimes it's just the safest way to go, because there is less blood loss. I don't know what I am going to do now."

What is this so-called partial birth abortion, and how did it happen that Congress and the Supreme Court are weighing in on medical procedures practiced by only a small number of physicians? To put this issue in context, about 90 percent of the approximately 1.2 million abortions in the United States occur in the first trimester of pregnancy. Nearly all of the remaining 10 percent occur in the second trimester, with only about 1 percent of all abortions occurring after twenty-one weeks of gestation. Of these second-trimester procedures, the vast majority are performed using a procedure called standard dilation and evacuation (D&E), in which the physician removes the fetus in pieces, which calls for inserting instruments into the uterus several times. An intact D&E abortion involves dilating the cervix, removing the fetus intact until only the skull remains in the uterus (because it is too large to pass through the cervix), then partially collapsing the skull so it can pass through the cervix safely for the woman. In certain situations, as Majors suggested, physicians deem this procedure safer than the alternative. The physician needs to make fewer passes into the uterus, the patient typically experiences less blood loss, and there is less risk of perforation. Sometimes the procedure is used in cases of wanted pregnancies that have gone horribly wrong, either because of severe fetal anomalies or because of threats to the pregnant woman's health or life. At the trials involving this procedure, medical experts testified that intact D&E may be the safest procedure for women with such conditions as uterine scars, bleeding disorders, and heart disease, among others. Another reason that this option is sometimes used is that it allows heartbroken parents to be able to hold and grieve for a partly intact fetus wrapped in a blanket.

The antiabortion movement has made political hay out of "partial birth abortion," or PBA, since the early 1990s, when one of their operatives infiltrated a medical conference and heard a presentation by one of the doctors who developed this technique. The decision to shift the debate over abortion from abstract moral principles to an actual description of abortion techniques was undeniably a brilliant strategy on the movement's part. The sensationalist campaign against this procedure, replete with pictures on the Senate floor of a full-term fetus with scissors at its skull, led to legislation banning the procedure in many states. More important, the PBA campaign promoted the mistaken cultural perception that many abortions take place very late in pregnancy, when in fact recent innovations in abortion technology, such as medication abortion and the MVA, mean that more abortions are taking place earlier in the first trimester. That intact D&E is used infrequently, is held by physicians to be the safest method in some situations, and is sometimes used for compassionate purposes—all this got lost in the shouting.

One way to comply with the Court's ruling is for providers to cause fetal demise before commencing the abortion. Some doctors already do this, by injecting a chemical agent, digoxin, into the woman's abdominal and uterine wall. However, this practice has not been uniformly accepted; some physicians believe that such injections are unnecessary, carry no medical benefit to the woman, and carry risks, however slight. "I'm going to have to subject my patient to something she doesn't need, just to comply with a law made by politicians," I heard one frustrated doctor say at a gathering called to discuss the decision. Nevertheless, providers who have not in the past used digoxin or similar agents are now doing so.

What will be the lasting impact of the *Gonzales v. Carhart* decision? Although we do not yet have hard data, anecdotal evidence from colleagues makes me believe that second-trimester abortion services are being cut back in some locations and are becoming even harder to find. But I fear that the impact of the decision will go beyond second-trimester provision and will have a chilling effect on abortion provision as a whole. Young physicians, even those contemplating offering only first-trimester abortion, have no doubt observed the hyperpoliticized nature of this branch of medicine, in which medical colleagues are threatened with huge fines and jail time. All but the most committed might reasonably conclude that taking on the identity of an abortion provider is simply not worth it.

There are other very unfortunate aspects of this Supreme Court decision. In a stunning upset of precedent, for the first time since 1973 and the *Roe* decision, the Court found constitutional a law restricting abortion that did not contain an exception to protect the health of the woman. The decision does state that the ban does not apply in cases where a woman's life is at stake. But it is not always so clear-cut in medical situations as to what constitutes a genuine "threat to a woman's life," and here too politics can be expected to intrude. Some abortion providers understandably fear what an anti-abortion physician might claim in a courtroom about the likelihood of a particular patient's death if the banned procedure had not been performed. An ob-gyn in South Dakota—a state that, as we have seen, has become intensely polarized around abortion—gave a forecast of the nightmare scenarios that might well arise in the operating suite: "If someone has a 10 percent chance of dying, is that what they mean? Or is it 30 percent or 50 percent or 80 percent? By the time you figure out that somebody is at a high risk of dying, they're probably going to die."

The abortion rights movement was also dismayed that in its majority decision, the Supreme Court for the first time legitimized the highly contested notion of "post-abortion syndrome." Though he conceded that "no reliable data" exist on the subject, Justice Kennedy nonetheless cited the "regret" and "severe depression and loss of self-esteem" that can accompany abortion. He argued that such regret would be exacerbated if women who underwent intact D&E learned only after their abortions the "details" of the procedure that had been used.

Justice Ruth Bader Ginsburg, who wrote the dissent to *Gonzales v. Carhart,* took the unusual step of reading her eloquent dissent aloud from the bench. She expressed her dismay that the majority was willing to ban a procedure "found necessary and proper in certain cases" by medical experts. She worried about the future of legal abortion itself: "The Court's hostility to the right *Roe* and *Casey* [a subsequent Supreme Court decision on abortion] secured is not concealed." Most poignantly, in light of Ginsburg's career-long advocacy for women's equality, she decried the paternalism inherent in the majority's willingness to protect "fragile" women from possible "regret" over the details of the particular procedure used in their abortion: "This way of thinking reflects ancient notions about women's place in the family and under the Constitution—ideas that have long since been discredited."

When all is said and done, many of the regulations governing the provision of abortion are not what one would reasonably expect of regulations in the health-care world: actions taken to safeguard the health of patients. Rather, many of the regulations I have discussed in this chapter are designed to make abortion care onerous and costly for patient and provider alike. As Linda, my clinic director friend from the South, said while talking about the latest "reg" mandating that doctors tell patients things that are untrue: "Dude, where's my country?"

V

HOSPITAL-BASED ABORTIONS

Chaos, Cruelty, and Some Accommodation

"I groveled and flattered him as much as I could. I sweet-talked him. Finally he caved." The speaker was Dr. Margaret Riley, a vibrant and witty ob-gyn in her forties, who is the medical director of a free-standing clinic on the East Coast. I recently heard her talk at an academic conference on abortion. In a just world, I thought, a woman like this should not have to grovel before anyone, but Dr. Riley does what she has to do. In this case, she had been advocating with the medical director of an insurance company on behalf of a very sick patient who needed an in-hospital abortion.

Dr. Riley's description of her pleading immediately took me back to an interview I conducted a long time ago with another feisty woman doctor, who similarly had to grovel before a male colleague on behalf of a patient. As Dr. Ethel Bloom recounted this incident to me, "I actually went down on my knees begging him—but I think he felt he had been doing too many lately, and his hospital had been breathing down his neck. I walked out of there shaking."

But here the similarities *should* end. The case Dr. Bloom talked about took place in the 1960s. She was trying to obtain an abortion for a young patient from an ob-gyn colleague who occasionally took risks and did abortions in his hospital, violating the rules of that time by falsely claiming "medical necessity." In contrast, the incident described by Dr. Riley took place in 2007, thirty-four years after *Roe!* Why does she have to "sweet-talk" someone in the medical system for what should be a routine approval for a patient in a very serious condition? Dr. Riley's remarks at that conference speak volumes about the chaos, and indeed cruelty, that characterizes abortion care for women who are too ill to be seen in freestanding clinics.

I was so intrigued by Dr. Riley's comments—I had not been fully aware of the particular difficulties of women too sick for clinic abortions—that I called her and asked for a follow-up interview. Keeping the patient's name and other details confidential, she described the case in question, which concerned a seventeen-year-old with a history of recurrent pulmonary embolism (blood clots in the lungs). When the young woman became pregnant, her hematologist suggested termination as the safest course, as pregnancy could dangerously exacerbate her condition, possibly leading to death. With the hematologist's backing, Dr. Riley arranged to perform the abortion in a local hospital. The young woman was admitted and prepared for surgery. Literally as Dr. Riley was leaving for the hospital to perform the abortion, someone from the patient's insurance company called to announce that the company refused to authorize payment for the procedure, which would cost thousands of dollars—money the family did not have.

Riley immediately called the medical director of the company. "He said they would only pay if 'the condition is life-threatening.' Of course I wanted to shout, 'You moron! Don't you know that pregnancy in a patient with pulmonary embolism *is* life-threatening?' But I restrained myself. I calmly kept telling him how sick she was." Riley did not feel she should have to justify the patient's pregnancy, and recalled being quite offended when the other physician questioned why the patient had not used birth control. Nonetheless, she gritted her teeth and explained to him that the patient had initially been on the pill, but oral contraception and other hormonal methods were contraindicated, as they could exacerbate her condition. The patient had gotten pregnant using a condom. "Finally, the breakthrough came when I got the hematologist to call him and confirm how sick she was. Then he agreed. Of course he thought that I, the abortion doctor, was doing this just for the money—but a hematologist, well, that was a different story."

This case is just one of several that Dr. Riley discussed with me that reveal the challenges she faces when advocating for women who are too sick for clinic abortions. Most hospitals, including Dr. Riley's, do not provide routine or, as they are often called, "elective" abortions, but exceptions are sometimes made for pregnant women who are very ill. While the reluctance of the medical director of the insurance company to approve an abortion may have been driven as much by a desire to cut costs as by antiabortion sentiments, in other instances Dr. Riley and her patients face unmistakable hostility. She told me of the case of a pregnant woman in her early twenties with deep vein thrombosis (DVT), or a blood clot in the leg, which can be life-threatening. With all the names crossed out, Dr. Riley showed me a three-page summary of all the negotiations with various doctors who had cared for the patient and whose approval had been necessary in order to clear the patient for an in-hospital abortion. At one point the summary read: "Ms. X [the patient] called with the news that Dr. Y [her primary-care provider] stated if she was not continuing the pregnancy she was no longer his patient." When the patient was briefly admitted to the hospital before her scheduled abortion because of a flare-up of her DVT, her obstetrician attempted to persuade her to continue this high-risk pregnancy and even made her take a tour of the newborns' nursery! In the end Dr. Riley was able to perform the requested abortion—a full month after the patient's original request.

Dr. Riley told me of a nurse who visited the bedside of another abortion patient when she was recovering from her procedure: "She copied the patient's chart—completely unauthorized!—and started talking to the patient about suing for malpractice" (which the patient did not do). Riley also shared with me a letter she wrote to the hospital complaining about treatment of a nineteen-year-old patient who was hospitalized after suffering a uterine perforation at the clinic. At the patient's request, the clinic's director stayed with her in the ER while she was waiting for her surgery. A nurse approached, informed the young woman that she "had to tell her family," even though she was not a minor, and in the state in question, minors are not actually required to receive parental consent for an abortion. The nurse also demanded that the clinic director leave, even though she was there at the patient's request, to serve as her advocate, and no medical procedures were then under way.

As egregious as these incidents were, Margaret Riley's situation is in some respects considerably better than that of her fellow clinic abortion doctors in other areas. She operates in a fairly liberal state and over the years has worked out an "understanding" with a local hospital that usually lets her perform abortions for very ill patients. Conflicts such as the ones mentioned above, maddening as they are, usually get resolved, because Riley, as she put it to me, is willing to "bite her tongue" and engage in as many negotiations as it takes to receive authorization to perform an abortion.

In fact, another dimension to Dr. Riley's abortion provision in her local hospital warrants mention. One of the open secrets of contemporary mainstream medicine in the United States is the deeply ambivalent relationship to abortion, and especially to abortion providers, on the part of other physicians. Any doctor who takes care of women of reproductive age is going to be confronted with patients with unwanted pregnancies, and some portion of them will seek abortions. The majority of these patients can simply be referred to the nearest freestanding clinic (which may in fact be several hours' drive away, or in another state). But some patients, like those described here, will have pregnancies that threaten their health, even their lives, or will be carrying fetuses with severe anomalies. In a power reversal of sorts, the patients' primary-care physicians will then call on abortion providers like Margaret Riley to perform the procedure. For example, Riley told me of performing an abortion at twenty-two weeks of gestation—a gestational age that she does not do on an elective basis—for a woman with terminal cancer, at the request of the patient's oncologist.

Many of the abortion providers with whom I have spoken over the years have commented on the jarring combination of exclusion and sudden calls for help from medical colleagues. As Gary McPherson, an abortion provider in the Midwest, once said to me, with some bitterness, "All the pro-life doctors in my town, they treat me like a pariah—until they need me to come to take care of their very sick patients." But even in these cases, when the request for a hospital abortion comes from a referring physician, not the patient herself, there are often still obstacles from those in the hospital who refuse to permit an abortion, no matter how sick the patient is.

Such refusals are a problem in general, but they are particularly salient in Catholic hospitals. The problem has been compounded lately because of the recent trends of hospital mergers, which has meant that many secular hospitals are now affiliated with Catholic institutions. As of 2008, the Catholic health-care system operated about one out of six hospital beds in the country. Catholic hospitals (including secular ones involved in mergers) and their employees are bound by the guidelines within the "Ethical and Religious Directives for Catholic Health Care Services," a document produced by the National Conference of Catholic Bishops. These directives prohibit abortion, as well as sterilization, birth control, assisted reproduction, and the dispensation of emergency contraception (though some Catholic hospitals do permit the latter for rape victims if it can be proven that these women are not pregnant when they take the medication).

The Catholic Church's opposition to abortion is well known, and no informed person would go to a Catholic hospital for an elective abortion. But what happens when pregnancies are life-threatening, as with ectopic pregnancies? Ectopic pregnancies occur when a fertilized egg implants outside the uterus, usually in a woman's fallopian tube, and they are the leading cause of first-trimester maternal mortality in the United States. Since the 1990s, a common treatment of ectopic pregnancies, as documented in the medical literature, is to administer methotrexate, a drug mainly used for cancer treatment but that also causes fetal demise (methotrexate is gradually replacing salpingectomy, a surgical treatment for the removal of an ectopic pregnancy).

Similarly, what happens with women whose uterine pregnancies suddenly go terribly wrong—for example, when the water membranes burst prematurely, putting the woman at risk of chorioamnionitis, an infection of the uterus that can cause high fever, is associated with sterility, and can be life-threatening? In such cases the woman starts to miscarry, a process referred to medically as a "spontaneous abortion." The crucial question for her physician is whether she will miscarry before infection sets in, which can occur within a matter of hours. Therefore, the preferred medical treatment for ruptured membranes is to evacuate the pregnant woman's uterus as quickly as possible.

But both of these medically preferred treatments run into obstacles at Catholic-owned or -affiliated hospitals. The Catholic health directives do state, albeit vaguely, that an abortion may be performed in certain situations. For instance, directive 47 reads: "Operations, treatments and medications that have as their direct purpose the cure of a proportionately serious pathological condition of a pregnant woman are permitted when they cannot be safely postponed until the unborn child is viable, even if they will result in the death of the unborn child." But what does this directive actually mean when it needs to be interpreted in Catholic institutions, often very quickly, in emergency situations? Pregnant women with failing pregnancies can show up at a Catholic hospital—sometimes the only hospital in a given region—which then compounds their tragedy by refusing to provide the treatment that is the medical standard of care for their condition.

I have learned that this directive is subject to different kinds of interpretations, often reflecting the bias of whichever member of a hospital's ethics committee is on call when these difficult situations arise. The sociologist Lori Freedman uncovered a number of disturbing cases in Catholic-affiliated hospitals where physicians' medical judgments were overruled because of a strict interpretation of directive 47. In these cases, which occurred in hospitals in different regions of the country, doctors were forbidden to terminate doomed pregnancies in cases where a fetal heartbeat could be detected. One such case was detailed to Freedman by an ob-gyn in the Midwest: "She [patient] was very early, 14 weeks. She came in . . . and there was a hand sticking out of the cervix. Clearly the membranes had ruptured and she was trying to deliver. . . . There was a [fetal] heart rate . . . we called the ethics committee and they said, 'Nope, can't do anything.' So we had to send her to [University Hospital, ninety miles away]." This solution, in which the patient was sent to another hospital because her physician felt that that was a safer proposition than hoping the fetus would die before infection and excessive blood loss set in, has become such a common occurrence in the abortion-providing world that it has launched a new term: "ambulance cases."

To avoid such dangerous delays, Freedman discovered, doctors will sometimes break the hospitals' rules on behalf of their patients. Hearing of these cases, I was yet again reminded of how contemporary abortion care has become eerily reminiscent of the pre-*Roe* world I researched earlier. Then too some "physicians of conscience," as I termed them, would bend the truth or violate established protocols in order to help their desperate patients, often undertaking considerable personal risk in doing so. For example, Dr. Ethel Bloom, the physician who begged a colleague in vain to perform an illegal abortion for her patient, ultimately solved the problem by claiming that her patient had tested positive for rubella. Rubella in pregnant women was just becoming recognized in the 1960s to have a strong association with fetal anomalies, and in Bloom's state constituted grounds for an authorized abortion. The test at that time was so expensive that Bloom gambled, correctly, that the hospital authorities would not demand a retest. Unlike Bloom, however, Freedman's interviewees are practicing medicine in a context in which abortion is legal, yet they are compelled to cheat to perform tragically necessary terminations on behalf of patients whose pregnancies were wanted.

One such case of rule-breaking involved an ob-gyn in the South, Dr. G., as Freedman referred to her, who already had a history of frustrating encounters with her Catholic-affiliated hospital over the treatment of pregnant women in distress. In this instance she decided simply not to follow the usual protocols: that is, she did *not* consult the ethics committee and did *not* check for a fetal heartbeat. The patient in question, fourteen weeks pregnant, had burst membranes and was in the process of miscarrying. As with other cases of ruptured membranes, Dr. G.'s overriding objective was to evacuate the uterus before infection set in. When the patient came to the emergency room, Dr. G. immediately transferred her to an operating room and began the uterine evacuation. But there she ran into trouble with the attending nurse. "So we went to the operating room and the nurse kept asking me, 'Was there heart tones, was there heart tones?' I said, 'I don't know.' Though I kind of knew there would be. But she said, 'Did you check?' I said, 'I don't need an ultrasound to tell me that it [fetal demise] is inevitable, the membranes are hanging out of the cervix. . . . You can just put [on the patient's chart] "the heart tones weren't documented" and they can interpret that however they want to interpret that.'"

Another case of rule-breaking involved Dr. S., a physician in the Northeast, who was treating a patient nineteen weeks pregnant who was in the process of a very prolonged miscarriage. The patient was already septic—that is, infection had set in—and she had a temperature of 106 degrees. But Dr. S. was prevented by the hospital ethics committee from evacuating her uterus, again because of the presence of a fetal heartbeat. As he later told the story to Freedman: "This woman is dying before our eyes. I went in to examine her and I was able to find the umbilical cord through the membranes and just snapped the umbilical cord . . . so I could put on the ultrasound—

'Oh, look! No heartbeat. Let's go.' She was so sick that she was in the ICU for about ten days and very nearly died. . . . Her bleeding was so bad that the sclera [the whites of her eyes] were red, filled with blood."

Though no disciplinary action was taken against Dr. S., the incident was deeply upsetting to him. As he recalled his feelings at the time of this crisis, "I just can't do this. . . . This [job] is not worth it to me." He shortly thereafter resigned his privileges at that hospital and took a position at a secular medical center.

Dr. Debra Stulberg is a brilliant young family medicine physician at the University of Chicago who has also completed advanced study in medical ethics. I have learned much from my discussions with her about contemporary bioethical issues in reproductive health. She initially brought to my attention a very controversial case regarding the handling of a patient with an ectopic pregnancy at a hospital outside Chicago. West Suburban Medical Center, where Stulberg had been a resident, had recently been acquired by a Catholic health organization, Resurrection Health Care, and now was subject to the above-mentioned directives. When a woman arrived at the hospital with a diagnosis of an ectopic pregnancy of less than ten weeks gestation, she was not offered methotrexate, which is what the doctors at West Suburban would have done before the hospital was acquired by Resurrection. Because the patient's fetus had a heartbeat, the physician on call did not even consult the hospital's ethicist. As she told a local newspaper, she already knew that treatment via methotrexate would not be permitted. "We offered her, because of the religious directives, the opportunity to sign out as if she were going home and to go to a different hospital where they could possibly offer her medical management."

Discussing this case with me afterward, Dr. Stulberg recalled how appalled she and her fellow residents had been, but she did not second-guess the doctor on call who made the decision to transfer the patient. "One thing everybody learns in medical school is that ectopic pregnancy is a true emergency. Delaying treatment can cause the patient to bleed internally and die. . . . She [the doctor on call] wanted the patient to be at a hospital where she could have all treatment options available to her. . . . It's crazy that a woman might unknowingly . . . end up at a Catholic hospital with a life-threatening obstetric emergency and not be offered all medically reasonable treatments."

My conversation with Dr. Stulberg about this case also led me to comprehend the wide gulf—both linguistic and philosophical—that exists between the medical approach to an ectopic pregnancy and that of the Church. "Medically, we never talk about the treatment of an ectopic pregnancy as an 'abortion,'" Dr. Stulberg said. "I think any ob-gyn would accept that the goal of treating an ectopic is terminating the pregnancy that has developed in a pathological way so as to threaten the woman's health. It's just so straightforward—fetus is nonviable, woman could die—that it's not even on the spectrum of abortion. It's just talked about as the treatment of a dangerous condition. When we want to know if the treatment has been effective, we ask if the ectopic pregnancy has 'resolved.'"

But while the treatment of an ectopic pregnancy may be straightforward for physicians, this is not the case for the ethics committees that oversee the treatment of such cases in Catholic-affiliated hospitals. In some cases the woman's fallopian tube is removed, satisfying the principle of Catholic medical ethics of not directly ending the life of the fetus but of course resulting in a possible compromise to the patient's future fertility. In other cases, presumably when doctors determine that the patient may be close to death, and when there is a more liberal ethics committee, the fetus is directly aborted as quickly as possible. In still other cases, like the one at West Suburban, the patient is sent elsewhere. In the controversy that ensued after this incident and another ambulance case (this one involving ruptured membranes) at West Suburban became public, the Reverend Thomas Nairn, a professor of ethics at the Catholic Theological Union in Chicago, suggested in an interview with a local newspaper that the doctor on call had overreacted. "In regard to tubal pregnancy, a fetus can be removed so that it does not constitute a direct abortion . . . as long as the intent is to manage a threat to a mother's life rather than to perform an abortion." But Nairn also acknowledged that other Catholic ethicists would view such cases of ectopic pregnancies differently.

After learning about these various cases, I have come to realize that it boils down to a matter of luck as to which Catholic or Catholic-affiliated hospital a woman with a doomed pregnancy happens to go to, if she is to receive treatment consistent with prevailing medical standards of care. Some of these hospitals have more liberal ethics committees, others ones that are more rigidly orthodox. Some may have doctors willing to take chances, possibly putting their careers at risk, and break rules on behalf of their patients, as we have seen. But others won't.

To be sure, it is not only in Catholic hospitals that women too ill for clinic abortions have problems. Ambulance cases occur in secular hospitals as well. Dr. Margaret Riley had numerous problems with performing abortions in her community hospital, as we saw. Though the Catholic directives on health care pose a particular challenge for women and their doctors, some of the issues that Riley has confronted, such as inappropriate behavior on the part of hospital staff members, reveal that abortion politics at its ugliest is very much an issue in secular American hospitals.

HEALTH WORKER REFUSALS

Another problem that occurs in hospitals with abortion services connects to a larger phenomenon in contemporary health care in the United States: so-called health worker refusals. This issue first began to receive widespread attention in the case of emergency contraception, when some individual pharmacists and drugstore chains began to refuse to fill prescriptions, claiming that EC was an abortifacient and it would violate their beliefs to agree to distribute this drug. Some pharmacists even began to refuse to fill prescriptions for regular oral contraception, on the same grounds. Since then there have been well-publicized refusals in various other areas of health care— for example, some doctors have refused to offer assisted reproductive services to lesbian couples or single straight women. In a startling study of a nationwide sample of doctors published in 2007, researchers found that a "substantial minority" of the physicians surveyed said they felt no obligation to inform patients of treatments to which they themselves had moral objections. An even larger group of respondents in this study felt that they did not have to refer patients to other doctors who did provide care that they themselves objected to. The authors of this study estimate that about 40 million Americans are seeing physicians whose values preclude them from informing patients of a full range of treatments, and as many as 100 million have doctors who do not feel a need to refer patients for treatments they are unwilling to provide.

But long before the phenomenon of health worker refusal had a name, the problem of some health workers' objections to participating in abortion was well known. As mentioned in chapter 2, shortly after the *Roe* decision, Congress passed legislation stipulating that no doctor employed in a public facility had to participate in abortion work, a principle reaffirmed some years later when opt-out provisions for routine training in abortion for ob-gyn residents were established. But doctors are hardly the only health workers with objections to working in an abortion service. Over the years of researching this field, I have come to see that auxiliary staff, especially nurses, can sometimes be a larger obstacle. Indeed, one of the major original rationales for the establishment of the freestanding clinic model in the early 1970s was the ability to hire only staff members who were supportive of abortions. In the years leading up to *Roe* there were plenty of stories in circulation of nurses' insensitivity—sometimes outright cruelty—to patients who received authorization for in-hospital abortions, and the problem has not gone away. Because doctors have such clear-cut rules for opting out of abortion training and provision, by the time a patient gets to a hospital for an abortion, she is likely to see someone with the ideological commitment of a Dr. Riley. However, the rules for participation in abortion-related services for nurses, medical assistants, receptionists, schedulers, and so on are more ambiguous, and there are often staff conflicts when hospitals provide abortions.

IRIS'S STORY

At the suggestion of a physician on the East Coast, Dr. Sylvia ("Sylvie") Shore, I conducted a long interview with Iris Foyle, a nursing manager in the family medicine department in which Dr. Shore was a professor. The department in which the two women worked was affiliated with a major medical center and served a low-income, ethnically diverse urban population. Dr. Shore thought it would be useful both for her purposes and for mine to have this interview, because of Iris's involvement in the early abortion service the physician had recently initiated. Dr. Shore informed me that Iris was "strongly anti-abortion" and the initial negotiations around her involvement in the new abortion service had been strained and even difficult. But, she told me, these deliberations had ended on a professional and amicable note. Given how many of her peers elsewhere had similar problems with nursing staff when abortion care was being introduced into a hospital-based clinic, Shore's reasoning was that my interview might shed light on what had made the initially resistant nurse cooperate with the new service.

Iris Foyle, in her mid-fifties, was born on a small Caribbean island and came to the United States as a teenager. I greatly enjoyed my interview with her, and not only because I learned so much about the problem under discussion. Over the years I have conducted hundreds of interviews, and the best ones, for me, are those in which the interviewee does not conform to my preconceptions. In other words, although Iris was strongly opposed to abortion, she did not fit my idea of a stereotypical "right-to-lifer," that is, a staunch right-winger who is both religious and very conservative. Several times during our interview she spoke critically of "corporate America" and the ways in which health-care management was becoming "corporatized." She spoke wistfully of the days (the 1960s and 1970s) when "social medicine" as a concept flourished in progressive medical circles and health workers were seen as potential agents of change. She clearly was distressed at the current state of health care, in which so many were uninsured or underinsured. Though she was raised in a Pentecostal household, she told me that she did not consider herself especially religious and only rarely went to church.

At the same time, Iris told me that abortion "repulsed" her and that she would refuse to go into the room when a procedure was under way. So how does someone with such strong feelings manage to live up to her professional responsibilities when they call for some degree of participation in an abortion service? Things had gotten off to a rocky start. Iris had been hired around the same time that abortion care was being established in the family medicine clinic, but this fact simply had not come up during her interview. She was stunned when she discovered that the ultrasound machine that had recently been purchased by the department was to be used for abortions. (Ultrasonography is widely used to determine gestational age in abortion care.) As a nurse manager, she had duties that included assigning the nurses under her supervision to work in the abortion service and assuring that the necessary equipment and supplies were in place. She briefly considered resigning: "I had to go back and really examine how I felt. I [realized] I'm going to have to be involved in this if I stay, or I could choose to go someplace else." Significantly, her initial dismay over the thought of being involved in abortions came not only from her personal opposition to the procedure. She was also very apprehensive of the controversy she thought this new service might bring. "I know this community [surrounding the hospital] . . . I know there are people with very strong feelings against abortion. I was thinking of the potential for people lining up outside, protesting, and I was not ready for that!"

Despite her reservations, Iris struggled to find a way to comply with the fact that abortion was being offered in her department. Soon after taking her new position, she had a serious talk with Sylvie Shore and made clear to the physician her personal philosophy on abortion. "I said, Sylvie, you need to know I am pro-choice, but that for me, this really means just that—a right to choose and to direct our own paths. . . . I strongly believe that people have a choice [to choose abortion], but I also believe just as strongly that you don't have a right to impose your choice on me, or force me into a position to have to act in a way that I don't want to."

Iris also communicated to Sylvie the line she drew between what she felt incapable of doing personally and what she was willing to do as a nursing professional. "From a personal standpoint, I will not step in that room and assist you in any way with that abortion. . . . But I will, in my role, get you [the equipment and supplies] that you need." (Iris's statement that she would never directly assist at an abortion has to be seen as a symbolic statement, given that as a supervisor she did almost no clinical work.)

Iris's other major concern was figuring out which of the nurses under her supervision were willing to be involved. Hospital policy, reinforced by Iris's supervisor, was that nurses and other hospital employees had to do a variety of related tasks, such as scheduling, prepping the patients, and providing aftercare, but could choose not to be in the room while an abortion was taking place. Making the nursing assignments was less problematic than she feared. "I went to each nurse one at a time . . . to find out, how did they feel about abortion. . . . I asked, 'Could you assist with one?' Before this, I had no idea how they felt about that issue." As it turned out, two of the nurses had no objections to this work, while one did. The willingness of these two was an enormous relief to Iris, as she realized she was certainly in no position to insist that her nurses take on responsibilities she herself was unwilling to do.

But the real emotional breakthrough in Iris's ability to participate in this work in a professional manner came with an important gesture on Sylvie Shore's part. Besides reassuring Iris that the abortion service would be offered only to the department's regular clinic patients and not to the community as a whole, Sylvie offered to take on the task of ordering the various supplies needed for the MVA service, acknowledging Iris's discomfort with that. The nurse was deeply moved by this offer by the doctor, and also by Sylvie's overall response to her feelings about abortion. "Sylvie expressed to me, 'I understand where you are coming from. . . . [W]e will do everything we can to make this as painless as possible for you as we put in the service.'" In the end, Sylvie researched all the items that were needed and Iris did the actual ordering.

Reflecting on her interactions with Sylvie about a year or so after they occurred, Iris commented on the importance of the "honesty and dialogue" that had transpired between the two women. When I asked her if she thought that Sylvie's behavior was typical in today's health-care environment, she answered, "No. People [in health care] act the way they do in corporate America—'This is the job, get me what I need'—and then they expect it to happen, never exploring how people really feel about such a charged issue." Then, in a comment that surprised me because of its frankness, she continued, "And when you don't take the time to explore, you're going to get a fiasco. You know what happens? People will just sabotage you. I could have easily sabotaged this whole project . . . because of my influence over the staff. . . . I'm bright enough to know how to sabotage."

But Iris did not sabotage the abortion care offered by the family medicine department. Both she and Sylvie felt that the service was going very well—though to be sure, their criteria for "going well" differed. For Sylvie, it meant that those of her patients who desired abortions could be seen by their own doctor in the same clinic where they got the rest of their health care, and that these patients were treated in a supportive manner by all concerned. For Iris, "going well" meant that no one who was opposed to abortion was forced to participate directly in its delivery and that she had enough nurses who were willing to participate. Staffing issues did not become a crisis. But "going well" for Iris also implied that one of her major fears did not materialize—namely, that the department's outpatient clinic would become an "abortion mill," or, to use another phrase that came up in our interview, that "the floodgates" would open.

The main lesson here, I believe, is a startlingly simple one: that sheer human decency (and emotional intelligence) can make a big difference. By genuinely listening to Iris, by offering to take on some of her abortion-related tasks, by communicating to her what would and would not happen with the new abortion service, Sylvie Shore was able to help the nurse achieve an acceptable comfort level with this work. As simple as this might seem, in the harried world of many of today's hospitals, even well-meaning physicians do not always think to take the time to listen to their nurse colleagues in this way.

I have heard similar deeply moving stories of abortion rights physicians taking steps to acknowledge the differing views of co-workers. A family medicine resident on the West Coast told me that shortly after her residency program began offering early abortion in its clinic, a receptionist beloved of many of the residents asked to be transferred to another floor on the day of the abortion service. When this request was overlooked by the busy clinic director, a group of residents marched to his office to demand that her request be honored. Once satisfied that this would be done, the young physicians proceeded to perform abortions.

I am not so naive as to believe that all abortion conflicts in the modern hospital can be managed so readily. There is an important distinction to be drawn between health workers who refuse direct involvement in abortion work for themselves, like Iris, and those who don't want *anyone* to do abortion work. I have no illusion, for example, that the nurse mentioned at the start of this chapter who stealthily copied the chart of one of Dr. Riley's patients and urged the patient to sue would change her views even if she engaged in dialogue with the physician. But having learned how abortion politics frequently manifests itself inside the hospital setting in inappropriate ways, I take comfort in realizing what the Sylvie Shores of the world can accomplish. Even in this most polarized of worlds, it seems, emotional intelligence still can make a difference.

VI

ABORTION PATIENTS
AND THE "TWO AMERICAS"
OF REPRODUCTIVE HEALTH

"It's a sad calculus. . . . It helps if they are farther along in pregnancy [rather] than earlier. Or if they are living with their batterer, and he would know if they'd pawn anything. Or if they are homeless. . . . Like, we got this call last week from a woman whose house burned down and her three children were taken away. We were able to get some money for her."

A few years ago I spent some time with the staff of the hotline of the National Abortion Federation. Sandy, the case manager, was explaining to me what kind of triage can occur in the effort to help desperate women raise money for abortions they can't afford. Most of the hotline's one hundred or so callers per day are simply looking for a referral to an abortion provider in their area. But a sizable minority are seeking the hotline's assistance in raising money to pay for their abortions.

The situation of low-income women and public funding for abortions is this: in 1976, Congress passed the Hyde Amendment, the first legislative victory of the antiabortion movement. This measure excludes abortion from the comprehensive health-care services (including prenatal care) provided to the poor through the Medicaid program. The Hyde Amendment does allow abortion funding in cases of rape, incest, and threats to the life of the pregnant woman. Thirty-five states have followed Congress's lead in restricting public funding of abortion, but the rest do allow their Medicaid programs to pay for abortions for low-income women.

During my visit, I watched as Sandy and her coworkers attempted to help women in need of financial assistance. Some money was available from patient assistance funds managed by NAF and similar organizations. But of course there are never enough funds to meet the needs of all who request help, and simply being poor is not always enough of an "extenuating circumstance," as Sandy put it.

Not surprisingly, rape is one extenuating circumstance that the various abortion funds do prioritize. But if state governments were obeying the law, the hotline would have to raise far less money for rape victims, nearly all of whom are on Medicaid, and would be able to allocate these funds to others.

The problem, however, is that numerous state Medicaid programs simply refuse to enforce this provision to pay for the abortions of women who meet the exceptions permitted under the Hyde Amendment. Fighting with antiabortion state bureaucrats often drags on indefinitely and pushes women later into pregnancy, making the procedure even more expensive and a provider more difficult, if not impossible, to find. In a recent year, nearly 28 percent of the money raised by this hotline went to those who were theoretically eligible for state funding because they had been raped, were incest victims, or faced life-threatening conditions.

But as I learned in the day I spent with the hotline's staff members, even women who are high enough on the extenuating-circumstances spectrum to qualify for financial aid often don't get enough to pay for their abortion. As I sat and listened to Sandy work the phones nonstop, I realized that much of what she was doing was a unique and challenging form of financial counseling. Her task was to instruct her often indigent callers in the delicate art of fundraising.

"Could you ask your friends for forty dollars? If they say no, maybe ask for twenty, or even ten," I heard her say in a calm voice. Later she told me that that particular caller had been evicted from her house for not paying the rent and was crashing with her three children at a friend's place. To another caller I heard her say, "Well, do you have anything you might pawn? Some jewelry? A TV set?" And to another, "Is it possible you could postpone your car payment until after the abortion?"

Sandy's case management is strikingly labor-intensive. She told me she averages about fifteen phone calls per case—with the client, with the various abortion funds, with the clinic that is the potential site of the abortion—whether the woman successfully obtains enough money for an abortion or not.

After blocking callers' names and other identifying information, Sandy showed me some of the intake forms from the previous month. The meticulously kept log of each call made and received hinted at lives lived on the edge. For example, in response to the items on the form that ask about whether funds might be raised from the "man involved with the pregnancy," I saw the stark one-word response "Crackhead," recorded verbatim by a hotline staffer. "No idea where he is," read another response, and a third, "Has nothing." The hotline staff assured me, however, that there are numerous instances of "good guys"—fathers and husbands and boyfriends—who actively participate in the search for funding.

In response to the question about "items to pawn," one form's entry read, "No TV." Another simply said, "House robbed, nothing left." There were numerous references to domestic violence and an overrepresentation of pregnancies resulting from rape. (Nationally, about 1 percent of all abortions occur because of rape.)

Sometimes the grim realities of the callers' lives mean that even seeming victories can include defeats. Consider, for example, the case of a woman from a southern state, a mother of five, who lived in a mobile home. Believing herself to be fifteen to sixteen weeks pregnant, she obtained a tentative appointment at a clinic, which informed her that the cost of an abortion would be $450. Through a combination of Sandy's calls to various funds and the patient's own fundraising (I saw a notation about "yard sale" in the file) they were able to cobble together the necessary money. Reading this, I visualized Sandy and Rebecca, the hotline's director, pumping their fists in the air and yelling "Yesss!" But in the chart I noticed a subsequent, chilling entry: "Patient called to leave message—said she lost her ride to the clinic." By the time the woman did make it to the clinic, according to Sandy's crisp notes, "Pt sono'ed [had an ultrasound] at 18 weeks and clinic raised cost by $440. Pt decided to continue pregnancy since she didn't have sufficient funds to have abortion."

When I spoke with Sandy and Rebecca about this case, they confirmed that it was not an uncommon occurrence. Many hotline callers are without cars and are dependent on sometimes unreliable friends and relatives to get them to their appointments. The problem of "sono'ing over," as the hotline staff put it, is a serious one. Either the patient's pregnancy has advanced past the point where the facility in question performs abortions, or, as in this case, the cost becomes prohibitive. (While some might find the clinic's response coldhearted, in fact abortion costs have remained remarkably flat since 1973, while the costs of operating the clinics, especially with regard to security measures, have gone way up. Moreover, many clinics offer a considerable amount of subsidized care.)

To be sure, I learned of some unqualified triumphs as well during my visit to the hotline. Some patients manage to beat the odds with a combination of luck and tenacity. Sandy told me of a woman from a mid-Atlantic state with a mind-numbing series of problems. Already the mother of several young children, she was in the midst of a difficult divorce from an abusive husband, against whom she had obtained a restraining order. "My husband would kill me if he found out I was pregnant," she told the hotline staff. She was about to be evicted from her home because of difficulty in paying the rent. She had become pregnant after being given a date-rape drug. The woman had duly reported the rape to police and was determined to get the state's Medicaid program to pay for her abortion.

This involved an enormous effort on her part. Though she was so poor that her phone had been disconnected (talks with the hotline took place via a neighbor's phone), she managed to find a public Internet connection and download the necessary form for a Medicaid abortion involving a rape. Then she embarked on a surreal series of phone calls with state Medicaid officials, all of whom seemed determined to prevent approval of her abortion. With the help of a public-interest lawyer in the hotline's network, the patient was finally able to reach someone high enough—and sympathetic enough—in the Medicaid hierarchy to approve her request.

The next obstacle was to find a provider in her rural area who would accept a Medicaid-paid abortion. Neither her antiabortion primary-care doctor nor her equally antiabortion ob-gyn was any help. Finally, after much frantic calling around, with the hotline's aid she located a clinic that performed her abortion. "And all this calling and arranging happened in just four days!" Sandy marveled.

The stories of women I heard and read about that day at the NAF hotline suggested to me situations so challenging that affordable abortions would hardly solve these women's problems. In the long run, it was clear, only in a society that provided what is now lacking in contemporary America—affordable housing, living wages, better child care, better domestic violence programs, and above all universal health care—would these women and their children have a shot at a better life.

In the short run, however, accessible and affordable contraception and abortion would make an enormous difference to these women and to the children they already have. Indeed, some improvement did occur shortly after my visit to the NAF hotline. An anonymous donor made a sizable contribution to help pay for abortions for poor women. This donation was directed specifically at women in the thirty-five states that do not allow Medicaid funds to be used for routine abortions (that is, those not related to rape, incest, or threat to life). This new infusion of funds has made an enormous difference to the beneficiaries. Annie Moses, who runs a clinic in the Deep South, has a particularly impoverished clientele. She shared with me some of the letters she received from those who acquired such funding.

> I had my first baby at the age of 18 and I take care of him without the help of his dad because he is in jail now and I just could not [have another child] all alone without any help and a baby is a lot of money that I don't have.

> I would like to thank the Funder that helped me pay for this. I could not afford it myself. I lost my job, me and my husband separated and I had just begun school trying to better myself but if it wasn't for the Funder that helped me pay for this I don't know what I might have done. I have two kids already, living with my parents.

> I have to have an abortion because of my heart condition. After I had my twins my heart became weak and I was told it would be best if I don't have any more children.

> I thank you for the chance to receive help in paying for this procedure because I know I could not afford it without

your help. I came to the realization that if I could not afford this procedure, then how could I afford this child? I am currently unemployed.

But for the poorest of the poor, who are disproportionately represented among all abortion recipients, paying for the procedure is only part of the challenge of having an abortion. The problems facing the most vulnerable women needing abortions was made even clearer to me when I visited another reproductive health hotline, this one in Oakland, California.

California is one of the most progressive states with respect to abortion. It allows the use of Medicaid funds to pay for abortions for low-income women. Its voters are predictably supportive of abortion rights in presidential and statewide elections. (In November 2008, for the third straight time, a ballot initiative that would have complicated minors' access to abortion was defeated.) In the major metropolitan centers—Los Angeles and San Diego in the south, the San Francisco Bay Area in the north—first-trimester abortion services are fairly plentiful. For the most part, clinics in these urban centers are free of the aggressive picketing and harassment that occurs elsewhere. But 40 percent of California's counties have no known abortion providers, and some of these counties are located far from the urban areas that do offer abortion services. For women without cars or the money to pay for gasoline, just getting to a clinic and paying for incidental expenses such as food and housing can be extremely difficult. My visit to the Access Hotline made this very clear.

Access receives about twelve hundred calls a year, I was told by Destiny, the hotline's engaging director, who exudes both competence and compassion. Many of these calls are from women who are simply seeking a reliable referral in their area. Some calls are about a range of topics related to pregnancy and reproduction: Where can one get a free pregnancy test? Can the caller, a father, force his daughter to get an abortion? ("No!" he is told.) Can the hotline recommend a good couples' counselor? But many callers are women who need help financing an abortion. One of the first things that the staff members do for these callers is assess whether they are eligible for Medi-Cal, the state's Medicaid program, and then explain to those who are qualified how to enroll. But often that is just the start of the interventions the staff must undertake.

As I looked through the hotline's detailed records, one case in particular grabbed my attention, that of a Latina whom I shall call Monica. Her case was especially striking both because of the number and length of phone calls that were recorded and because Monica's saga led me to a visceral realization of the herculean efforts it takes for some women to obtain an abortion successfully. Monica was in her twenties, lived in a farming town in California's vast Central Valley, and at the time of her first contact with Access was already in her second trimester of pregnancy. Even in a liberal state such as California, there are not that many options for women needing abortions in the second trimester.

The Women's Options Center at San Francisco General Hospital is one of the major providers of second-trimester abortions in the central and northern part of the state, and Access refers many of the callers seeking these procedures to this facility. The WOC, like the public hospital in which it is located, is well known for the humane care it extends to its patients, many of whom, because of their indigent status, are, as one physician put it to me, "those patients nobody else wants." (Access staff told me of a particularly distraught patient who missed her bus and was late for her appointment on the afternoon of Christmas Eve; WOC staff quickly assembled a team that was willing to work late and perform the patient's abortion.) Besides its physicians, all of whom are affiliated with the Department of Obstetrics, Gynecology, and Reproductive Sciences at the University of California, San Francisco, the center employs dedicated nurses, counselors, and administrative staff members, a number of whom have worked there for many years and have been hired for their sensitivity to abortion patients.

But making a referral to the WOC for Monica was only the beginning. The call log revealed conversations about getting on Medi-Cal. I also saw a notation about transportation: "We looked up bus schedules for her." This came after a previous phone call about whether the hotline could help with the purchase of gasoline if Monica found a friend to drive her. Ultimately Monica did take a bus, one that left at 5:30 a.m., because that was the only way she could make it to San Francisco in time to have an afternoon appointment at the WOC.

The calls to Access continued even after Monica bought the bus ticket, with the help of the hotline. When she arrived at the bus station in San Francisco, she called again, under the incorrect impression that someone was going to meet her at the station. She did not have enough money to take a cab, so a staff person told her how to reach the hospital by bus. Monica called again after her appointment, not having realized (or, more likely, not having remembered) that, as with many second-trimester abortions, her procedure was a two-day affair (the first appointment being used to insert lamineria, an agent that gradually dilates the patient's cervix overnight).

So now, quite late in the workday, Monica needed housing. The staff quickly went into gear and contacted people on its lists of volunteers who have agreed to take in abortion patients who cannot afford overnight housing. A couple whom staff members later told me were "star" volunteers agreed to house Monica for the night, and I noted a flurry of additional calls arranging a rendezvous for Monica and her hosts. The final notation I saw in this long file was a message from the WOC staff to the Access staff mentioning that at the end of this two-day procedure, after Monica's abortion was successfully completed, the patient realized she had no money to return to the bus station, so the staff chipped in to give her cab fare.

THE "TWO AMERICAS" OF
CONTRACEPTION AND ABORTION

The experiences I had at the two hotlines I visited, witnessing the obstacles that Monica and other poor women face in obtaining abortions, are reflected in disturbing data that have recently emerged about the wide gulf in reproductive health events between poor and nonpoor women. While there has been much notice in the past several years of a dramatic decline in the overall number of abortions occurring in the United States—the record high since legalization was 1.61 million in 1990, but by 2005 the number was 1.2 million—this overall decline masks profound differences among American women. So striking are these differences that researchers at the Guttmacher Institute have spoken of the "two Americas" of women's reproductive health. The institute's studies show that a poor woman is four times as likely as a higher-income woman to experience an unplanned pregnancy. Not surprisingly, this fact in turn leads to vastly different abortion rates. The rate among women living below the federal poverty level ($9,570 in 2006 dollars for a single woman with no children) is more than four times that of women at 300 percent of the poverty level (forty-four as opposed to ten abortions per one thousand women).

These wide differences in abortion rates can also be expressed in racial terms. African American women obtain about 37 percent of the abortions in the United States, white women 34 percent, Latinas 22 percent, and "others" (Asians, Pacific Islanders, and Native Americans) the remaining 8 percent. The bottom line is that African Americans, who make up about 13 percent of the overall population, and Latinas, who make up about 15 percent, are considerably overrepresented among abortion recipients.

This striking disparity between white women and women of color, and especially the high rate of abortion for black women, has attracted much attention. Opponents of abortion have pounced on these data and attempted to revive long-standing accusations of genocide against the African American community on the part of the family planning establishment in general and Planned Parenthood in particular. In spring 2008 a group called Issues4Life, a faith-based organization, wrote to the Congressional Black Caucus, denouncing Planned Parenthood for its "racist" goals and calling on the caucus to propose withdrawing the federal funds Planned Parenthood receives for family planning purposes (a step the caucus did not take). Other antiabortion activists have claimed that the high rate of abortion among black women is due to "aggressive marketing" by providers in minority communities, a charge echoed in conservative newspapers such as the *Washington Times*.

There is no question that the history of reproductive politics in this country includes numerous episodes of what can only be understood as a racially motivated targeting of women of color: coercive sterilizations of African American and Latina women, the disproportionate placing of the first generation of publicly funded family planning clinics in African American communities, the still hotly debated controversies about Margaret Sanger's dealings with eugenicists early in her career. But I do not believe that the higher abortion rates among minority women are a function of any racist intentions on the part of the contemporary Planned Parenthood organization. (I do believe, as I shall explain, that these differential rates are in part the consequences of living in a racially and economically stratified society.) But with respect to the allegation of the Issues 4Life group, I agree with the statement that the Guttmacher Institute posted on its Web site: "No conspiracy theories [are] needed." The institute reiterated the argument that higher abortion rates among women of color are a direct consequence of higher rates of unintended pregnancies.

But why do African American and Latina women have so many more unintended pregnancies? The major reason is different access to and use of contraception. The notion of the "two Americas" fits here as well. Drawing on Guttmacher data, here is a thumbnail sketch of what we know about contraceptive use and access in the United States (the data are from 2006, the most recent year for which information is available).

As a cultural value, use of contraception is very deeply embedded in American society. One government study stated that 98 percent of heterosexually active American women have used a method of birth control at some point in their lives. But this figure, of course, does not account for significant differences in regular usage. For example, Guttmacher data reveal that 46 percent of women who have abortions did not use a contraceptive method during the month in which they became pregnant. About 10 percent of sexually active women do not regularly use contraception, and these nonusers are disproportionately young, poor, black, or Hispanic. Predictably, this group accounts for nearly half of all unplanned pregnancies. Overall, of the 6 million pregnancies that occur each year, nearly 3 million are unintended, giving the United States one of the highest rates of unintended pregnancy in the industrialized world.

There are further differences in the kinds of contraception different groups of women use. More affluent women (which means a greater proportion of white women) are likely to be users of oral contraception ("the Pill") and to have partners who have had vasectomies. Black and Hispanic women are more likely to rely on three-month injectables (Depo-Provera) or condoms. In addition, the more affluent women are more likely to have jobs that offer health insurance that covers prescription contraception (though not all health plans do). Pills have a higher effectiveness rate than condoms. Hormonal injectables are very effective, but users have to be able to renew them every three months, either with their own funds or through public programs.

How much contraception is publicly provided? According to a 2008 Guttmacher Institute report, about 36 million American women are in need of contraceptive services—that is, women who are fertile, heterosexually active, and do not wish to become pregnant at the moment. Of this number, about half, 17.5 million women, are dependent on publicly funded contraceptive services and supplies because of poverty or age. (Twenty-nine percent of this group was below the age of twenty, and 71 percent had incomes below 250 percent of the federal poverty level.)

Public funding for contraception, which totaled $1.85 billion in 2006, comes from a variety of sources. Medicaid is the chief source of funding for family planning services, accounting for 71 percent, while Title X of the Public Health Service Act, the only federal program devoted specifically to this purpose, accounts for about 12 percent. The remainder of the funding comes from additional contributions from some states and other sources. Of the 17.5 million women mentioned, only 7 million—41 percent—received contraceptive services from publicly funded clinics in 2006. When I asked a Guttmacher staff person about the contraceptive status of the remaining 59 percent, she acknowledged that the institute did not have a precise answer to that question, although this matter is under investigation. But she was quick to point out that one should not assume that all these remaining women do not receive help. For example, she said that some may be getting services from a private doctor using Medicaid funds, and others are relying on methods they or their partners purchase, mainly condoms. Nevertheless, it is reasonable to conclude that current levels of public funding of contraception are woefully inadequate to meet the needs of a considerable number of poor women.

These figures also mask important differences that have consequences for women depending on where they live. For example, Medicaid is a joint endeavor between the federal government and the states; states have the discretion to decide how much of their Medicaid funds they wish to allocate for family planning. Some states, responding to extremist political forces engaged in a campaign to redefine contraception itself as abortion, have clamped down on family-planning funding from Medicaid and other sources. For example, Texas and several other states have in the past few years reduced state spending for family planning and redirected these funds to crisis pregnancy centers, facilities that counsel against abortion, preach abstinence, and do not offer any education or services relating to contraception. In Texas, some $5 million previously allocated to family planning services was sent instead to CPCs by the state legislature. A major motivation of this legislation apparently was to "defund" some Planned Parenthood clinics in the state that had provided these services. The action also led to the closing of a family planning program at a University of Texas health center in Dallas. When the transfer of funds was announced, doctors at the health center warned that as many as 11,000 women would lose access to services.

Let's put a human face on these kinds of cutbacks. Here is a first-person account by a Latina woman named Tanya, written on the day that these cuts went into effect in Texas and later posted on a Web site. Tanya and other women at a Planned Parenthood clinic typically received not only birth control pills but also annual exams, including screenings for cervical cancer (which is presumably why the sixty-five-year-old woman mentioned was there).

> So this morning I dragged myself out of bed before dawn to be at planned parenthood at 730 and wait in the freezing morning shade until 9 for my annual exam. At 930, myself and the 25 other women (of color) grumbled in solidarity and confusion, wondering why we were still waiting and shivering, finally an employee opened the doors, and corralled us inside just to inform us that there would be no walk-in exams today. or tomorrow. or ever. Boys at the texas state legislature cut pp's funding by 40% last Friday. I stood at the office stunned, while 3 mothers began to cry. Another woman, at least 65 years old, turned to me and asked, "que dijo?" (what did she say?). as I tried to explain what I still didn't understand, I began to feel my anger swell. Overnight one of the safest, most reliable, most critical social services

vanished. all patients over 24 years old have to seek new clinics, all birth control now costs $35/month, all annuals $125,
all pregnancy tests $30.

Tanya's poignant story reminded me of an experience I had several years ago. I was checking into a hotel in Phoenix for a national
conference on women's health issues. As I was completing my reg-
istration, a friend, a doctor, came over and greeted me. He told me
enthusiastically that he had just been to a session whose topic was
making oral contraception available over the counter for medically
eligible women, and thus presumably cheaper and easier to obtain (a
situation that has not yet come to pass). Suddenly the young woman
checking me in, with whom I had probably not even made eye contact, broke excitedly into our conversation: "Oh, wow! When is this
going to happen?" She went on to tell us that she was in her early
twenties and had three children. Even though she worked at the hotel, she could not afford to be on the pill, her preferred method of
birth control. That incident made a deep impression on me. This
hotel clerk probably made too much to qualify for Medicaid but not
enough to be able to afford the pill on her own, especially given the
expense of raising three children.

The stories of Tanya and the hotel clerk (and the millions of
women in similar situations) make it very clear that some women
simply can't afford birth control without some degree of public funding. Inability to afford the pill, one of the most reliable forms of contraception—$35 a month in 2006 dollars, which was beyond Tanya's
reach—is a major reason for the great divide, the "two Americas" I
have been describing. Lack of money for contraception is just one
indication of a larger problem that exists along racial and income
lines: the significant disparity in health care more generally. Black
women, for example, are less likely to have health-care coverage and
less likely to live in safe and clean neighborhoods than white women.
Not only do African American women have worse sexual and reproductive health outcomes—higher rates of unwanted pregnancies,
higher rates of sexually transmitted infections (STIs), and higher incidence of low-birth-weight babies—they also have higher rates of
diabetes, obesity, heart disease, and other conditions.

Dr. Melissa Gilliam, an African American ob-gyn at the University of Chicago, also rejects the "far-flung conspiracy theories" about black women's abortion rates. Rather, she connects these rates squarely to the larger health-care disparities I have mentioned. In a widely distributed opinion piece, she listed a number of sensible steps to bring down the rate of unplanned pregnancies among black women. Citing the well-documented failure of abstinence-only sex education, she called for "better sexual health literacy," pointing out that "only one in three sexually experienced African American males and fewer than half of African American females had received formal instruction about birth control before they first had sex." She also advocated an expansion of Medicaid eligibility for family planning services and increased funding for Title X services. The latter program, notably, provides subsidized contraception and also tests for and treats STIs in both men and women. Yet Title X has been under continual attack from social conservatives since its inception, and its defenders wage a constant struggle merely to keep it from being abolished altogether.

While the inability of many poor women to afford contraception and the inadequacy of public funding for this purpose are the main reasons for high rates of unintended pregnancies, there are other reasons as well. One of these is an antagonistic relationship between the sexes, including domestic violence. I am thinking here of the many stories I have been told over the years by clinic workers of the sabotage of women's use of contraception by people in their networks. I've heard stories of women whose partners (or in some cases parents) beat them if they discover them using birth control. I recall being told of cases of angry boyfriends or husbands flushing birth-control pills down the toilet or poking holes in condoms. I still gasp when I remember several different health professionals telling me of cases in which male partners yanked out women's intrauterine devices (IUDs). "You could consider that sexual assault," one nurse practitioner said to me.

Though no precise figures are available on how large a part these kinds of actions play in women's inability to use contraception, they are widespread enough for the topic of birth-control sabotage to merit its own entry in Wikipedia. This seems to be a particular problem for teenage women. One study of 474 teenaged mothers in the Chicago area found that more than half had experienced domestic violence during the past twelve months, and the same number experienced at least one form of birth-control sabotage. More mundanely, even in the absence of violence, many women have to negotiate condom use with their partners. As those who run abortion clinics know better than most, too often women fail in these negotiations.

As these cases show, it is precisely because birth-control use is a social as well as a medical act, connected both to the very public world of politicians and to the private world of intimate relationships, that this subject has been so fascinating for me and other social scientists. But for women in the real world, of course, getting contraception and being able to use it is not an academic exercise. For an unknown number of women, the ability to use contraception is a struggle not only against poverty and right-wing lawmakers but also with their sexual partners.

STIGMA AND THE ABORTION PATIENT

How does the intense politicization of abortion that I have been discussing throughout this book actually affect women who are receiving abortions? I have discussed the polarized debate about the mental health consequences of abortion and the repeated conclusion of experts that there is no evidence to suggest that abortions cause mental health problems. Nevertheless, providers report that many women who are showing up for abortions these days are not immune to the gross misinformation and stigma that now surround the procedure. This appears to be true of women from both Americas.

The depth of the contemporary negative mythology about abortion was brought home to me very clearly by a story told by Dr. Suzanne Poppema, a veteran abortion provider. After performing an abortion on a teenaged patient who "seemed very calm and together," Poppema left the room, examined the tissue, and returned to tell the patient, as was her custom, that the procedure had gone smoothly and there would be no problem if the patient someday wanted to have children. Poppema was astonished to hear the patient ask, "When are you going to use the steel ball with the knives on it?" The young woman went on to say that she had been told by a counselor at a CPC of such a steel ball with "tiny razorlike knives that would spin around in my uterus." The main point of this story for

Dr. Poppema—and me—was not that egregious lies about abortion are told at many CPCs. The misinformation routinely given to young women at CPCs is a well-known fact, the subject of a congressional inquiry. Rather, it is that in the face of such terrifying information, as Poppema put it, "she *still* came for her abortion!"

Indeed, I have heard many stories over the years of women's determination to get abortions no matter what. Several years ago, when a major earthquake hit the Seattle area, half of one of the clinics in a nearby suburb was literally reduced to rubble, with just a gaping hole open to the elements where a wall had once stood. As the staff assembled to start the cleanup and assess the damage, they were startled to see women showing up for their scheduled appointments! As a staff member wryly said later, "If you don't want to be pregnant anymore, a small thing like an earthquake is not going to stop you."

Clearly neither gruesome scare tactics from the antiabortion movement nor natural disasters will stop some women from trying to get the abortions they need. But this doesn't mean that abortion patients do not internalize larger cultural messages about the procedure. In a number of ways, I have seen how the current stigma affects the behavior and self-image of abortion patients. One example is insurance coverage of abortion, an issue that is by definition more likely to affect women who have higher incomes than the poor do. A handful of states forbid private insurers from covering abortion services except in cases of life endangerment, and more prohibit such coverage for public employees. No surprise there. What is surprising is the number of women whose insurance policies do cover abortion but who choose not to use their coverage. One study, done at UCSF, surveyed 212 patients who had received a medication abortion and found that only a tiny fraction of those with health insurance used it to pay for their abortion. Similarly, numerous clinic administrators have told me of patients' preference to pay cash for their abortions, even if they have insurance coverage. The reason? These women do not want a paper trail of their abortions to exist. In some cases they do not want family members to find out; in other cases they wish to keep this knowledge from their employer or their primary-care provider.

The reluctance on the part of some women to have their "regular" physician learn of an abortion is particularly interesting to me, since it seems at odds with the efforts of some primary-care physicians to incorporate abortion into general practice. This hesitation stems from an often well-founded fear of disapproval, but also from patients' shame over having an abortion. In a recent small study in which I participated as a consultant, Kate Cosby, a public-health researcher at UCSF, interviewed twenty abortion patients—most, though not all, low-income women—in three clinics in "heartland" states (conservative midwestern states) in which abortion was highly regulated. Some of the patients had traveled considerable distances. When Cosby asked if they would have preferred to have their own physician perform the procedure, only a small minority said they would. Some stated flatly that they knew what their doctor's reaction would be if they raised the topic: "He would have tried to talk me out of it." More poignantly, some women spoke directly of the tainted identity they felt as an abortion recipient and their consequent desire to keep the abortion secret. As one, the mother of two children, said, "I don't think I would be comfortable going to my ob-gyn for an abortion, knowing that's the same man that delivered my children. . . . I would think he would think of me differently. . . . I mean, he sees me in one light, and that's the way I want him to see me."

To be sure, patients' fears about their regular doctors' disapproval are not unfounded in some cases. But we can speculate that for many primary-care clinicians, the issue is not actual opposition to abortion but rather obliviousness of it. As Christina Hernandez, a clinic administrator in the South, said on a provider Listserv, "Every week, without fail, at least one patient tells me how mortified she was when her family physician or ob-gyn gave her the results of her pregnancy test, cheerfully congratulated her on the baby to come and immediately began setting her up for prenatal care without any consideration at all for how she might feel about it." Hernandez went on to write, "The patient will then ask me what she can say to her doctor to conceal the fact that she had an abortion, and whether the doctor will be able to tell at her next exam. I suggest that instead of worrying about that, she should be more concerned that her doctor didn't care about how she felt about her pregnancy in the first place—and then I dig into my referral files and help her find a pro-choice physician in her area."

So strong is the desire of many women to keep the fact of their abortions secret that in many of the facilities I have visited—clinics, hotlines, doctors' offices—the staff makes a notation next to the patient's name if they can leave a message using the facility's name. Even though traveling for several hours to obtain an abortion can be very difficult, many women fear that if they receive an abortion in their own community, they might run into an acquaintance in the waiting room. (I recall an especially touching tale of a policewoman who was scheduled to have an abortion at a clinic that received many protesters and who was terrified that some of her fellow officers would be on duty the day of her procedure.) The antiabortion movement has long recognized the power of outing abortion patients as a means of discouraging other potential patients. This explains the movement's numerous efforts to photograph the license plates of cars in clinic parking lots and film those entering and leaving the clinics.

To return to the abortion recipients interviewed by Cosby in the heartland states, the palpable sense of isolation and corresponding lack of solidarity with other abortion patients were for me one of the most interesting things to emerge from this study. "I am a Christian—I am not doing this casually," one woman said, clearly suggesting that others in the waiting room were not so thoughtful or moral. Another woman said, "I think that people should be held accountable for their actions, and a lot of times it's the convenience of the situation that makes it easy . . . to get an abortion, and if I wasn't the person that I was, I mean, this would be real easy, just real simple." Perhaps the starkest example of isolation came from one woman's response to the question of whether she would "ever consider being part of a group that supports people who get abortions." Her answer was an emphatic no. As she put it, "I wouldn't support them because . . . it [might become] a habit for everyone." The speaker was a twenty-year-old mother of one, about to have her second abortion.

What should we make of these attitudes? None of these women felt that abortion should be illegal. (This is, by the way, not true of all abortion recipients; virtually every provider with whom I have ever had contact told me of the occasional protester who grimly arrives at the clinic for an abortion for herself or her daughter. The provider community wryly describes this unique patient group as "the women whose three acceptable exceptions for an abortion are 'rape, incest, or mine.'") Cosby's respondents felt that their abortions were necessary, but having to take on the identity of an abortion patient made them feel both sad and shameful. Necessary, because they were getting abortions for the same reason women always do: they recognized that they could not adequately care for a child at this moment in their lives. This seemed especially true for the more than half of the interviewees who already had children. Sad, because the abortions they sought seemed to symbolize for them their failure to achieve the lives they wished they had. As one woman said wistfully, when asked if there were circumstances under which she would not have had the abortion, "If my old boyfriend would still be with me, not caring if I was pregnant . . . or if I had the money and my own house, my own car, maybe I wouldn't care about having a man beside me, and I could just move on with my kids."

And finally, why the shame about abortion, and the seeming necessity to differentiate themselves from other women in the same position? Whatever else of a personal nature these women brought to the abortion experience—for example, religious beliefs—they live in a society, as I have argued from the first pages of this book, in which abortion has been relentlessly stigmatized by its opponents. It's not all that surprising that they have internalized negative messages about abortion. I was particularly struck, though, by the lack of empathy with other abortion recipients that some of these women expressed.

I can't help reflecting how different the situation was in the 1970s, when abortion was first legalized in the United States. Then, many women seeking abortions felt connected to a larger movement. "Second-wave" feminism was flourishing, and women's health issues were a central focus of that movement. People still had fresh memories of the days when abortion was illegal and thousands of women had died or been injured from unsafe abortions. Rather than being ashamed, many abortion patients in those immediate post-*Roe* years felt both relieved and entitled to have this once dangerous procedure done in a professional, woman-centered setting.

My point is not that there no longer exists a movement for abortion rights. Today there continues to be an extremely hardworking, multifaceted reproductive rights movement. As I document in this book, dedicated health-care providers resolutely go forward each day to provide abortion care, often risking their personal safety. Brilliant lawyers at the ACLU, the Center for Reproductive Rights, and elsewhere work tirelessly to stem the tide against the various restrictions imposed by judicial and legislative bodies. Advocates such as those I've described at NAF, the Access hotline, and similar groups help vulnerable women who need abortions and other reproductive services in numerous ways.

The problem, rather, is that there is a clear gap—of class and of education—between those who work in this increasingly professionalized movement and the majority of women now getting abortions. Yet another challenge for this beleaguered movement is to make the isolated women in the heartland waiting rooms feel that they are part of the struggle.

VII

"EVERY WOMAN IS DIFFERENT"

What Good Abortion Care Looks Like

Every woman that comes through is different. Every experience is different. Her counseling is different, her pain management is different. With one you may tell jokes, with one you tell stories, with another you cry.

—DAVID BENNETT, MD, veteran abortion provider

What really happens in abortion clinics or providers' offices, beyond the actual fact of the abortion procedure itself? The antiabortion movement relentlessly disparages abortion-providing facilities as "mills," where women are treated in a brusque and unsafe manner. Opponents also revile the "abortion industry," whose only objective, they claim, is to make as much money as possible. One of the most explosive charges made against abortion providers is their alleged callousness about what they are doing—specifically, their lack of regard for the fetus within the body of the pregnant woman.

This characterization of abortion care is very different from what I have learned during the years I've spent within this community. The providers I have interviewed and observed and the conversations I have monitored on-line have revealed an unusual level of compassion for patients and dedication to the mission of women's health. Does this mean that I believe there are no substandard facilities or individual providers who are incompetent and/or uncaring? Sadly, no. What can only be described as "rogue clinics" periodically surface in the news, usually after the injury or, more rarely, the death of a patient. These clinics—or, in some cases, individual doctors—typically prey on women in low-income immigrant communities. These facilities have inadequate medical standards and often egregious ethical practices as well. For example, in 2008, the sisters Bertha and Raquel Bugarin were arrested for practicing medicine without a license at a string of clinics they owned in Southern California. Their clinics served mostly poor Latinas, many of whom were probably undocumented immigrants. A number of lawsuits have been filed against the sisters, for both injuries and a wrongful death. The doctors hired by the Bugarins had dubious medical backgrounds and seemingly little training in accepted methods of abortion provision. One of them had a record of sexual exploitation of abortion patients; another was on probation for performing medical procedures while under the influence of alcohol when he began work at these clinics.

Inept and unethical abortion providers remind me, of course, of the era before *Roe*. I find it outrageous that so many years after the legalization of abortion, vulnerable women are still subject to such unacceptable medical care. While the antiabortion movement seizes upon these instances of rogue care to tarnish the entire abortion-providing community, I draw quite different lessons from these incidents. That such clinics can flourish until the inevitable disaster occurs strikes me as a "perfect storm" caused by the marginalization of abortion care from mainstream medicine, the lack of universal health care in the United States, and the particular difficulties facing undocumented immigrants in obtaining health care. Put simply, if the women who went to the Bugarins' clinics had had a primary health-care provider, and if they had not been embarrassed to ask for an abortion, and if they had been able to receive an abortion from their primary provider or a referral to an appropriate responsible abortion facility, these tragedies would not have occurred.

Fortunately, the overwhelming majority of abortion facilities in this country are very different from the rogue clinics. Abortion is the most scrutinized branch of American medicine, and the overall excellent safety record of the procedure has been established in numerous studies. But what does good abortion care actually mean, beyond safe provision of the abortion itself? In the pages that follow I offer instances of what I believe to be the essential element of high-quality abortion care: the acceptance of nuance, and the realization that all abortion patients cannot be treated the same, as the epigraph to this chapter suggests. I also show that the indifference to the fetus that abortion providers are frequently accused of simply does not exist.

One of the providers from whom I have learned the most is Dr. Julia Miller, a family medicine physician and one of the national leaders in the effort to incorporate abortion provision into primary-care practice. Miller, one of the hardest-working people I know (I have gotten e-mails from her sent at 1 a.m.), is actively involved in training residents and, where legally permitted, advanced practice clinicians such as nurse practitioners, midwives, and physician assistants. She works tirelessly to get relevant medical organizations like the American Academy of Family Practice to recognize abortion care as a legitimate part of family medicine. In order to reach a wide audience of family medicine and other primary-care clinicians with similar interests, she cofounded a Listserv, to which she frequently contributes. Many on this Listserv are not yet as actively involved in abortion care as Miller; her posts offer an ongoing seminar of sorts on the gratifications and challenges of bringing this procedure into a family practice. Here are portions of some of her messages, which illustrate a range of patient needs and Miller's responses.

> I had such a sad patient come in today for an abortion. She'd come in a week ago but was so tearful we could hardly talk, so I asked her to come back after thinking some more.... [After more counseling and discussion of the options, including adoption, the patient decided to proceed with the abortion.] She asked me if she could have the pregnancy. I thought it might help her to see that it was only a tiny sac, so I washed it off and brought it back to her.... I gave it to her in a jar.... [S]he wanted to put it in the —— River, at a place she knew that felt special to her. I told her I thought a good-bye ritual like that would help her move on. We had a long long hug before she left. I plan to encourage more counseling when she comes back next week.

In the next post, Miller shares "an interesting and heartwarming follow-up experience," one concerning a patient who had come to her for an abortion just as she was about to move out of town with her fiancé.

She came back today. The relationship with the fiancé had crashed despite her efforts at counseling. She moved back here to where her support network waited. . . . What was such a wonderful part of her visit to me was the way she discussed her abortion. As a family doctor I have processed abortion guilt with so many women. But this was totally different. She spoke of it matter-of-factly. She told me she was completely thankful, given the way the relationship turned out, that she had made the decision she made. And she talked about wanting to have children with her new partner when she was sure the relationship was solid.

The following post describes Dr. Miller's gratification at being able to provide in-office ultrasonography for a patient who had experienced some bleeding and feared she was having a miscarriage. The patient's husband and five-year-old son were able to accompany her during this office visit. It is fairly unusual for family physicians to have ultrasound machines; Miller had such a machine because of her abortion provision. If she had not had this technology, the patient would have had to wait longer to be scheduled for an ultrasound at an off-site facility.

We did the sonogram. . . . The sono showed a small embryo, with the visible flicker of the fetal heart. . . . Everyone was overjoyed. Hugs all around. She wants me to do her prenatal care and it was all in all one of those happy family medicine moments. One that I could make possible because of my abortion training!

Three patients, three different situations, three equally heartfelt hugs passing between doctor and patient. These vignettes from Dr. Miller's practice capture the essence of what good abortion care means. In each instance Dr. Miller, to use a phrase common in the abortion-providing world, "met the patient where she was at." In the case of the first abortion patient, she acknowledged the patient's emotional pain, urging her to take more time to decide, to consider the option of adoption, to conduct a meaningful burial ritual, and to think about post-abortion counseling. In the case of the second, she affirmed the patient's sense of having made the right decision at a difficult time. In the case of the woman who feared a miscarriage, Miller shared in the elation that this wanted pregnancy was viable.

These brief glimpses of Miller's responses to the different needs of her patients reminded me of another instance where the principle of "meeting the patient where she is at" could not have been clearer. I was observing at an ultrasound training workshop in the Pacific Northwest. The workshop was for primary-care clinicians who were beginning to offer medication abortion in their practices and were planning to use ultrasonography to date their patients' pregnancies precisely. (Ultrasounds are not required as part of the medication abortion regimen but are widely used for this purpose and in abortion care more generally.) As is common in this kind of medical training situation, the host clinic had recruited two pregnant patients to serve as volunteers so the trainees could practice using an ultrasound machine. In return, the patients were to receive a certain amount of free medical service from the clinic.

After a lecture, it was time for the trainees to enter the procedure rooms with the waiting volunteers. Before this happened, the group was informed that the first room contained a woman who was planning to continue her pregnancy and the second, one who was planning to terminate. Immediately after the training session, we were told, one of the clinic's doctors was going to perform the second woman's abortion, at no cost.

When I entered the first room with the group of about six trainees and two trainers, I sensed a high energy level, and there was a lot of jovial banter between the clinicians and the volunteer, including thanks for her service. When the embryo (about five weeks gestation) was first located on the ultrasound, the trainer enthusiastically pointed this out to her. As different trainees took turns finding the tiny embryonic sac, others kept up a steady stream of small talk, asking how the pregnancy was going, how the patient was feeling, and so on. The group left with wishes for a successful pregnancy and birth.

The mood changed immediately when we entered the second room. People became far more subdued. The patient was graciously thanked for her volunteer service, but there was none of the buoyancy that I had just witnessed with the first patient. When the embryo was initially located on the screen, the trainers quietly pointed it out to the trainees and did not call it to the woman's attention. I noted that she did not look at the screen at all for the forty-five minutes the group was in the room. Some of the trainees, waiting for their turn at the ultrasound, made small talk with the patient about neutral topics such as the beauty of her hometown. When everyone was finished, the patient was again thanked for her helpfulness, and the group quietly left the room.

At this point, you might well think "Duh!" It's only common sense, after all, that a group of health professionals would react differently to women in different situations. It may be common sense, but as we have seen, common sense does not always prevail when politicians or some clinicians become involved in the decisions of pregnant women. Whether it is antiabortion legislators demanding that all abortion patients be read the same "informed consent" scripts or mandating the showing of ultrasounds to these patients, or oblivious physicians assuming that a positive pregnancy test is always welcome news, the fundamental mistake is the belief that a "one size fits all" policy is appropriate for women with unplanned pregnancies. What I have learned repeatedly from observing the abortion-providing world is that good care is incompatible with treating all women alike.

"OWNING" THE ABORTION DECISION

Realizing that not all women who are present in an abortion clinic are necessarily appropriate candidates for an abortion—at least at that moment—is one key way in which providers make distinctions among patients in their waiting room. The cardinal rule of abortion provision has not changed since I started observing this field in the 1970s: no woman should get an abortion unless it is truly her decision. Providers are aware that some small portion of patients are there against their will, because either a male partner or a parent has demanded an abortion. As we saw in chapter 4, a great deal of state regulation focuses, via parental notification or consent laws, on parents' abilities to *prevent* a teenager's abortion, and tragedies can result when young women are driven to take matters into their own hands. But I have heard of numerous other unhappy situations where parents and teenagers came into conflict because the parents demanded an abortion that the young woman refused to undergo. At a meeting where a group of counselors discussed such conflicts, I heard one particularly heartbreaking tale from a counselor in the Midwest: when a mother learned that the clinic would refuse to do an abortion unless her teenage daughter consented, she became so angry that she shouted to everyone present that she was through with her daughter and the pregnant young woman could not return home. The shaken staff was left with no option other than to call Child Protective Services to arrange emergency housing for the teenager.

But it is not just coercion from others that abortion providers worry about. To use the language I often hear from clinicians and counselors, the woman must "own" her decision. That is, she must enter into the abortion experience with both a knowledge and an acceptance of what she is doing. I heard this principle articulated once again in the fall of 2008 at a workshop called "Promoting Post-Abortion Well-Being." I was somewhat surprised to see among the other workshop participants Dr. Leroy Carhart and his wife, Mary—surprised only because I knew that this couple had been involved in abortion care for many years. I was moved that these veterans still felt there was more for them to learn.

Lee Carhart is a very well-known figure in reproductive rights circles. He is named in two Supreme Court cases, *Stenberg v. Carhart* and *Gonzales v. Carhart,* a reflection of his tireless efforts to challenge congressional attempts to impose a ban on a particular method of second-trimester abortion. I heard of Dr. Carhart many years ago, before I had the chance to meet him, because the violence that had befallen him and his family was particularly appalling. In 1991, though abortion was only a small part of his practice in Nebraska, antiabortion extremists burned down his house and his stables, killing his seventeen cherished horses and household pets and destroying virtually everything the Carharts owned. As he has told journalists, the fire was a turning point in his life; he determined "not to cede a victory to the antis" and began to provide abortions full-time. Mary Carhart works with her husband in his Omaha-area clinic.

At the workshop in question, both Carharts elaborated on the idea of a woman "owning" her decision. Like Dr. Miller, who sent an ambivalent patient home to reflect further on the abortion decision, both Lee and Mary don't hesitate to send a patient home to reconsider—"a few every week"—if she appears to be conflicted about having an abortion. At their clinic, each patient is asked to fill out a ten-item questionnaire. One of the first items asks, "Whose decision was it for you to have an abortion?" But even if pressure from others is not at play, other factors can act as a red flag. For example, the patients are requested to circle words that best describe how they are feeling—words ranging from *relieved* and *resolved* to *numb* and *ashamed*. They are also instructed to anticipate how they will feel after the abortion. They are instructed to list their concerns about the coming procedure, and one choice is "not sure of my decision to have an abortion." Patients whose answers suggest a worrisome level of conflicted feelings are questioned further by a staff member. Additionally, patients' behavior on the procedure table can act as a warning that the abortion should not proceed—at least, not then. Julia Miller told her Listserv colleagues of a patient who "got a little hysterical when I had just put the speculum in. I told her I can only do the procedure for women who want it, and that her tensing up gave me a message that she had not really made up her mind." (The patient subsequently calmed down and the abortion proceeded uneventfully.)

Why make such attempts to weed out patients who express a high degree of indecision, or at least to delay the procedure? Lee Carhart is concerned about the emotional aftermath of an abortion for such patients. Although he agrees with the general research finding that relief is the major post-abortion reaction, he believes that a small number of patients may experience genuine regret. His mantra, when faced with deeply ambivalent patients, is "She doesn't have to decide today." Most of those he sends home return to the clinic, sure of their decision. Others don't.

Deciding who is not an appropriate candidate for an abortion is, of course, a delicate and imperfect process. Patients express a broad range of emotions at the time of an abortion. Some patients express sadness, often as much about the circumstances that made the abortion necessary, such as a failed relationship or lack of money to raise a child, as about the abortion itself. But this sadness is often mixed with certainty that the patient is choosing the best course for herself at this moment. Younger patients sometimes reveal a great deal of anxiety, but this often reflects concern about the physical aspects of the procedure ("Will it hurt?") rather than their feelings about the abortion. Though different clinics and clinicians use different methods of patient appraisal, the central question remains: is the patient truly okay with the decision?

Some of the patients who have the hardest time "owning" the abortion decision, not surprisingly, are those who have strong anti-abortion beliefs. Miller shared an account of a patient who "was unhappy about being pregnant but did not believe in abortion." This patient returned three times and anxiously queried Miller and the junior physicians working with her about the possibility of birth defects, looking for a medical justification for an abortion—a justification that simply didn't exist in her case. In short, this patient wanted a doctor to make the decision about the abortion on her behalf. Others on the Listserv acknowledged similar cases of women who attempted to put the decision in the clinician's hands. One of those responding to Miller's post first allowed that perhaps the "pendulum has swung too far" in the direction of humanist physicians' reluctance to give direct advice because of fears of appearing too "paternalistic." But in the abortion case, she continued, this reluctance is appropriate: "No other medical treatments involve so much potential guilt and regret as the decision to have a child/not have a child, and that is one decision where I feel that patients really need to take responsibility. It's more than treatment for yourself for cancer—it's a lifelong commitment to another human being or the loss of the opportunity for that commitment."

DEALING WITH THE FETUS: MEETING THE WOMAN WHERE SHE IS AT

But even when it is clear to providers that patients truly are "owning" their decision and are suitable candidates (which describes the vast majority of women seeking abortions), there are still interesting, often challenging policy decisions that providers have to make. For example, what is the appropriate language to be used in counseling? Counselors and clinicians tend to use the terms *pregnancy* and *fetus;* in contrast, many patients use the term *baby,* which makes some providers uncomfortable. Similarly, how should providers respond to the occasional patient who asks to see her ultrasound before her abortion, or, afterward, the *product of conception* (another term used far more by providers than by patients)?

It is in situations like these that I am most struck by the wide gap between the "one size fits all" policies of antiabortion legislators and the nuance that is so fundamental to good abortion care. Here, for example, is Lydia, an administrator in a midwestern clinic, in conversation with colleagues on a provider Listserv, discussing the issue of appropriate language in the abortion context:

> Patients who have a wanted pregnancy and lose it, or choose abortions because of fetal anomalies, always call it "the baby." It is a baby to them, developed or not. . . . Some women never "connect" to the pregnancy. . . . [F]or them, it is nothing like a baby. It is just there, they want it removed. They would hate the word "baby" and do not use it. I have also seen women somewhere in the middle. Our job is to meet the woman where she is and provide her with accurate information. I do not feel it is my job to correct her terminology as long as she has a thorough understanding of the facts.

Many abortion providers maintain a similar policy of flexibility with respect to ultrasounds. Ultrasounds have become one of the latest weapons in the regulatory war waged by foes of abortion. A number of states have passed laws that make mandatory ultrasound viewing part of the informed-consent process. Forcing women to view ultrasounds they don't want to see strikes me as, at best, a gimmick that antiabortion legislators can use to please their constituents, and at worst, a step that imposes unnecessary cruelty on vulnerable women. The meanness—not to mention the absurdity—of state ultrasound mandates became especially clear to me when I looked at the text of a recently passed Oklahoma law (under legal challenge at the time of this writing). This law requires abortion providers to perform an ultrasound on all patients and, among other things, to "provide a medical description of the ultrasound images, which shall include the dimensions of the embryo, and fetus." The law, however, stipulates that "nothing in this section shall be construed to prevent a pregnant woman from averting her eyes from the ultrasound image." I looked in vain to see if the woman was also allowed to cover her ears. Besides the imposition on women of "unwelcome speech by the government in a private setting" (which is the argument made by the Center for Reproductive Rights in challenging this law), the ultrasound requirement, if it goes into effect, will probably force the closing of the women's health clinic bringing the suit because of the increased costs the law would impose. This is a clinic, incidentally, that also provides contraceptive services and adoption counseling.

The Oklahoma law has the added perverse feature of preventing a woman from suing her doctor if he or she intentionally withholds other information about the fetus, such as the information that it has an anomaly. So women are forced to hear something they may not choose to hear but are not entitled to information that would presumably be of critical importance to them. This is what public policy looks like when it is in the hands of antiabortion fanatics.

But some women do wish to see the ultrasound. Most providers with whom I am familiar do the commonsensical thing: they respond to the requests of individual women. That is, women who ask to see the ultrasound are shown it, but unless the abortion is taking place in states that mandate ultrasound viewing, no one is forced to. Similar policies are used for showing patients the products of conception after the abortion. While some people involved in abortion work are hesitant to do this, feeling that the later in gestation the abortion occurs, the more upsetting it might be to see the product, others have come to "trust women," as veteran abortion providers often put it. Renee Bancroft, a long-time provider, works in a clinic that does a fair number of second-trimester procedures. In a Listserv discussion of the pros and cons of showing patients products of conception, Bancroft posted the following:

> I remember an incident from before I was totally convinced that women know what is right for themselves in this regard: I did a 16-week vacuum aspiration and the woman asked to see the POC [product of conception]. After telling her what she would see, I brought it in in a little pyrex dish. . . . She held it near her face and touched some of the parts with her finger. Meanwhile I was thinking to myself, "She's going to start

crying hysterically, I shouldn't have showed her POCs that are so big, I did the wrong thing." . . . After a few minutes she handed it back to me, and with a look of great relief on her face, she said, "Thank you. I'm so relieved it's so small." And there ended my assumption that I could know what would be best for any given woman in this situation.

Another provider contributed this comment to the discussion: "I agree with full disclosure. . . . [W]e have to give women credit for being able to handle the information. A fundamental part of the anti-choice worldview is that women are not able to be moral actors in their own lives; [we need to] treat all women as persons able to morally reason and make choices." She then added yet another compelling reason to respond to patients' wishes in this realm: "They may feel worse if they see a mangled 28-week fetus on a picketer's poster and think this is what their POCs looked like."

ABORTION PROVIDERS AND CONTRACEPTION

A discussion of birth control with patients occurs in most abortion-providing facilities (and virtually all those that I observed in researching this book). Initiating such discussion is the standard of care governing clinics and private practices affiliated with the National Abortion Federation and Planned Parenthood, which together account for well over half of all abortions performed in the United States. Some clinics, if they are able to afford it, send women home with a month's supply of pills or another birth-control method. Christina Hernandez told me of "schmoozing with our drug company reps, hatching schemes to get our patients enough pills" to carry the often desperately poor women served by Hernandez's clinic until they can somehow come up with the money for contraception themselves.

At the most superficial level, this practice may sound contradictory. Indeed, some contributors on the Listservs I frequent occasionally make joking reference to "putting ourselves out of business" when this subject comes up. More seriously, though, there is no contradiction in abortion providers' promotion of contraception. As public health proponents, members of this group believe as fervently in the goal of preventing unwanted pregnancies as they do in the right of women to decide to end such pregnancies.

The real irony is that these clinicians, who have been defending abortion for thirty-five years, increasingly have to defend contraception as well. The steadily escalating attacks on contraception by sectors of the antiabortion movement have become a new, and to me surreal, front in the abortion wars. I remember well when contraception represented common ground between supporters and opponents of abortion in Congress. Passage of the first bill providing federal funding for contraception occurred in 1970, shortly before the *Roe* decision. One of the key sponsors of this legislation was the first President Bush, who as a young congressman from Texas was nicknamed "Rubbers" because of his enthusiasm for condom distribution. But as the religious right gained strength as a political force, this common ground began to dissolve. Contraception began to be denounced in some conservative circles as "supportive of the abortion mentality." Several years ago the Pro-Life Action League, an antiabortion group in Chicago, hosted a conference called "Contraception Is Not the Answer." The following statement was posted on the group's Web site after the conference: "The entire edifice of sexual license, perversion and abortion is erected upon the foundation of contraception."

Eventually, to its opponents, contraception became the *equivalent* of abortion. This occurred through a novel redefinition of when pregnancy begins, and therefore what constitutes an abortion. The medical community has long defined a pregnancy as beginning with the implantation of a fertilized egg in the wall of the uterus. In contrast, religious right activists claim that pregnancy begins with the fertilization of an egg by a sperm. This claim is highly problematic. There are a number of compelling scientific reasons that implantation is the medical marker for pregnancy: there is actually no way to know if a woman is pregnant before implantation; fertilization is a process that can take up to twenty-four hours; and anywhere from one third to one half of all fertilized eggs never begin or complete implantation.

The religious right's redefinition of contraception was first deployed in a fierce battle over EC, with opponents claiming that the emergency-contraception drug (a higher-than-normal dose of oral contraception) causes an "abortion." More recently other contraceptive methods, including regular birth control pills, have come under attack. Even though most scientists believe that these hormonal methods work by preventing ovulation and hence conception, it cannot be proved beyond a doubt that they never prevent implantation.

What is the impact of this new attack on contraception for women? We have already seen how certain state legislatures are cutting funding for contraception and redirecting these funds to crisis pregnancy centers that offer no contraceptive supplies or even education. Spurred by a group called Pharmacists for Life, many drugstores, including, for a time, the Wal-Mart chain, announced that they would not stock EC. Soon some pharmacists refused to fill prescriptions for regular birth-control pills as well. Abortion providers, as we have seen, are left trying to fill in the gaps. This is the case for Annie Moses, whose southern clinic serves poor women from particularly conservative areas. Mentioning to her colleagues how many calls she was getting from women who were seeking not abortions but EC, she commented on the "irony that we seem to be the only ones dispensing EC in this area."

BEYOND THE MEDICAL IN ABORTION CARE

For health professionals who work in abortion care, performing abortions is first and foremost a medical act, one to be done safely and in a respectful manner. But a combination of such factors as the poverty of many of their patients, the bitter social conflicts surrounding abortion, and the opposition to abortion of many in the patients' immediate circles means that abortion care cannot be contained in a solely medical framework. Much of what I have seen in abortion-providing facilities speaks to staff responses to the social circumstances of their patients. Two quite different incidents reinforced this understanding of abortion care for me.

The first involved a young woman of sixteen who was receiving a medical abortion from Sylvie Shore, the family medicine doctor who has incorporated early abortions into her practice in a large teaching hospital. I was spending the day observing Dr. Shore in her office, and with the patient's permission I was able to witness this interaction between doctor and patient. Shore had previously told me that the patient's mother, on the hospital's housekeeping staff, knew of the pregnancy and had encouraged her daughter to come to Shore for an abortion.

The patient—I'll call her Laura—seemed quite composed for a sixteen-year-old. Shore, who was very warm and welcoming, reconfirmed with Laura her wish to end her pregnancy. The doctor reaffirmed as well the mother's knowledge and support of this decision. She then explained exactly what the two-step procedure would consist of: Laura would take the mifepristone right then and would go home with a second medication, misoprostal, to be inserted inside her cheek the following day. After Shore handed Laura the mifepristone tablet and Laura swallowed it, the doctor resumed casual conversation for a few moments.

She then turned to the issue of the misoprostal, which Laura needed to take in twenty-four hours. She informed Laura that in the hours following the insertion of the drug in her cheek, she would be going to the bathroom frequently. Seemingly as an afterthought, Shore then asked the teenager how many bathrooms there were in her house and who else would be home in the afternoon, when Laura returned from school and was to take the misoprostal. Laura replied, without much elaboration, that her father would be there. Upon further gentle questioning from Shore, she acknowledged that he had not been told of either the pregnancy or the abortion. Doctor and patient then engaged in a strategy session as to how best to handle this situation. At the end of this encounter, Shore mentioned that she looked forward to seeing Laura for her follow-up visit, which would include prescribing a birth-control method.

Admittedly, there is nothing particularly dramatic about the incident I just recounted. But Dr. Shore told me later of her knowledge of conflicts between the girl's parents and the mother's fears that her husband would find out about Laura's situation. The doctor also pointed out to me, in a follow-up e-mail, how suited her field of family medicine is to handle complex cases such as this one. Stating that her goal was "to support the patient's strengths in the face of the conflict at home," Shore went on to say that "I, like many family docs, often know some of the 'back story' ahead of time, so we can frame our questions in a way that allows the story to come out from the patient, and then problem-solve with them."

The second incident involves a more challenging situation that confronted Annie Moses and the staff of her clinic (a facility that for various reasons gets far more than its share of extreme hardship cases). As Moses recounted to colleagues on a Listserv: "A very pregnant 11-year-old. Imagine, blond, blue eyes, and small. A child . . . this little one was too far in the pregnancy for us to help. Broke my heart. I needed to spend some time with this family trying to figure out what to do."

Ultimately, the path chosen was one that Moses and her staff (and clinics across the country) had been on numerous times. The young patient, impregnated by a relative, was referred to George Tiller, a Kansas physician who performed later abortions than most other providers. As Moses wrote, "The staff gave this very poor family some 'traveling money' out of their own pockets. And off they went on a very long road trip to receive abortion care." Tiller performed the abortion at a substantially lowered cost, and the eleven-year-old returned home, no longer pregnant.

For years, until his brutal murder by an antiabortion fanatic in May 2009, George Tiller was one of the best-known—and most controversial—abortion providers in the country. Because his clinic in Wichita was one of only a handful in the United States known to offer later abortions, including third-trimester care for women with fetal anomalies and serious health conditions, he had become the preeminent target of antiabortion extremists in the United States. He had been relentlessly hounded for years by opponents who have stalked him at his office, his home, and his church. His clinic was bombed in 1986 and was blockaded for six weeks in the summer of 1991. In 1993 he was shot (though not seriously injured) by a member of the so-called Army of God. (After this 1993 shooting, Tiller made it a point to return to the clinic the very next day.) Dr. Tiller had been repeatedly subjected to various legal actions brought by Phill Kline, the former attorney general of Kansas and a leading religious right activist in that state. Kline's accusations ultimately came to nothing, and his failure to win reelection can be at least partially attributed to his single-minded obsession with abortion in general and Dr. Tiller in particular. In March 2009, a jury took just forty-five minutes to acquit Tiller of charges, brought by Kline's successor, that the doctor had violated a technical aspect of a Kansas law that regulates late-term abortions. Immediately after his acquittal, the Kansas Board of Healing Arts, which regulates the licenses of physicians, announced that it would investigate a similar charge against him—a charge brought, notably, by an Operation Rescue operative, who herself had served time in jail for antiabortion violence and who had a history of contacts with Scott Roeder, Tiller's murderer.

Within abortion-providing circles, however, Tiller was a beloved figure, honored both for his technical proficiency with the more complex abortion procedures and for his generosity to women and their families in often very difficult situations. Indeed, he was frequently referred to by the community as Saint George, precisely because of his frequent willingness to help out his colleagues across the country with some of their most challenging cases, medically and socially, like the eleven-year-old mentioned above.

Tiller's practice had long been of interest to me. When I first began studying this field, I became aware of his pioneering efforts to incorporate spiritual assistance for patients into his practice. I recall being deeply moved at a national meeting when I saw slides of the space set aside at Tiller's clinic for grieving parents, many of whom had just gone through the abortion of a much-desired pregnancy. In this space—the Quiet Room—people could choose to be counseled by a chaplain on Tiller's staff and could participate in rituals such as a baptism or blessings for the aborted fetus. Shortly after Dr. Tiller's death, his family announced that his clinic would be closed permanently.

Other abortion facilities have gradually been adopting the practice of incorporating spiritual elements into abortion care for interested patients. As in Tiller's practice, a number of clinics have set aside space as sanctuaries or meditation rooms, sometimes including religious materials from a variety of traditions as well as nondenominational materials. These sanctuaries often contain material from the Religious Coalition for Reproductive Choice, an organization of clergy who support women's decision to have an abortion. From some providers I have heard stories of women bringing their own clergy with them to the initial visit to an abortion clinic. I also recall a conversation I had with a Protestant minister old enough to have been active, in the pre-*Roe* era, with a network of clergy who helped women find safe abortion providers. Now much of his abortion-related activity, he told me, is praying with women who "fear they will go to hell" because they have had an abortion.

Dr. Julia Miller's encouragement that an anguished patient perform a good-bye ritual for her fetus is but one illustration of the numerous ways in which spiritual elements are being incorporated into abortion care. But such offers of spiritual practice are just that—offers. Not all women wish to partake of them. Even those who do wish for some spiritual component as part of their abortion will want quite different things. Once again we see that the essence of good abortion care is not to treat all women the same way.

ADDRESSING THE ABORTION STIGMA

In recent years I have seen abortion providers attempt to grapple with another issue that affects the emotional status of some of their patients: the stigma surrounding abortion. In the last chapter I offered a few indications of how this stigma sometimes manifests itself in patients sitting in clinic waiting rooms, citing their isolation and lack of empathy with other patients and their concern that others, such as their primary-care physicians, will learn of the abortion. Providers realize that the consequences of the stigma can be problematic. As one physician put it at a workshop I attended, "Even if our patients don't feel bad about abortion, they *think* they should." A counselor at the same event spoke of patients' expectations of being criticized for having an abortion, pointing out that in some situations, "women can't talk to the people closest to them about this important thing that happened to them."

What these providers are saying is that emotions have a social as well as a psychological component. Arlie Hochschild, a professor emerita of sociology at the University of California, Berkeley, is one of the pioneers of the sociology of emotions. She has written of the "framing rules" and "feeling rules" that govern particular situations and experiences at a given moment in society: in short, the way we are "supposed" to think and feel about certain issues. She highlights the struggles among various groups "to assert the legitimacy" of their favored frames and feeling rules in contested areas. She writes as well of "emotion work," the efforts people make to cope with the prevailing feeling rules governing various issues.

Drawing on Hochschild's concepts, I see the current state of the abortion conflict in the United States as one in which the emotional rules put forward by the antiabortion movement—that abortion is an immoral and selfish act and that a woman should feel ashamed of having one—are dominant for many people, including abortion recipients. To gain a sense of how these rules have changed significantly over time, consider this passage from a recent essay by the Reverend Katharine Ragsdale, an Episcopal priest, and Susan Yanow, a longtime reproductive rights activist: "Thirty years ago abortion was seen as a positive advancement—medically, socially and religiously. Medically, abortion was seen as a solution to a public health problem. Safe abortion reduced maternal mortality and morbidity. Socially, access to abortion gave women the ability to order their reproductive, family and professional lives. From a religious perspective, abortion enabled women to be responsible stewards of their God-given gifts and talents—to make decisions about how to order their lives so that they could best use those gifts to serve God and the common good."

In the current environment, though, as Ragsdale and Yanow put it, women are succumbing to "obligatory guilt." What steps are abortion providers taking to address this? Or, to use Hochschild's terms, how are providers attempting to challenge the currently dominant "feeling rules" about abortion? While the abortion-providing community recognizes, of course, that this is a huge task that they cannot accomplish alone, I have been heartened to note two recent innovations that acknowledge the difficulties some patients have with getting an abortion in such a divided society. The first, occurring at the abortion facility itself, involves attempts to "validate and destigmatize" the abortion experience, to borrow from the language of a new training program that Planned Parenthood has instituted for all of its workers who interact with abortion patients. I have begun to see staff, at Planned Parenthood clinics and elsewhere, use some version of the following messages when talking with patients: "You are not alone—nearly 50 percent of pregnancies are unplanned"; "One out of three women in the United States has an abortion"; "The main reason that women have abortions is that they know they are not ready to be good mothers to a child at this point in their life."

Second, I have noted among providers a newfound endorsement of the usefulness of talk after the abortion. Some clinics are in a position to offer post-abortion counseling to patients who desire it, but many are not. But far more than when I first began study-ing this field thirty years ago, various external options exist for pa-tients to process their abortion experience in a nonjudgmental way with others, and the provider community seems more willing than in the past to recommend them. One of the best known and most often recommended of these post-abortion groups is an organiza-tion called Exhale. The group was founded by Aspen Baker, who was surprised, after her own abortion in 1999, at how hard it was to find a satisfactory counseling agency that accepted her decision to have an abortion while enabling her to talk about the complex feelings that the abortion had aroused. In 2002, she and others started a "talk line" for women—and men—who wished to discuss abortion. Though Baker and others connected with Exhale support legal abortion, the organization is studiously apolitical, calling itself "pro-voice." I was not surprised to learn that Baker, a warm and engaging woman in her thirties, had majored in peace and conflict studies as an under-graduate at Berkeley. As she explained to me, "Pro-voice is a peace-waging strategy to end the domestic culture war around abortion. We believe that the debate has gotten far removed from the real, lived experiences of women who have had abortions and their loved ones. It is time to stop, listen, and learn the full truths of each person's unique experience, offer them support and respect, and ensure that their voices lead public discussion about abortion."

The Exhale talk line is staffed by volunteers from the Bay Area, who undergo fifty-four hours of training and whose role is mainly to listen to whatever callers wish to say. (The one topic that is off-limits is politics.) These volunteers are trained to work with callers (from all over the country and even abroad) to identify potential options for healing and self-care and to make appropriate referrals to profes-sional mental-health services for those who appear to need them (a minority of their callers, according to Baker).

How many abortion patients come to clinics with negative feelings about abortion and negative feelings about themselves for obtaining one is impossible to say. There are, of course, variations among women's responses to abortion according to religion, geogra-phy, age, personal history, and so on. Moreover, we have no precise way of knowing how beneficial the efforts of clinics and of external groups like Exhale are in dealing with the feelings of stigma experienced by some patients. The provider community must tread lightly in the attempt to help patients with "emotion work," being careful not to impose unwanted services or referrals on women who neither need nor want such attention. But I have no doubt that if it is offered carefully and thoughtfully, this encouragement to find safe spaces for some patients to talk about their abortion experience is a positive step in the evolution of abortion care.

WHAT KIND OF AMERICA
DO WE WANT?

The sexual and reproductive regime that the religious right has sought to impose on the United States for nearly forty years is not what most Americans want. Most Americans want abortion to remain legal. An even greater number of us deeply value contraception. That 98 percent of heterosexually active American women have used birth control reveals how far out of the mainstream the escalation of the abortion wars to include contraception lies. Most Americans, more-over, believe that when they go to a pharmacy, their prescriptions should be filled, whatever the personal views of individual pharmacists. Most Americans want schools to teach comprehensive sex education, a curriculum that includes but goes beyond abstinence counseling. Most Americans don't think their government should lie to them about important health matters (or indeed, about any matters), and decry the politicization of science that has taken place to advance the religious right's agenda.

But if most of us don't want the America of the religious right, what kind of country do we, the majority, want, with respect to sexuality and reproduction? This is not as easy a question to answer as it might seem, because so much energy since the 1970s has been consumed by the abortion wars. This point became poignantly clear to me recently, when I met with Lynne Randall, a friend and colleague who has spent her adult life working in the field of reproductive health. Currently she is a vice president in the national office of Planned Parenthood, in charge of the organization's abortion services. Lynne men-tioned a recent trip to the Netherlands, where she had met with a counterpart of sorts, a health ministry official who also works in re-productive health. Lynne spoke with undisguised envy of her Dutch colleague's situation: "The unintended pregnancy rate is very low, the government is completely supportive of reproductive health care, contraception is widely available, abortion is free, and yet the Dutch have one of the lowest abortion rates in the world." Lynne told me of some of the innovative projects the Dutch official was undertaking. She then said to me, with a sigh, "After meeting her, I thought to myself, 'This is what my work day *could* be like—thinking up ways to improve the health-care situation of women.'"

Lynne's work life certainly involves creativity, but too much of her time is taken up fighting rear-guard actions to enjoy the freedom to be as proactive as her international colleagues. I share her regret that the immense amount of time and money that the reproductive rights movement in this country has been forced to devote to defending abortion has meant a huge loss of opportunities to work on other issues. Think of the millions of dollars spent in security upgrades at clinics that other medical offices typically don't need—bullet-proof glass, for example. Or think of the energy and dollars consumed in fighting the endless court battles over restrictions and the many ballot measures about abortion. And then think of how these resources might be spent in improving American women's health care.

In a similar conversation, another valued colleague, Lynn Paltrow, suggested that abortion serves as a "brilliant distraction" from a serious confrontation with the full range of reproductive health needs of American women. Paltrow, a lawyer, directs an organization she founded called National Advocates for Pregnant Women. The organization's mission is "to promote the rights and human dignity of all women, particularly pregnant and parenting women."

NAPW's advocacy has focused on the numerous ways in which pregnant women are controlled by authorities. The organization staunchly supports abortion rights, but it has deliberately sought to connect this issue to reproductive struggles in other terrains. The range of issues with which NAPW engages is a reminder that the abortion wars may be the most visible reproductive wars taking place, but they are hardly the only ones. Paltrow and her coworkers have fought on behalf of women who are forced to have cesarean sections, pregnant women who are jailed (as opposed to being given treatment) for drug problems, incarcerated women who are made to give birth while shackled, and so on. Not only have the abortion wars distracted from larger conversations about the many other issues facing pregnant women and their families, Paltrow argues, they distract as well by their ability to polarize. Women who otherwise have a great deal in common—because of the failures of both government and the private market to meet many families' needs—are separated by their positions on abortion. "Even people who are profoundly anti-choice don't have health insurance and are losing their pensions and can't send their kids to college. . . . [B]ut conservatives' focus on abortion and 'bad mothers' has led to a situation where it is more acceptable to deny welfare to 'bad mothers' and where it is more acceptable to have the U.S. be the only industrialized country without paid parental leave."

My conversations with these two women reminded me of other areas of sex and reproduction that have been distorted by the abortion wars. Take the issue of teen sexuality. A full discussion of this complicated subject is well beyond the scope of this book, but I am struck by the extent to which the religious right has defined the terms of the ongoing debates on this issue. The concern that many people across the political spectrum have about adolescents' sexual behavior transcends the polarizing battles over abstinence-only sex education and laws mandating parental notification and consent for abortions. Even those with liberal views on those questions are troubled by how teenage sexuality plays out in a society that is simultaneously squeamish about sexuality and dramatically oversexualized. While I am sympathetic to the pressures on all adolescents, research suggests that younger female teenagers are the most vulnerable to poor outcomes from premature sexual activity. In particular, I have been disturbed by what the data tell us about young women who become sexually active before the age of sixteen; they are more likely than older teens to report that their first intercourse was forced, more likely to have an unintended birth, and more likely to have sexually transmitted infections. I remember from my first days in this field a particularly compassionate nurse practitioner describing her interaction with a teen of about fifteen who had come to a clinic for birth-control pills: "She was so rigid, even a pelvic was impossible. We talked, and she told me she hated sex. It didn't occur to her that she didn't have to do it."

I believe that we as a society are failing teenagers by insisting on such ineffective strategies as abstinence-only sex education, which treat mature seventeen-year-olds the same way as immature thirteen-year-olds. Wouldn't it be better to have a broad social consensus in the United States, as there is in many European countries, that sexual activity should not start until sixteen or later (though appropriate supports should be available for those who start sooner)? What if this consensus included provisions for giving all adolescents the information they need to make the decision as to when to initiate sexual activity thoughtfully? "Information" in this case refers not only to information about pregnancy and disease prevention but also to a discussion of expectations about what sexual intimacy with a partner would mean, how one might express sexual feelings even if one does not feel ready for intercourse, and how society's messages about gender expectations play into sexual decisions. I have seen such conversations take place in family-planning clinics that have special services oriented to teenagers, including males, and I have witnessed very moving exchanges between teens and staff members in which some young people were affirmed in their decision to become sexually active and others were equally affirmed in their decision to postpone such activity. Helping young people to discern what they truly want and learn how to say yes if they really mean yes and how to say no if they really mean no would be a gift of clarity amid this society's conflicting messages about sexuality. As with good abortion counseling, the rule that the best sex educators follow is that each young person is unique and "one size fits all" approaches make no sense.

Another casualty of the abortion war and its spillover into teenage sexuality is that we are nowhere near having such nuanced discussions with young people in public schools. To borrow the title of a feminist collection on sexuality published some years ago, sex involves both "pleasure and danger," but most American schools seem capable of focusing only on the dangers. Worse, even these dangers are often not presented truthfully. In a report prepared for Congressman Henry Waxman of California on federally funded abstinence-only programs, investigators found that "over 80 percent of the abstinence-only curricula . . . contain false, misleading, or distorted information about reproductive health." These curricula contain such patently false statements as "sweat and tears can lead to HIV transmission" and "5 percent to 10 percent of women who have

abortions will become sterile." The issues raised by adolescent sexuality are indeed challenging, but blatant lies are not the way to meet
these challenges. That is not the America we want.

PUTTING ABORTION IN CONTEXT

Though I have argued that the abortion wars have served to distract from fully identifying an appropriate sexual and reproductive
agenda, I nonetheless think that the basic elements of what many
Americans want have been known for quite some time. In simplest
terms, people want the supports they need to achieve the intimate
lives and families they wish for. Think back to some of the women
seeking abortions whom we met in chapter 6. These women clearly
need better contraceptive services and education, but they need a lot
more as well: child care, health care, domestic violence services, jobs
that pay living wages, affordable housing—a depressingly familiar
list of the unmet needs of too many Americans. Universal health care
is a particularly crucial component of this list. One of the reasons
that European countries have such better indicators of reproductive
health—fewer unintended pregnancies, lower infant mortality rates,
and so on—are the national health-care systems, which offer everyone routine preventive health care.

Much of this expansive agenda goes back to the early days
of the women's movement of the 1970s. There was a recognition at
that time, which I remember from studying the child-care issue, that
abortion was only one part of a much larger platform. One of the
earliest abortion rights groups was the Committee for Abortion
Rights and Against Sterilization Abuse (CARASA), a response to
the practice in some states of physicians' sterilizing poor, often non-
English-speaking women without their knowledge. When the National Organization for Women (NOW), the first mass organization
to emerge from the 1960s rebirth of feminism, issued its Women's
Bill of Rights in 1967, support for child care and maternity leaves was
as prominent as support for abortion.

Work on behalf of this agenda has been significantly derailed because of the necessity to defend abortion against the powerful back-
lash that sprang up immediately after the *Roe* decision. Although
I understand and support the decisions made by various feminist

groups, I believe that in the long run abortion is best defended when it is seen as just one part of a larger mosaic of reproductive and sexual rights and services, as women's health activists in the 1970s understood. One of the most eloquent expressions of this connection between abortion and other reproductive events was made by Rachel Atkins, a physician assistant who was for many years the director of the Vermont Women's Center. In a frequently quoted statement that she originally made to a *New York Times* reporter, Atkins noted, "There aren't two different kinds of women sitting in our waiting room—women who have abortions and women who have babies. They're the same women at different times in their lives." (Atkins's statement contains a slight exaggeration: not all of those who have an abortion go on to become mothers, but most do. Indeed, 60 percent of abortion recipients already have children.)

My call for an expansive sexual and reproductive agenda comes at the beginning of 2009, as the United States faces its most serious economic crisis since the Great Depression of the 1930s. This crisis, which is unfolding as I write, has relevance for this broad agenda in at least three different ways. First, the scope of the crisis will inevitably push the realization of some of the items on this agenda, such as sufficient employment and affordable housing, even further out of reach for some Americans. Second, times of economic crisis lead to significantly increased demands for both contraceptive and abortion services. The main lesson that scholars of reproductive health learned from the Great Depression is that when people realize the impossibility of caring for a child (or another child), they make significant efforts to control their fertility. At a time when both contraception and abortion were still illegal, birthrates fell considerably, suggesting widespread use of withdrawal, condoms when they could be found, and illegal abortion. Similarly, the current economic crisis has already made itself dramatically evident to the abortion-providing community. By early 2009, staff members at abortion funds and individual clinics across the country were reporting an unprecedented number of calls—a "hair-raising number," as one fund administrator put it—from desperately poor women seeking help to pay for their abortions. "You have no idea what we're seeing now, just how many calls we are getting from women who have lost their jobs, their homes, their safety net," one clinic administrator told me. In spite of their best efforts, the abortion-rights community cannot meet this huge demand for subsidized abortions on its own. I am not alone in fearing a rise in illegal and unsafe abortions in the foreseeable future.

Third, this predictable increase in the demand for abortions may make more visible an often overlooked, and for many Americans quite difficult, aspect of reproductive politics: the right of poor women to *have* children. The government's official policy, we can reasonably conclude, is that there is no such right. The critical policy choice occurred in 1996, when a Democratic president, Bill Clinton, and a Republican-led Congress overturned sixty years of precedent and passed a welfare reform measure that abolished Aid to Families with Dependent Children (AFDC). AFDC was a program of financial support for families with children under eighteen where there was no employed parent. (Notably, AFDC had its roots in the New Deal of Franklin D. Roosevelt, which was implemented during the Great Depression.)

AFDC was replaced by a welfare program called Temporary Assistance to Needy Families (TANF), with *temporary* being the key word. TANF for the first time limited the total time that adult recipients, mainly single mothers, could spend on welfare (two years in some states, up to five years in others). Like many other observers of social welfare, I have been dismayed by these time limits and the hardships they impose on the poor, especially in dire economic times like the present. TANF's results, after more than ten years, have been decidedly mixed. For some participants the program has worked as intended; welfare recipients have transitioned to the paid labor force and have managed to achieve economic independence, albeit precariously. For too many others, however—and the numbers will only get worse in the immediate future—the withdrawal of this safety net has put them and their children into what economists call "deep poverty," defined as those living below 50 percent of the official poverty line. In 2007 the official poverty level for a family of four was an income of $21,027, so imagine such a family trying to exist on approximately $10,500. A November 2008 report from a Washington think tank, the Center on Budget and Policy Priorities, predicted that as a result of the current economic crisis, the number of Americans in deep poverty will rise by as many as 8 million and those in "regular" poverty by as many as 10 million.

Beyond my concern for the financial hardships imposed by TANF, I find the legislation both fascinating and alarming because of the unprecedented level of regulation of sexual and reproductive behavior in a welfare bill. The political atmosphere leading up to the bill's passage was dominated by what can only be described as hysteria coming from the right over the issue of illegitimacy. In a famous 1993 op-ed piece entitled "The Coming White Underclass," published in the *Wall Street Journal,* the influential conservative author Charles Murray proclaimed, "Illegitimacy is the single most important social problem of our time—more important than crimes, drugs, poverty, illiteracy, welfare, or homelessness, because it drives everything else." Murray's policy prescription could not have been clearer: "End all economic support for single mothers."

TANF did not go as far as Murray and other conservatives, many affiliated with the religious right, wished. But the bill did attempt to address out-of-wedlock pregnancy in several ways. It permits states to impose "family caps" that deny additional funds for any child born to a woman after she has been certified as a TANF recipient. The bill for a time had another odd feature for a welfare measure: competition among the states for "illegitimacy bonuses," to be given to those states that reduced illegitimacy rates without raising abortion rates. (This competition was eventually stopped as it became clear that many states had no reliable ways to measure either abortion rates, as women frequently went to other states for the procedure, or the number of children actually born out of wedlock.) The bill provided an additional infusion of cash to existing abstinence-only sex education programs. Finally, states were encouraged to make "marriage promotion" activities part of their welfare efforts, a strategy that received hundreds of millions of additional dollars during the Bush administration. Such efforts rested on the idea that the quickest and best route out of poverty for a poor woman was marriage.

Each of these items in the welfare reform bill strikes me as misguided. The family cap provision in particular created a very rare moment of convergence between antiabortion and abortion-rights groups. The National Right to Life Committee and the National

Conference of Catholic Bishops broke with other partners in the religious right and opposed this policy, fearing that it would lead to more abortions among poor women (and indeed, as we saw in chapter 6, abortion rates among poor women in recent years have far outstripped those of women who are not poor). NARAL Pro-Choice America and NOW also spoke out strongly against family caps, stating that they represented an assault on reproductive freedom.

Abstinence-only sex education, as we have seen, has repeatedly been shown to be ineffective. Moreover, teenagers make up only a relatively small portion of those on welfare or of those having out-of-wedlock births, contrary to popular beliefs. Toward the end of the Bush presidency, officials announced a "clarification" that these abstinence-only programs were also geared toward those aged eighteen to twenty-nine, the age group that in fact has the most out-of-wedlock births. This announcement led James Wagoner, a longtime advocate for comprehensive sex education, to say of these officials, "They've stepped over the line of common sense. To be preaching abstinence when 90 percent of people are having sex is in essence to lose touch with reality."

The marriage-promotion efforts strike many critics as futile and a wasteful and improper use of government funds. As these critics point out, people usually marry those in similar social and economic situations. Therefore, if a woman living below the poverty level marries a man in the same situation, their marriage will not lift this couple out of poverty. I agree with critics who argue that such efforts, under the wrong leadership, could encourage women to stay in unhealthy relationships. The fact that many of the contracts for these marriage-promotion programs were given to conservative religious organizations with very traditional views on gender makes me wary. (In surely one of the most bizarre instances of marriage-promotion efforts, a group connected to the Unification Church— the Moonies—received federal funding to offer such a program in Oakland, California. Many people, including myself, wondered what a group known for huge mass weddings in stadiums, with marriage partners chosen by the leader of this church, was doing offering advice on marriage.)

If done well, however, marriage promotion could give poor couples the same benefits of counseling that many other couples are able to purchase privately or with the help of insurance policies. Given that a recent large study of poor women revealed that one of their major complaints about their male partners is emotional neglect, if not abuse, this kind of counseling might be very helpful. We simply do not know enough at this point to say what the results of these marriage-promotion programs have been. It strikes me as a safe guess to say that some of the welfare poor have strengthened their bonds with husbands and partners because of these programs, and that is a good thing. But it is simply wishful thinking to imagine that marriage in itself can solve the problem of poverty, especially since poverty among children is not confined to single-parent families.

Ironically, these marriage-promotion efforts have been made at a time when marriage itself is becoming increasingly a privilege of those who are not poor. A number of sociologists have investigated the high degree of nonmarriage among the poor with children and have concluded that marriages are postponed simply because people feel economically unable to take this step. Paula England and Kathryn Edin have written about the financial bar that poor couples feel prevents them from marrying: "Couples who hadn't married four years after their baby's birth, but hadn't broken up either, still clung to this bar as a major reason they hadn't married yet. What parents meant by this economic bar was usually something like wanting one or both of them to have a good job so they didn't need family or friends or the government to give them money to pay all their bills each month."

Moreover, those who are not poor are more likely both to marry *and* to be insulated from criticism for having children out of wedlock. As it happens, I am writing these words on the day that newspapers announced a "first"—the pregnancy of an unmarried member of Congress. Linda Sanchez, a thirty-nine-year-old legislator from California, announced that she intended to marry at some point after the birth of her child. The lack of a scandal surrounding this pregnancy confirms that we are becoming a society that accepts a variety of family forms, at least among those who are economically independent (though I suspect that if this politician had chosen an abortion and if that had become publicly known, there would have been more of a furor among her constituents).

Most Americans still value marriage, and the majority, for the foreseeable future, will follow the conventional pattern of marrying before having children. An increasing number, though, will have children first and marry later; some will have children and never marry, mostly because of economic barriers, but others on philosophical grounds. Currently about 40 percent of all births in the United States occur to unmarried women. Many of these women have ongoing relationships with the fathers of their children, often in a cohabiting situation.

Some single women, hearing their proverbial biological clocks ticking, will opt to become pregnant through donor insemination. Some, whether single or married, will adopt. By the time this book appears, one hopes that more progress will have been made toward recognizing the marriage rights and the adoption rights of gay Americans, both of which received setbacks in the fall 2008 election. For me, the increasing social acceptance of this variety of family forms is a positive development, for which the feminist movement of the 1960s and '70s can take at least partial credit. More tolerant attitudes toward childbirth outside of marriage on the part of Americans are among the factors that have reduced the abortion rate in recent years.

But what of the poorest Americans, for whom the current economic crisis will only intensify the impossibility of rearing children adequately without external support? Economic hardship, as I have said, has already increased the demand for contraception and abortion. But is that the only response a compassionate society wants to make to those who can't afford children? There is a widespread consensus in the United States that child-rearing is essentially a private affair and people should have only the number of children they can afford. In contrast, most other industrialized countries see children as both a public and a private responsibility, and grant children's allowances, a universal cash subsidy in support of parenthood. But the reality is that some Americans will never be able to afford parenthood on their own, and I fear the number in this category will only grow in the near future. Should parenthood, which for many is one of the most profoundly gratifying of all human experiences, be denied to some solely on the basis of income?

A direct answer to this question comes from the reproductive justice movement, a coalition of activists of color that has put forward an important reframing of "reproductive rights." Loretta Ross, the national coordinator of a group called Sistersong, has articulated how this approach differs from that of traditional abortion rights groups: "[Reproductive justice] offers a new perspective on reproductive issue advocacy, pointing out that as Indigenous women and women of color it is important to fight equally for (1) the right to have a child; (2) the right not to have a child; and (3) the right to parent the children we have, as well as to control our birthing options, such as midwifery. We also fight for the necessary enabling conditions to realize these rights. This is in contrast to the singular focus on abortion by the pro-choice movement."

LOOKING AHEAD: A PARTIAL TRUCE IN THE ABORTION WARS?

This book is being completed during the first one hundred days of Barack Obama's presidency. Thinking about what this new administration might imply for the main subject of this book, the abortion wars, I find myself cautiously (quite cautiously) optimistic. I am reminded of a quote from an essay by the distinguished American historian Carroll Smith-Rosenberg. In a comparison of the bitter conflict over abortion in the 1980s with an earlier one in the nineteenth century, which led to the criminalization of abortion, Smith-Rosenberg wrote:

> At times the issue of abortion lies quiescent. . . . But at other times, forces within a society catapult the issue of abortion to a position of political and moral centrality, transferring the acts of the bedroom and the doctor's office to the most public political arena. At such times decisions surrounding abortion become the central drama of a culture, a play dealing with basic fissures in the social structure, one that raises fundamental issues concerning the distribution of power and the nature of the social order.

I wonder if it is reasonable to hope that abortion will someday soon stop being the "central drama" in U.S. domestic politics. Will it decline as a key factor in foreign policy as well? Is it possible that abortion could eventually be perceived by Americans as just one of a number of reproductive health services that women and their families may need at some point?

My cautious optimism stems from several sources. First, the role of abortion in the presidential campaign of 2008 differed in some significant ways from its role in previous elections. The Republican ticket was more strident than usual in its opposition not only to abortion but to contraception as well. John McCain famously squirmed and stammered, "I'll get back to you" when asked by a reporter if he felt it was reasonable that some insurance policies pay for Viagra but not for birth control. His running mate, Sarah Palin, expressed opposition to abortion even in cases of rape and incest. McCain made what was widely considered to be a serious gaffe when, in the last preelection debate, he referred contemptuously to "women's health," even using air quotes, in discussing when a contested abortion technique might be medically indicated.

In contrast, Barack Obama and his running mate, Joe Biden, forcefully defended legal abortion. Significantly, Obama went further on reproductive and sexual matters than other recent candidates from his party, who tried to avoid these potentially explosive topics. At the debate where McCain appeared to mock the health concerns of women, Obama eloquently called for a restoration of common ground for this divisive issue. His defense of abortion was made in the context of a larger agenda, in which he endorsed efforts to reduce unintended pregnancies and to make adoption more feasible. Notably, the then-candidate spoke of "helping single mothers if they want to choose to keep the baby."

Obama's sensible approach to these politically charged issues received support in unexpected quarters. Several high-profile figures from the religious right, including the influential evangelical pastor Joel Hunter, broke ranks and announced support for Obama, saying that his policies would do more to reduce abortions than those of McCain. Significantly, Hunter and other evangelicals also supported Obama because of their concerns about poverty and the environment, suggesting a welcome broadening of issues important to at least some in this group. Obama also received very public support from well-known conservative pro-life Catholics, who also expressed the belief that the Democratic candidate would do more to reduce the incidence of abortion than the Republican one. Obama gained a higher percentage of Catholic votes than the previous Democratic candidate, John Kerry, himself a Catholic.

To be sure, "common ground" in the world of reproductive politics has often proved more elusive and complicated than many proponents from both sides originally imagined. In a piece written shortly after the election, the Reverend Debra Hafner, a Unitarian Universalist minister and one of the leading supporters of reproductive justice within progressive clergy circles, welcomed support for Obama from conservative Christians. But she cautioned readers to distinguish between reducing abortions and reducing unintended pregnancies, which implies an unapologetic defense of contraception. She argued that the latter is not only the better public health position, "it is a faithful and moral one as well." In one of the most eloquent religious statements on behalf of contraception that I have seen, Hafner wrote, "The sanctity of human life is best upheld when we assure that it is not created carelessly."

While presumably both sides of the abortion wars can find common ground on adoption, this too has proved problematic because of the opposition of some religious right figures to adoption by gays or single individuals. In any event, though adoption under certain circumstances can be an excellent choice for all concerned, and ongoing efforts to help low-income people adopt are commendable, only about 1 percent of American women with unintended pregnancies decide to pursue this option.

These cautions about the difficulties of common ground notwithstanding, what the 2008 election may foretell is a recapturing not only of common ground but of common sense on the prevention of unintended pregnancy. This consensus, I have argued, was lost when fanatics, at the height of their powers in the George W. Bush years, sought to redefine contraception itself as abortion. Indeed, I believe that overreaching by the religious right on this matter was a factor in the movement's lack of influence in the election cycles of 2006 and 2008. The ability to control fertility, to space one's children, and to decide not to have children at all are core values for Americans. Put another way, to challenge a practice that is used, at least occasionally, by 98 percent of heterosexually active women is a doomed strategy.

Another reason that I think abortion will recede as the central drama of American society is that the current economic crisis will take over that role, and properly so. To return to Smith-Rosenberg's formulation, I cannot think of anything that more reflects "basic fissures in the social structure, [and] that raises fundamental issues concerning the distribution of power and the nature of the social order," than the subprime mortgage disaster and the various attendant dramas, including enormous numbers of home foreclosures for poor and once middle-class people, revelations of obscene profits for hedge-fund managers, huge bailouts for banks and other industries, and as yet unknown numbers of jobs lost. This crisis is where the attention of our political leaders should be, and abortion, I think it is reasonable to assume, will no longer serve as the "brilliant distraction" that it did during the presidency of George W. Bush.

The severity of the economic crisis has led to a reconsideration of the proper role of government on the part of many Americans, including our political leaders. Ever since Ronald Reagan famously said in 1981 that "government is not the solution to our problem, government is the problem," our political culture has been dominated by a worship of the market free from regulation and a corresponding mistrust of any government initiatives in the realm of social policy. Recall how easily conservatives were able to derail President Clinton's attempt to provide universal health care in the 1990s. The simple phrase a "big government program" could effectively be used as a damning epithet. But the devastating failure of the mortgage market after Republicans succeeded in assuring no meaningful government oversight and the spectacle of industry executives going to Congress to beg for bailouts have changed the equation: proactive government is again becoming a respectable idea.

This carries two implications for the issues I have been discussing here. First, social provision to poor families may again become politically acceptable. Obama's words at the debate—"helping single mothers if they want to choose to keep the baby"—may not seem especially remarkable, but since the welfare reform measure of 1996, providing increased assistance to poor women in this situation has been virtually absent from political discourse.

Also, the economic crisis has served to intensify a broad-based desire for universal health-care coverage among the American people. Barack Obama has pledged to make this happen, and he will be doing so in a context quite different from that of the 1990s. What the actual outlines of this program will be are unclear as of this writing. Quite possibly they will involve an expansion of Medicare that permits uninsured people to enroll in that program, or perhaps in a new government one that will compete with existing insurance plans. As always in discussions of universal health care, the coverage of contraception and abortion will be sticking points, possibly deal-breakers for some of the constituencies, such as Catholic health institutions, that have to be brought on board. Some insurance programs will hopefully continue to cover these items; some won't. But the thought that the 45 million or so currently uninsured Americans would have access to good health care can only mean better outcomes in terms of overall health, including reproductive health.

Even if abortion is no longer the central drama of our culture in the Obama years and beyond, it would be naive to think that the abortion wars will end completely. To be sure, some of the fronts in this war will see welcome changes. Most encouraging to me are the changes that have already occurred at the presidential level, and will doubtless continue. In his inaugural address, the new president forcefully announced that "science will have a rightful place" in his administration, a message particularly meaningful to the reproductive health community. In his first days in office, the new president (as expected) overturned the controversial global gag rule, which prevented USAID from funding family-planning services in countries and agencies that use their own resources on abortion-related activities. Obama also announced that the United States would once again honor its commitment to contribute to the United Nations Population Fund (UNFPA), a commitment breached during the Bush years. Elated UNFPA officials said that the contributions withheld by the Bush administration could have prevented nearly 2 million unwanted pregnancies and nearly 800,000 abortions each year. Hillary Clinton, President Obama's choice for secretary of state, quickly made clear through personnel changes that the administration would change the tenor of its global AIDS policies and discard the high priority given to abstinence promotion. The new president also overturned the Bush administration policy that forbade use of federal funding for stem cell research.

Though not all of the new president's appointments are in place at the time of this writing, it is clear that unqualified ideologues will not be named to important positions within health agencies. Moreover, President Obama's nominations to the judiciary, at the Supreme Court and lower levels, will offer some degree of balance to those made by Bush, although the ideological makeup of the Supreme Court is not expected to change in the near future.

But neither the religious right nor the single-issue antiabortion organizations will be going away. If we know anything about social movements, it is that defeats can often reenergize them. We witnessed a deeply sad reminder of this, some five months into the Obama presidency, with the slaying of Dr. George Tiller by an individual with a long history of ties to the most extreme wing of the antiabortion movement. Perhaps significantly, this murder came shortly after President Obama gave a commencement speech at the University of Notre Dame, where he called for common ground on the abortion issue and urged that both sides address each other with "Open hearts. Open minds. Fair-minded words." The president's appearance at Notre Dame was itself protested vigorously on the college campus by leading figures within radical antiabortion circles.

At the political level, in spite of the setbacks during the last few elections, the religious right will remain a potent force in the Republican Party. Even before Barack Obama was inaugurated, there was word of a Republican hopeful for 2012 making automated calls to antiabortion activists in Iowa, the state with the first presidential caucus. In Congress, in the first week of the new Obama administration, Republican leaders made clear that opposition to both abortion and contraception would still be a weapon in the party's arsenal. John Boehner, the Republican leader in the House, ridiculed the fact that the president's stimulus package included a modest provision that allowed states to expand use of Medicaid funds for family planning, and he successfully pressured the administration to have this provision removed. In certain states and localities, abortion opponents will still wield considerable power, and they will continue to impose onerous restrictions on abortion provision.

Mainstream medical institutions will continue to be an extremely consequential front in the abortion wars. In a new political atmosphere, one hopes, these institutions will live up to their responsibility to make abortion training a routine part of medical education in the most relevant specialties. Similarly, the predicted rise in demands by patients for contraception and abortion as a result of the economic crisis will, I hope, soften senior physicians' objections to their partners' performing in-office abortions.

A significant challenge that individual hospitals and medical societies will continue to face in the years ahead is how to deal with the health-worker-refusal movement, which represents one of the newest tactics of sexual conservatives. A parting gift by the Bush administration to its religious right allies was the successful imposition by the Department of Health and Human Services of a "conscience clause" for all workers in the thousands of health-care institutions across the country that receive federal funding. This clause goes beyond abortion and allows workers to refuse to be involved in virtually any activity they object to. When HHS first announced this policy, the agency received an unprecedented 200,000 letters from health professionals and others opposed to this move. This regulation could create havoc, particularly in the delivery of contraceptive and assisted-reproduction services. Though the Obama administration is now in the midst of overturning this particular regulation, health-worker refusals will undoubtedly remain a favored tactic of the religious right. Medical institutions—and political ones—need to devise ways to assure that the public gets access to legal health-care services, no matter what objections individual practitioners may have.

What of the stigma that I have argued is such a strong feature of the abortion story in the United States? Can we expect this to diminish in light of the changing political and economic circumstances that lie ahead? Two things that I think are especially important for destigmatization to occur are the normalization of abortion within health-care circles and greater attention to the circumstances of actual abortion patients.

I saw the positive results of both these factors in an unexpected place. With colleagues at UCSF, I have been conducting interviews with "opt-outs," doctors in ob-gyn and family medicine residencies who exercised their legal right to opt out of abortion training in programs where others were routinely trained. Though these young physicians were not required to perform abortions, they did do auxiliary tasks, such as counseling and ultrasounds, which brought them into contact with patients. My interviews show that these doctors' contacts with women getting abortions changed their views on the subject. The opt-outs, many from conservative religious backgrounds, spoke of receiving a much greater understanding of the reasons that women seek abortions. These doctors also told me of their increased respect for colleagues who did take on the challenges of abortion care. As one young doctor, a Mormon, said to me, "I used to think abortion was a black-and-white issue. . . . Now I am seeing the many, many shades of gray." These interviews reinforce the importance of the numerous efforts that are under way within the advocacy community to get the stories of abortion recipients told to a larger audience.

Even assuming a renewed commitment to preventing unwanted pregnancies in the years ahead, reducing the stigma of abortion is critical, because there will always be a need for some abortions. Some contraceptive failures will inevitably occur over the thirty years or so that most women are at risk of pregnancy. Some women will be unable to afford the most effective contraceptive methods. Some wanted pregnancies will turn into unwanted ones, because of the pregnant woman's illness or a tragic turn in the health of her fetus or a change in social circumstances such as the breakup of a relationship or a devastating economic setback. And there will always be the issue of human frailty. Some couples simply won't use contraception, or they won't use it regularly. Some women who wish to use contraception will be unable to persuade their partners to do so.

Though I finish this book heartened by recent political changes that might diminish the obstacles to abortion care, I have learned that this care, in the final analysis, is always dependent on local factors. What restrictive measures state legislatures will pass, which of these measures the courts will find acceptable, how responsive to protesters police in a particular community will be, how cooperative local hospitals will be with clinics needing backup care for their patients, how tolerant medical practices will be to junior members who wish to incorporate abortion care, whether local contractors and vendors are willing to service clinics—all these factors will help determine the fate of abortion provision in particular settings. I do know that the abortion providers you have met in this book will make every effort within their power to continue offering care to the women who come to them.

Toward the end of this project, I had a phone conversation with a clinic director in a state especially hostile to abortion. As I talked with her about the latest regulation imposed by the state legislature and upheld by the courts, she sighed and said, "No one likes it, it is dumb, it is annoying, but we'll adapt. We'll do what we have to do."

"ABORTION IS A PERFECTLY PROPER NOUN"

The Association of Reproductive Health Professionals (ARHP) is a Washington-based educational organization with a national membership of about 11,000. Its membership is composed of doctors, nurses, midwives, and others who work in all areas of reproductive health, including abortion. Each year since 2005, ARHP has presented at its annual meeting a Preserving Core Values in Science Award to an individual "who has raised public awareness about scientific integrity in policy decision-making." It is hardly surprising that this organization would make scientific integrity a central issue. As we have seen, reproductive health has been a major battleground in which an ideological war against science took place in the Bush years.

In the fall of 2008, ARHP presented this award to two medical librarians and a young physician. The trio was honored for their whistle-blowing actions in the Popline scandal. Popline is the world's largest database in the field of reproductive health; it has long been funded by the U.S. Agency for International Development, and it is administered at the School of Public Health at Johns Hopkins University. One day in the spring of 2008, Justin Diedrich, a physician researcher, and Gloria Won, a librarian, both at UCSF, were puzzled that they could not access any references from Popline with the word *abortion* in the title, although they had done so in the past. Popline was known to have about 25,000 references on abortion. When Won and her supervisor, Gail Sorrough, e-mailed the Popline manager about this, the response was that *abortion* had been made a "stop word," similar to *and* and *the*. *Abortion* was no longer a searchable term. With surprising candor, Debra Dickson, the manager, went on to justify this decision by saying, "As a federally funded project, we decided this was best for now." Dickson suggested to the two librarians that they use other terms, like *fertility control, postconception* and *pregnancy, unwanted.* Dickson and her colleagues took this highly unusual step, according to the *New York Times,* apparently in reaction to "concern" expressed by AID officials after finding two abortion-related articles (out of 25,000!) that pertained to abortion "advocacy," as opposed to pure research. Why those two articles were not removed and the other 24,000-plus items left intact can only be answered in terms of the fanaticism that characterized government agencies in the Bush years, as I have argued.

As librarians, Won and Sorrough were deeply offended by this brazen interference with the flow of knowledge and information. Encouraged by Justin Diedrich, they e-mailed news of this policy to medical librarians across the country, who in turn alerted other sectors of the medical, academic, and library communities. In a very short time, thousands of people voiced their objections to the step taken by the Popline staff and there was widespread media coverage of the incident. The dean of the School of Public Health at Johns Hopkins quickly denounced this censorship and demanded an immediate restoration of *abortion* as a searchable term on Popline.

At the ARHP award ceremony, Gail Sorrough explained her decision to challenge Popline's action by saying, "Abortion, after all, is a perfectly proper noun." Her double meaning, I am sure, was fully intended.

The actions of the three whistle-blowers honored at ARHP reminded me that in the fight to destigmatize abortion, we have allies in many different occupations and in every segment of society. These allies recognize that the struggle for reproductive freedom is part of a much larger struggle for a truly free and open society.

THE LEGACY OF GEORGE TILLER

The slaying of George Tiller on May 31, 2009, showed that the fanatical and violent elements of the antiabortion movement—which many, including myself, had thought to be in decline—are still very much with us. Dr. Tiller's murder will inevitably affect the issues discussed in this book, though in ways not entirely clear as I write these words, a mere ten days after his death. Some potential abortion providers will understandably be deterred from entering this field. But just as the organization Medical Students for Choice was formed in response to the first killing of an abortion provider in 1993, some young physicians will quite likely enter this field, precisely so as not to cede a victory to the terrorists. The political fallout—for the movements on both sides of the abortion divide, for the Obama administration and its efforts to reach some common ground on this issue—is unknown as well.

One thing, however, has become very clear in the days following Dr. Tiller's death: women in desperate situations will now face much harder times. Abortions that occur after twenty-one weeks' gestation make up barely 1 percent of the 1.2 million abortions that are performed each year in the United States yet are among the most harrowing—and necessary— for the women involved. Those women (and their partners) who came to Tiller's clinic for the later abortions for which he was so reviled were typically carrying much-wanted pregnancies that had gone horribly wrong. In many cases these were women who had set up cribs and had their baby showers. Some of these women had fetuses with heartbreaking anomalies that were discovered only late in pregnancy, such as anencephaly, a lethal birth defect in which most of the brain and parts of the skull are missing. Other women had themselves become very ill in the course of a pregnancy, for example, with the onset of cancer, which demanded a course of chemotherapy.

In the aftermath of Tiller's murder, some of his patients have broken their silence and spoken out publicly about the tragic situations that necessitated these late abortions, and of the extraordinary kindness and respect with which they were treated by the doctor and his staff. These women's stories have begun to change the national conversation about why some late abortions, including those in the third trimester, take place. It is now more difficult for antiabortion spokespeople to continue, with any credibility, with their practice of making snide comments about late abortions occurring for the most trivial of reasons.

Most important, Tiller's death has also led many to ask why, with his clinic now closed, are there only one or two other doctors remaining in the United States who have a practice similar to his? The answer lies in the factors discussed in this book: a combination of highly restrictive state laws and hospital regulations governing late abortions, inadequate training opportunities for these more complex procedures, the stigma that is particularly associated with later abortions, and, of course, the kind of unbearable scrutiny that likely awaits anyone willing to undertake this work.

One response to George Tiller's death, obviously, must be a serious commitment to end the unacceptable violence against abortion providers. The public must demand that the Obama administration and local authorities use every resource at their disposal to confront the violent wing of the antiabortion movement before yet another tragedy occurs. It was deeply upsetting to learn that Tiller's accused assailant had vandalized another Kansas clinic twice in the period leading up to the murder, including the very day before the event. In each instance, the individual's license plate was reported to local police and the FBI, neither of whom apparently took any action.

But another response to this killing must be a demand that the mainstream medical community acknowledge the reality that there will always be some women who need abortions later on in pregnancy. Local medical institutions must make provision for these cases—especially since these women can no longer be sent off to Kansas, out of sight and mind of "respectable" doctors and hospitals. In the abstract, late abortions are understandably distasteful to many. When considered in the context of real women's lives, however, these procedures are essential.

This is what George Tiller understood. This will hopefully be his legacy.

ACKNOWLEDGMENTS

My greatest debt is to those members of the abortion-providing community, most of whom appear in this book under pseudonyms, who have so generously shared with me their reflections on the challenges and gratifications of their work lives.

In my case, at least, it does take a village to write a book. The research village in which I am most fortunate to reside is the Bixby Center for Global Reproductive Health in the Department of Obstetrics, Gynecology, and Reproductive Sciences at the University of California, San Francisco. I am grateful to all my Bixby colleagues, and particularly to those in the Advancing New Standards in Reproductive Health (ANSIRH) program—my neighborhood in this village—for the many ways they have helped with this project. I especially thank Tracy Weitz, the director of ANSIRH, for inviting me into this vibrant community of clinicians and social scientists. Tracy and I have been engaged in a nonstop conversation from the day we met, and I have benefited enormously from her brilliant observations about abortion care and abortion politics. Also at ANSIRH, Michaela Ferrari was a wonderful research assistant in every way, including guiding me through various technological challenges with exquisite tact.

I am very grateful for a number of faculty research grants I received from the University of California, Davis, and I particularly appreciate the support I received for this project from Vicki Smith, chair of the Department of Sociology at Davis. Two visits I made to the University of California Center in Washington, D.C., were very important in both starting and finishing this book, and I thank the center staff members, who were so accommodating. I also thank Ellen Chesler, formerly of the Open Society Institute, for her early support of this research.

I am grateful to the following individuals who helped me in various ways to obtain needed information: Felisa Preskill, Bethany

Herrera, Maya Manian, Stanley Henshaw, Rachel Jones, Talcott Camp, Louise Melling, Diana Greene Foster, Lori Freedman, Frances Schwartz, Alice Abarbanel, Robin Rothrock, Marji Gold, Kristen Nobel, Jody Steinauer, Laura Castleman, and Linda Prine. I thank as well my cyberfriends at Reproductive Health Reality Check—Emily Douglas, Scott Swenson, and Amie Newman—for keeping me so well informed about political developments in this field, and also for providing me with a forum to try out some of the ideas presented in this book. I appreciate the excellent job done by Margo Rodriguez in transcribing my interview tapes.

Over a period of years I have been engaged in lively dialogue about reproductive and sexual politics with the following friends, all of whom have enriched this book: Rivka Gordon, Maureen Paul, Rosalind Petchesky, Debbie Rogow, Ruth Rosen, Judy Stacey, Barrie Thorne, and Susan Yanow.

I owe special thanks to Renee Fox, whose lifelong practice of sociological fieldwork serves as inspiration to me. I am particularly grateful to her for a pivotal lunch meeting that helped clarify for me the book I was most capable of writing.

At Beacon Press, it has been a pleasure to work with Amy Caldwell and Alexis Rizzuto. I greatly appreciate the always intelligent feedback I received from both of them, as well as their clear support of the book's purpose. Alexis's willingness to undertake repeated close readings of my manuscript, I am well aware, is hardly the norm at many contemporary publishing houses. Thanks as well to Liz Duvall for her excellent copyediting. At an early phase I also received useful editorial help from Tracy Ahlquist.

Turning to my family, I thank my sister, Jennifer, and brother-in-law, Joe, and my daughters, Miriam and Judith, for their constant love and encouragement. I am particularly indebted to my husband, Fred, who with his unique combination of intellectual rigor, good humor, and nurturance has helped with this book in ways too numerous to mention.

Finally, this book is dedicated to the memory of three very important people in my life, all of whom died as I was writing this book. Felicia Stewart, MD, beloved colleague and friend, was a visionary in the field of reproductive health. For Felicia, there was no contradiction between her firm belief in evidence-based medicine and her insistence that the values that inform this area of health care need to be articulated to the public. My mother, Anne Joffe, was very proud of my involvement in this field and deeply interested in the issues raised in this book. Once when I visited her in the hospital, we were discussing, at her request, the history of birth control in the United States. When I mentioned the 1965 Supreme Court decision that legalized birth control, she looked up at me with a puzzled expression and, with her usual common sense, asked, "They needed a law for that?" When this book was already in production, in May 2009, George Tiller, MD, who taught me so much about this field for the twenty years I knew him, was savagely murdered while attending church. His loss is enormous—to the family, friends, and colleagues who loved him, and to the women who came to him from all over the United States, and beyond, whom he treated with such respect and compassion.

NOTES

Preface

xi—eight members of the abortion-providing community: Data on violence against abortion providers are regularly tabulated and updated by the National Abortion Federation (NAF). See www.prochoice.org/pubs_research/publications/downloads/about_abortion/violence_statistics.pdf (accessed January 4, 2009). The Feminist Majority Foundation also has a project that tracks clinic violence. See feminist.org/rrights/clinic survey.html (accessed January 4, 2009).

xi—drug advisory panel: Chris Mooney, *The Republican War on Science* (New York: Basic Books, 2005), pp. 227–28.

xiii—a sitting U.S. senator: Charles Babbington, "Two Abortion Opponents Tapped for Senate Judiciary Panel," *Washington Post,* December 21, 2004.

xiii—"justifiable homicide": Gustav Niebuhr, "To Church's Dismay, Priest Talks of 'Justifiable Homicide' of Abortion Doctors," *New York Times,* August 24, 1994.

xiii—birth control is nearly universal: This information is from the Guttmacher Institute. See www.guttmacher.org/pubs/fb_ATSRH.html (accessed January 4, 2009).

xiv—the brutal assassination of Dr. George Tiller: Joe Stumpe and Monica Davey, "Abortion Doctor Shot to Death in Kansas Church," *New York Times,* May 31, 2009.

xiv—nearly half of all pregnancies: This figure is from the Web site of the Centers for Disease Control, www.cdc.gov/Reproductivehealth/Unintended Pregnancy/index.htm (accessed January 4, 2009).

I

The Stigma of Abortion

1—False information: Chris Mooney, *The Republican War on Science* (New York: Basic Books, 2005), 207–8. As Mooney perceptively points out, "Where religious conservatives may have once advanced their pro-life and socially traditionalist views through moral arguments, they now increasingly adopt the veneer of scientific and technical expertise" (208).

1—After the United States invaded Iraq: Rajiv Chandrasekaran, *Imperial Life in the Emerald City: Inside Iraq's Green Zone* (New York: Knopf, 2006), 91.

1—Several high-ranking officials: Marc Kaufman, "FDA Official Quits over Delay on Plan B," *Washington Post,* September 1, 2005.

1—Colorado's 2008 ballot: Wendy Norris, "Using 'States' Rights' to Restrict Abortion," *RH Reality Check,* May 15, 2008, available at www.rhreality check.org/blog/2008/05/14/origins-personhood-using-states-rights-restrict-abortion (accessed January 10, 2009).

1—the National Association for the Advancement of Preborn Children: Lois Uttley, "The Politics of the Embryo," Center for American Progress, July 19, 2005, available at www.americanprogress.org/issues/2005/07/b895399 .html (accessed January 6, 2009).

1—a routine confirmation: Rebecca Traister, "Fargo Fiasco," *Salon,* December 7, 2005, available at www.salon.com/mwt/broadsheet/2005/12/07/fargo/ index.html (accessed January 10, 2009).

1—In Waco, Texas: "Cookie Crumbles: Girl Scout Sex Furor Splits Texas Town," *USA Today,* March 3, 2004.

2—An increasing number of pharmacists: Rob Stein, "Health Workers' Choice Debated," *Washington Post,* January 30, 2006.

2—2007 Supreme Court case: Gonzales v. Carhart, 550 U.S. 124 (2007).

2—A South Dakota law: See www.ca8.uscourts.gov/opndir/08/06/053093P.pdf (accessed January 7, 2009).

2—"an attribute": Erving Goffman, *Stigma: Notes on the Management of Spoiled Identity* (New York: Touchstone, 1986 [1963]), 3.

3—"disqualified from full social acceptance": Ibid., preface.

3—3 percent of Planned Parenthood's services: Planned Parenthood Federation of America, Inc., "Planned Parenthood by the Numbers," November 2007, available at www.plannedparenthood.org (accessed December 15, 2008).

4—Gallup Poll data from 2008: See www.gallup.com/poll/1576/Abortion.aspx (accessed January 9, 2009).

5—use of the word choice: See Rosalind Petchesky, *Abortion and Woman's Choice: The State, Sexuality and Reproductive Freedom,* rev. ed. (Boston: Northeastern University Press, 1990), 1–17; Carole Joffe, "It's Not *Just* Abortion, Stupid," *Dissent* (Winter 2005): 91–96.

5—one out of three: Guttmacher Institute, "An Overview of Abortion in the United States," available at www.guttmacher.org/media/presskits/ 2005/06/28/abortionoverview.html (accessed December 15, 2008).

6—Catholic women have abortions: About 28 percent of American women are Catholics, and about 27 percent of those having abortions identify themselves as Catholic. See www.guttmacher.org/in-the-know/characteristics .html (accessed January 9, 2008).

6—evaluation commissioned by Congress: Mathematica Policy Research, "Impact of Four Title V, Section 510 Abstinence Education Programs, Final Report, April 2007."

6—"American taxpayers": Sharon Jayson, "Sex-Education Clash Churns over Grants," *USA Today,* April 16, 2007.

7—American Psychological Association: Report of the APA Taskforce on the Sexualization of Girls, 2007, available at www.apa.org/pi/wpo/sexualizationrep.pdf (accessed January 8, 2009).

7—*"sexual literacy"*: National Sexuality Resource Center, http://nsrc.sfsu.edu (accessed December 1, 2008).

7—*"A lot of people"*: Ellen Willis, *Beginning to See the Light: Sex, Hope, and Rock and Roll* (Hanover, N.H.: University Press of New England, 1992 [1981]), 217.

8—*the spread of ultrasonography*: Rosalind Petchesky, "Fetal Images: The Power of Visual Culture," *Feminist Studies* 13, no. 2 (1987): 263–92. This is a classic and still highly relevant article on the impact of ultrasounds and other fetal images on the abortion debate.

8—*this new branch of medicine*: Monica Casper, *The Making of the Unborn Patient: A Social Anatomy of Fetal Surgery* (New Brunswick, N.J.: Rutgers University Press, 1998), 168, 177.

9—*The religious right was set in motion*: One of the best books on the activities of this movement at the height of its power during the George W. Bush years is Michelle Goldberg, *Kingdom Coming: The Rise of Christian Nationalism* (New York: W. W. Norton, 2006).

10—*President Richard Nixon vetoed*: Richard Nixon, "Veto Message—Economic Opportunity Amendments of 1971," December 10, 1971, 92nd Congress, 1st Session, Document No. 92–48.

10—*"The opening shot"*: Onalee McGraw, *The Family, Feminism, and the Therapeutic State* (Washington, D.C.: Heritage Foundation, 1980).

10—*"battering ram"*: Petchesky, *Abortion and Women's Choice*, 242.

11—*the movement's "coming-out party"*: Esther Kaplan, *With God on Their Side: How Christian Fundamentalists Trampled Science, Policy, and Democracy in George W. Bush's White House* (New York: New Press, 2004), 70.

12—*"a superb pro-life résumé"*: Michele McKeegan, *Abortion Politics: Mutiny in the Ranks of the Right* (New York: Free Press, 1992), 67.

12—*"When it became possible"*: Bob Herbert, "In America, G.O.P. 'Big Tent' Is Shrinking," *New York Times,* May 1, 2000.

13—*A study by Congress found*: U.S. Congress, Committee on Oversight and Government Reform, *Federally Funded Pregnancy Resource Centers Mislead Teens about Abortion Risks,* July 17, 2006, available at http://oversight.house.gov/story.asp?ID=1080 (accessed January 10, 2009).

13—*"crass commercialization"*: Christopher Lee, "Bush Choice for Family-Planning Post Criticized," *Washington Post,* November 17, 2006.

13—*he abruptly resigned*: Christopher Lee, "Family Planning Official Resigns," *Washington Post,* March 30, 2007.

13—*this medication averted*: Guttmacher Institute, "Emergency Contraception Played Key Role in Abortion Rate Declines," December 17, 2002, available at www.guttmacher.org/media/nr/2002/12/17/nr_340602.html (accessed January 10, 2009).

13—*the "global gag rule"*: Center for Reproductive Rights, "The Global Gag Rule: Endangering Women's Health and Democracy," 2009, available at www.reproductiverights.org/hill_int_ggr.html (accessed January 10, 2009).

14—*PEPFAR:* Naina Dhingra, "PEPFAR Abstinence-Only Policies Come Under Fire," *RH Reality Check,* August 14, 2006, available at www.rhreality check.org/blog/naina-dhingra (accessed January 10, 2008).

15—*led to a year of jail time:* Joe Kafka, "School Contraceptive Measure Fails," *Aberdeen News,* February 7, 2006.

16—*"turned conservative churches":* Michelle Goldberg, "Palin and the Christian Right," *Nation,* September 28, 2008.

16—*Her mayoral race:* Ibid.

16—*When asked on national television:* See http://thinkprogress.org/2008/10/23/palin-abortion-clinic-bombers/ (accessed January 10, 2009).

17— *"aim[s] to stand up":* See www.cirtl.org/cmds.htm (accessed January 10, 2009). The Christian Medical and Dental Association is a separate but similar group that also strongly opposes abortion. See www.cmda.org/AM/Template.cfm (accessed January 10, 2009).

17—*"doctors of conscience":* Carole Joffe, *Doctors of Conscience: The Struggle to Provide Abortion Before and After Roe v Wade* (Boston: Beacon Press, 1996).

18—*antiabortion violence dramatically escalated:* "Violence and Disruption Statistics," National Abortion Federation, Washington, D.C., 2008, available at www.prochoice.org/pubs_rsearch/publications/downloads/about_abortion/violence_statistics.pdf (accessed January 10, 2009).

II
"You Need a Community with You"

25—*the number of abortion facilities:* Rachel Jones, Mira Zolna, Stanley Henshaw, and Lawrence Finer, "Abortion in the United States: Incidence and Access to Services, 2005," *Perspectives in Sexual and Reproductive Health* 40, no. 1 (2008): 6.

25—*one third of American women:* Ibid. Expressed another way, some 87 percent of U.S. counties are without an abortion provider.

26—*This group initially mobilized:* Carole Joffe, Patricia Anderson, and Jody Steinauer, "The Crisis in Abortion Provision and Pro-Choice Medical Activism in the 1990s," in Rickie Solinger, ed., *Abortion Wars: A Half Century of Struggle, 1950–2000* (Berkeley: University of California Press, 1998), 320–33.

26—*the Church Amendment:* Adam Sonfield, "Rights vs. Responsibilities: Professional Standards and Provider Refusals," *Guttmacher Report on Public Policy,* August 2005, available at www.guttmacher.org/pubs/tgr/08/3/gr080307.html (accessed January 13, 2009).

26—*an unprecedented intrusion:* Angel Foster, Jane van Dis, and Jody Steinauer, "Educational and Legislative Initiatives Affecting Residency Training in Abortion," *Journal of the American Medical Association* 290 (2003): 1777–78.

27—*advanced practice clinicians:* Diana Taylor, Barbara Safriet, and Tracy Weitz, "When Politics Trumps Evidence: Legislative or Regulatory Exclusion of Abortion from Advanced Practice Clinician Scope of Practice," *Journal of Midwifery and Women's Health* 54, no. 1 (January/February 2009): 4–7.

27—*researchers found in the early 1990s:* Mitchell Creinen and Philip Darney, "Methotrexate and Misoprostal for Early Abortion," *Contraception* 48, no. 4 (1993): 339–48.

28—*enabling more abortions in the United States:* Stanley Henshaw and Kathryn Kost, "Trends in the Characteristics of Women Obtaining Abortions, 1974 to 2004," Guttmacher Institute, 2008, 13.

33—*the role of champion:* In a study of nine family medicine residencies that had already integrated abortion training into their curriculums and seven that were exploring this step, the authors concluded that "the presence of a dedicated faculty champion was the most universal finding in our study." Christine Dehlendorf, Dalia Brahmi, David Engel, Kevin Grumbach, Carole Joffe, and Marji Gold, "Integrating Abortion Training into Family Medicine Residency Programs," *Family Medicine* 39, no. 5 (2007): 337–42.

35—*only 22 percent had provided:* Jody Steinauer, Uta Landy, Heidi Filippone, Douglas Laube, Philip Darney, and Rebecca Jackson, "Predictors of Abortion Provision Among Practicing Obstetrician-Gynecologists: A National Survey," *American Journal of Obstetrics & Gynecology* 198, no. 39 (January 2008): e1.39-e6, available at www.ajog.org (accessed September 19, 2008).

35—*In a smaller, qualitative study:* Lori Freedman, "Willing and Unable: Doctors' Constraints in Abortion Care," doctoral dissertation, Department of Sociology, University of California, Davis, June 2008.

35—*"Well, from now on":* Ibid., 112.

39—*more than ten times safer:* American Medical Association, Council on Scientific Affairs, "Induced Termination of Pregnancy Before and After *Roe v. Wade*," *Journal of the American Medical Association* 268 (1992): 3231.

39—*leading textbook:* Maureen Paul, E. Steve Lichtenberg, Lynn Borgatta, David Grimes, and Phillip Stubblefield, eds., *A Clinician's Guide to Medical and Surgical Abortion* (Philadelphia: Churchill Livingstone, 1999). A second edition of this work appeared under the title *Management of Unintended and Abnormal Pregnancy: Comprehensive Abortion Care* (Oxford, Eng.: Wiley-Blackwell, 2009).

III

The Clinics

48—*94 percent:* Rachel Jones, Mia Zolna, Stanley Henshaw, and Lawrence Finer, "Abortion in the United States: Incidence and Access to Services, 2005," *Perspectives on Sexual and Reproductive Health* 40, no. 1 (2008): 12.

48—The vacuum suction machine: A presentation on this new abortion technology was made at a 1968 conference on abortion at Hot Springs, Virginia, sponsored by one of the few abortion rights groups within medicine at the time, the Association for the Study of Abortion. The proceedings of this conference can be found in Robert Hall, ed., *Abortion in a Changing World,* 2 vols. (New York: Columbia University Press, 1970).

48—Studies done shortly after Roe: The noted biostatisticians Christopher Tietze and Sarah Lewit surveyed some 72,000 abortions in freestanding clinics after legalization and found that complication rates were lower for nonhospital clinics and also lower for hospital outpatient cases than for inpatients. Tietze and Lewit, "Joint Program for the Study of Abortions," *Studies in Family Planning* 3 (1972): 97–124.

49—The average price: Jones et al., "Abortion in the United States," 14. The average price of a first-trimester clinic abortion in the 1970s was about $147. Abortions done in hospitals can cost up to seven times as much as clinic abortions. Stanley Henshaw, personal communication.

49—Nearly 80 percent of larger abortion facilities: Stanley Henshaw and Lawrence Finer, "The Accessibility of Abortion Services in the United States, 2001," *Perspectives on Sexual and Reproductive Health* 35, no. 1 (2003): 16–24.

50—new legislation, FACE: U.S. Department of Justice, Civil Rights Division, Freedom of Access to Clinics Entrances (FACE) Act—Statute 18 U.S.C. §248, available at www.usdoj.gov/crt/split/facestat.php (accessed January 14, 2009).

50—"I lost my left eye": "Nurse Emily Lyons, Victim of a 1998 Abortion Clinic Bombing, Speaks About the Capture of Eric Rudolph," *Democracy Now,* June 3, 2003, available at www.democracynow.org/2003/6/3/nurse_emily_lyons_victim_of_ (accessed January 14, 2009).

51—a fire of "suspicious origin": Eleanor Bader, "Under a Pro-Choice President, Clinics Brace for Uptick in Violence," *RH Reality Check,* March 9, 2009, available at www.rhrealitycheck.org/blog/2009/03/02/under-a-prochoice-president-clinics-ready-uptick-violence.

51—began to receive letters: National Abortion Federation, "History of Violence: Anthrax Attacks," Washington, D.C., 2008, available at www.prochoice.org/about_abortion/violence/anthrax.html (accessed January 14, 2009).

56—the efforts of antiabortion contractors: Attempts by antiabortion contractors to organize boycotts within the construction industry of new Planned Parenthood facilities have taken place in Texas, Colorado, and Oregon, among other places. Typically the facilities do get built, although with often costly delays. These boycotts have in some instances been organized against facilities that did not intend to offer abortions—for example, a new clinic in Lufkin, Texas. The boycott organizer referred to Planned Parenthood as a "killing compound," which led to a sharp editorial reaction from the local paper, which called for a new facility to be built "as soon as possible." See "Waste of Time," *Lufkin Daily News,* January 7, 2007.

60—in the nursing home: I wrote about this incident at greater length in "Abortion Politics in the Nursing Home," AlterNet, February 25, 2008, available at www.alternet.org/reproductivejustice/77773/abortion_politics_in_the _nursing_home/ (accessed January 7, 2009).

IV
Regulating Abortion

62—*"Some will rob you"*: Words are from Woody Guthrie's ballad "Pretty Boy Floyd."

62—*state laws (of which there are more than four hundred)*: Center for Reproductive Rights, *"Roe v. Wade* in the State," New York, August 2007, available at www.crr.org (accessed September 15, 2007).

62—*[She] would be a rape victim*: Senator Napoli originally made this statement on *NewsHour with Jim Lehrer* on PBS; available at www.pbs.org/newshour/ bb/law/jan-june06/abortion_3-03.html (accessed January 17, 2009).

63—*Moiv's comments about clinic "regs"*: Moiv, "The Hidden TRAP Behind 'Safe, Legal, and Rare,'" *Daily Kos*, March 7, 2005, available at www.daily kos.com/storyonly/2005/3/7/21532/57642 (accessed January 17, 2009).

64—*"TRAP laws target"*: Center for Reproductive Rights, "Targeted Regulation of Abortion Providers (TRAP): Avoiding the Trap," New York, November 2007.

64—*"comparable complexity and risk"*: Bonnie Scott Jones and Tracy Weitz, "Legal Barriers Reducing Second Trimester Abortion Provision and Public Health Consequences," *American Journal of Public Health* 99, no. 4 (April 2009): 623–30.

65—*Yet 150,000 women*: Ibid., 624.

65–66—*Studies by social scientists*: See Theodore Joyce, Robert Kaestner, and Silvie Coleman, "Changes in Abortions and Births and the Texas Parental Notification Law," *New England Journal of Medicine* 354, no. 10 (March 9, 2006): 1031–38.

67—*Moiv, commenting*: Moiv, "The Hidden TRAP."

66—*In 1982 the President's Commission*: Cited in Rachel Gold and Elizabeth Nash, "State Abortion Counseling Policies and the Fundamental Principles of Informed Consent," *Guttmacher Policy Review* 10, no. 4 (2007): 5–6.

67—*In a rigorous review*: Ibid., 6–13.

67—*this allegation was displayed*: Chris Mooney, *The Republican War Against Science* (New York: Basic Books, 2005), 205–7.

68—*the written materials given to abortion patients*: Gold and Nash, "State Abortion Counseling Policies," 11.

68—*"vacuum aspiration during the first trimester"*: Carol Hogue, Lori Boardman, Nada Stotland, and Jeffry Peipert, "Answering Questions About Long-Term Outcomes," in Maureen Paul et al., *A Clinician's Guide to Medical and Surgical Abortion* (Philadelphia: Churchill Livingstone, 1999), 217.

68—*Given that studies show:* Gold and Nash, "State Abortion Counseling Policies," 11.

68—*medical experts say that pain receptors:* Susan Lee, Henry Ralston, Eleanor Drey, John Partridge, and Mark Rosen, "Fetal Pain: A Systematic Multidisciplinary Review of the Evidence," *Journal of the American Medical Association* 294, no. 8 (August 24, 2005): 947–54.

68—*"loaded language":* Gold and Nash, "State Abortion Counseling Policies," 9.

69—*"I have concluded in my review":* C. Everett Koop, *Koop: The Memoirs of America's Family Doctor* (New York: Random House, 1991), 276.

69—*A task force of the American Psychological Association:* The most recent APA task force report on this subject came in the summer of 2008. Brenda Major, chair, "Report of the APA Task Force on Mental Health and Abortion," American Psychological Association, Washington, D.C., August 13, 2008.

69—*"is a made-up disease":* Nada L. Stotland, MD, letter to the editor, *New York Times,* May 28, 2007.

69—*the most sensible statement:* Brenda Major, Catharine Cozzarelli, M. Lynne Cooper, Josephine Zubek, Caroline Richards, Michael Wilhite, and Richard Gramzow, "Psychological Responses of Women After First-Trimester Abortion," *Archives of General Psychiatry* 57 (2000): 777–84.

70—*"Appropriate, sensitive communication":* Anne Baker, Terry Beresford, Glenna Halvorson-Boyd, and Joan Garrity, "Informed Consent, Counseling and Patient Preparation," in Maureen Paul et al., eds., *A Clinician's Guide to Medical and Surgical Abortion* (Philadelphia: Churchill Livingstone, 1999), 25–26 (emphasis mine).

71—*doctors are specifically permitted:* Gold and Nash, "State Abortion Counseling Policies," 8.

72—*"These provisions mark":* Zita Lazzarini, "South Dakota's Abortion Script—Threatening the Physician-Patient Relationship," *New England Journal of Medicine* 359, no. 21 (2008): 2189–91.

72—*Thirteen states have laws:* Lauren Ralph and Claire Brindis, "Adolescents and Parental Notification for Abortion: What Can California Learn from the Experience of Other States?" Bixby Center for Global Reproductive Health, University of California at San Francisco, September 2008.

73—*Two recent tragedies:* Both these cases are discussed in Cristina Page, *How the Pro-Choice Movement Saved America: Freedom, Politics, and the War on Sex* (New York: Basic Books, 2006), 155–57.

75—*Texas has the second-highest rate:* A January 2009 Reuters report listed Mississippi as having the highest teen birth rate, followed by Texas (in a tie with New Mexico). Nationwide, teen birth rates in 2006 rose for the first time in fifteen years, a development many attributed to abstinence-only sex education programs. See www.reuters.com/article/domestic News/idUSTRE50679220090107 (accessed January 21, 2009).

75—*she found extraordinary disregard:* Helena Silverstein, *Girls on the Stand: How Courts Fail Pregnant Minors* (New York: New York University Press, 2007).

75—*the Colorado Court of Appeals:* Colorado Court of Appeals, "Upon the Petition of Jane Doe 2, Petitioner-Appellant," Court of Appeals No. 070CA1095, June 28, 2007, 1–10.

76—*"petitioner exhibited only minimal":* Ibid., 6–7.

77—*"abortionists and other people":* Ari Berman, "Meet the New Republican Senate," *Nation,* November 5, 2004.

77—*"The law need not give":* Gonzales v. Carhart, 550 U.S. 127 S. Ct. 1610 (2007) at 1636.

78—*"The decision vindicates":* Roe v. Wade, 410 U.S. 113, at 166.

78—*At the several trials:* Planned Parenthood Federation of America, et al., v. John Ashcroft, Attorney General, No. C 03-4872 PJH: United States District Court, Northern District of California (2004).

81—*"no reliable data" exist:* Gonzales v. Carhart, 127 S. Ct. at 1634.

81—*"found necessary and proper":* Ibid., at 1641, 1649, 1650 (Ginsberg, J., dissenting).

V

Hospital-Based Abortions

83—*feisty woman doctor:* Dr. Bloom's actions are discussed in Carole Joffe, *Doctors of Conscience: The Struggle to Provide Abortion before and after* Roe v. Wade (Boston: Beacon Press, 1996), 71–72. Some years after the publication of *Doctors of Conscience,* the physician I referred to as Ethel Bloom published a memoir, which includes an account of her use of rubella diagnoses to obtain authorized abortions for her patients. See Gertrude Copperman, MD, *I Was a Felon: And Other Stories from the Life of a Woman Doctor* (Xlibris, 2005), 49–51.

86—*one out of six hospital beds:* Catholic Health Association, "Catholic Health Care in the United States," Washington, D.C., 2007.

86–87—*"Ethical and Religious Directives":* National Conference of Catholic Bishops, "Ethical and Religious Directives for Catholic Health Care Services." 4th edition. Washington, D.C., 2001, available at www.usccb.org/bishops/directives.shtml (accessed January 21, 2009).

87—*common treatment of ectopic pregnancies:* Maureen Paul et al., *A Clinician's Guide to Surgical and Medical Abortion* (Philadelphia: Churchill Livingstone, 1999), 164–65.

87—*"Operations, treatments and medications":* This directive occurs in part four of "Ethical and Religious Directives," called "Issues in Care for the Beginning of Life." Interpretation of directive 47 is further complicated by the wording of directives 45 and 48, the latter of which refers directly to ectopic pregnancies: "Abortion (that is, the directly intended termination of pregnancy before viability or the directly intended destruction of a viable fetus) is never permitted" (dir. 45); "In case of extrauterine pregnancy, no intervention is morally licit which constitutes a direct abortion" (dir. 48).

88—a number of disturbing cases: The three cases discussed in the following pages are taken from Lori Freedman, Uta Landy, and Jody Steinauer, "When There's a Heartbeat: Miscarriage Management in Catholic-Owned Hospitals," *American Journal of Public Health* 98, no. 10 (October 2008): 1774–78.

90—a very controversial case: The only press account I could find of this case comes from a neighborhood newspaper, the *Oak Park* (Illinois) *Oak Leaves:* Chris LaFortune, "Hospital Rules Prompt Pregnancy Transfers," October 13, 2004, 5, 10.

91—"In regard to tubal pregnancy": Ibid., 5.

92—so-called health worker refusals: Rob Stein, a reporter with the *Washington Post,* was among the first to report on this phenomenon in the press. See his "Health Workers' Choice Debated," *Washington Post,* January 30, 2006, and numerous other articles, including "A Medical Crisis of Conscience," July 16, 2006, which cites the refusal of some ambulance drivers to transport abortion patients. Two of the advocacy groups that have been most active in documenting the impact of health refusals are the Mergerwatch Project (see www.mergerwatch.org) and the National Women's Law Center (see www.nwlc.org).

92—In a startling study: Farr Curlin, Ryan Lawrence, Marshall Chin, and John Lantos, "Religion, Conscience, and Controversial Clinical Practices," *New England Journal of Medicine* 356, no. 6 (February 8, 2007): 593–600.

94—stereotypical "right-to-lifer": I am aware of the various progressive currents within the contemporary antiabortion movement—for example, the "seamless web" position within Catholicism (a phrase associated with the late Cardinal Joseph Bernadin), which links opposition to abortion with opposition to warfare and capital punishment. Similarly, within Protestant evangelical circles, the Sojourners group (Christians for Justice and Peace) is opposed to abortion but identified with progressive positions on other social issues.

VI
Abortion Patients and the "Two Americas" of Reproductive Health

99—The Hyde Amendment does allow: American Civil Liberties Union, "Public Funding for Abortion," July 21, 2004, available at www.guttmacher .org/pubs/fb_contraceptive_serv.html (accessed January 22, 2009).

101—Nationally, about 1 percent: Rachel Jones, Jacqueline Darroch, and Stanley Henshaw, "Contraceptive Use Among U.S. Women Having Abortions in 2000–2001," *Perspectives on Sexual and Reproductive Health* 34, no. 6 (2002): 294–303, available at www.guttmacher.org/pubs/fb_induced_abortion. html#9 (accessed January 22, 2009).

104—40 percent of California's counties: Guttmacher Institute, "State Facts

About Abortion: California," 2008, available at www.guttmacher.org/
pubs/sfaa/california.html (accessed December 15, 2008).

106—*a dramatic decline:* Rachel Jones, Mia Zolna, Stanley Henshaw, and Lawrence Finer, "Abortions in the United States: Incidence and Access to Services, 2005," *Perspectives on Sexual and Reproductive Health* 40, no. 1 (2008):
6–16.

107—*the "two Americas":* Guttmacher Institute, "A Tale of Two Americas for
Women," May 4, 2006, available at www.guttmacher.org/media/nr/2006/
05/05/index.html (accessed January 22, 2009).

107—*denouncing Planned Parenthood:* Issues 4Life Foundation, press release,
"Issues4Life Foundation Demands Assault Against the Black Unborn
Stop," Union City, California, March 4, 2008, available at www.issues4life
.org/pdfs/press_release_dfpp.pdf (accessed January 23, 2009).

107—*"aggressive marketing":* Julia Duin, "Ignoring Issue of Black Abortions,"
Washington Times, January 11, 2009.

107—*racially motivated targeting:* On the coercive sterilization of African
American women, see Johanna Schoen, *Choice and Coercion: Birth Control, Sterilization, and Abortion in Public Health and Welfare* (Chapel
Hill: University of North Carolina Press, 2005). On Mexican American
women, see Elena Gutierrez, *Fertile Matters: The Politics of Mexican-
Origin Women's Reproduction* (Austin: University of Texas Press, 2008). On
the location of early family-planning clinics that stimulated charges of
black genocide in the 1960s, see Thomas Littlewood, *The Politics of Population Control* (Notre Dame, Ind.: Notre Dame Press, 1977). On the ongoing
controversy about Margaret Sanger and racial matters, see the discussion
in Ellen Chesler, *Woman of Valor: Margaret Sanger and the Birth Control
Movement in America,* 2nd ed. (New York: Simon and Schuster, 2007).

108—*"No conspiracy theories [are] needed":* Guttmacher Institute, news release, "No Conspiracy Theories Needed: Higher Abortion Rates Among
Women of Color Reflect Higher Rates of Unintended Pregnancy," August 13, 2008, available at www.guttmacher.org/media/nr2008/08/13/
index.html (accessed January 23, 2009).

108—*98 percent of heterosexually active women:* Guttmacher Institute, "Facts
in Brief: Facts on Contraceptive Use," January 2008, available at www
.guttmacher.org/pubs/fb_contr_use.html (accessed January 23, 2009).

108—*46 percent of women:* Jones, Darroch, and Henshaw, "Contraceptive Use
Among U.S. Women," 294–303.

108—*About 10 percent of sexually active women:* Guttmacher Institute, "Contraception Counts: Ranking State Efforts," *In Brief,* 2006 Series, no. 1. Available at www.guttmacher.org/pubs/2006/02/28/IB2006n1.pdf (accessed
January 7, 2009).

108—*More affluent women:* Susan Cohen, "Abortion and Women of Color:
The Bigger Picture," *Guttmacher Policy Review* 8, no. 3 (Summer 2008).

109—*about 36 million American women:* Guttmacher Institute, "Facts on Publicly Funded Contraceptive Services in the United States," August 2008,

1–4, available at www.guttmacher.org/pubs/fb_contraceptive_serv.html (accessed January 22, 2009).

109—*Public funding for contraception:* Ibid., 1.

109—*only 7 million:* Ibid., 2.

110—*In Texas, some $5 million:* Jordan Smith, "The New Texas Family Planning," *Austin Chronicle,* January 27, 2006.

110—*"So this morning":* "Why Tanya Cried," *Our Word,* December 16, 2005, available at http://ourword.org/node/775 (accessed January 22, 2009).

111—*the significant disparity in health care:* David Williams and Pamela Jackson, "Social Sources of Racial Disparities in Health," *Health Affairs* 24 (2005): 325–35.

112—*"far-flung conspiracy theories":* Melissa Gilliam, "Health-Care Inequality Is Key in Abortion Rates," *Philadelphia Inquirer,* August 10, 2008.

112—*One study of 474 teenaged mothers:* Center for Impact Research, "Domestic Violence and Birth Control Sabotage: A Report from the Teen Parent Project," available at www.impactresearch.org/documents/birthcontrol executive.pdf (accessed January 22, 2009).

114—*One study, done at UCSF:* Stephanie Van Bebber, Kathryn Phillips, Tracy Weitz, Heather Gould, and Felicia Stewart, "Patient Costs for Medication Abortion: Results from a Study of Five Clinical Practices," *Women's Health Issues* 16 (2006): 4–13. "Surprisingly, just 2 women (1%) reported that insurance was used to cover the cost of medication abortion. The most common reason given . . . was concern about confidentiality or privacy" (7).

115—*Some stated flatly:* The following quotes from patients in the heartland states are taken from Carole Joffe and Kate Cosby, "The Loneliness of the Abortion Patient," *AlterNet,* May 26, 2007, available at www.alternet .org/story/52386 (accessed January 23, 2009).

VII

"Every Woman Is Different"

120—*the sisters Bertha and Raquel Bugarin:* Tiffany Hsu, "Abortion Clinics Operator Is Charged," *Los Angeles Times,* February 8, 2008.

124—*The cardinal rule of abortion provision:* Anne Baker, Terry Beresford, Glenna Halverson-Boyd, and Joan Garrity, "Informed Consent, Counseling and Patient Preparation," in Maureen Paul et al., *A Clinician's Guide to Medical and Surgical Abortion* (Philadelphia: Churchill Livingstone, 1999), 25–38.

125—*"not to cede a victory":* Alexi Wright and Ingrid Katz, "*Roe* Versus Reality–Abortion and Women's Health," *New England Journal of Medicine,* July 6, 2006, 1–6, available at www.nejm.org (accessed August 1, 2008).

128—*a recently passed Oklahoma law:* State of Oklahoma, Enrolled Senate Bill No. 1878, "Freedom of Conscience Act," April 17, 2008.

128—*"nothing in this section":* Ibid., 13.

129—*will probably force the closing:* Barbara Hoberick, "Abortion Provider Sues to Halt Ultrasound Law," *Tulsa World,* October 11, 2008.

131—*the first President Bush:* George H. W. Bush's active promotion of family planning—until his "conversion" in the election of 1980—is described in Michele McKeegan, *Abortion Politics: Mutiny in the Ranks of the Right* (New York: Free Press, 1992). His congressional nickname is cited in numerous places, including a PBS documentary, "George H. W. Bush," *American Experience,* available at www.pbs.org/wgbh/amex/bush41/more/bush.html (accessed January 26, 2009).

131—*"The entire edifice of sexual license":* Pro-Life Action League, "Contraception Is Not the Answer," October 4, 2006, available at www.prolife action.org/home/2006/cinta3.htm (accessed January 27, 2009).

131—*fierce battle over EC:* This battle is recounted in Cristina Page, "No Plan B," in *How the Pro-Choice Movement Saved America* (New York: Basic Books, 2006), 99–119.

135—*Immediately after his acquittal:* Joe Stumpe, "Jurors Acquit Kansas Doctor in a Late-Term Abortion Case," *New York Times,* March 28, 2009. The role of Cheryl Sullinger, of Operation Rescue, in filing the charge with the Kansas Board of Healing Arts, is posted on the Web site of that organization: www.operationrescue.org/archives/two-tiller-complaints-progressing-says-ks-board-of-healing-arts/ (accessed June 10, 2009). Sullinger's history of contact with Scott Roeder, the accused murderer of George Tiller, including the fact that he had her phone number in the car in which he was caught, is documented in http://blogs.citypages .com/blotter/2009/06/doctor_killer_h.php (accessed June 10, 2009).

136—*"framing rules":* Arlie Hochschild, "Emotion, Feeling Rules, and Social Structure," *American Journal of Sociology* 85, no. 3 (1979): 551–75.

137—*"Thirty years ago":* Katharine Ragsdale and Susan Yanow, "Safe Abortion Should Be Embraced as Progress," *RH Reality Check,* July 14, 2008, available at www.rhrealitycheck.org (accessed January 27, 2009).

137—*"You are not alone:"* Lisa Littman, an ob-gyn in New York, has been one of the innovators in developing such messages to counter stigma. See Lisa Littman, "Threats to Healthy Coping after Abortion: Women's Perceptions and a Pilot Intervention Study," master's thesis, Mount Sinai School of Medicine, 2007.

VIII

What Kind of America Do We Want?

140—*when they go to a pharmacy:* On public responses to pharmacists' refusals, a poll conducted in May 2007 by Lake Research Partners found that 82 percent of adults and registered voters believed that "pharmacies should be required to dispense birth control to patients without discrimination or delay." From the National Women's Law Center "Pharmacy Toolkit," available at www.nwlc.org/pdf/Pharmacy%20Toolkit%20-%20Section%204 .pdf (accessed January 30, 2009). On parental preferences for comprehensive sex education, see Cynthia Dailard, "Sex Education: Politicians, Parents, Teachers and Teens," *Guttmacher Report on Public Policy* 4, no. 1 (February 2001), available at www.guttmacher.org/pubs/tgr/04/1/ gr040109.html (accessed January 30, 2009).

141—*NAPW's advocacy:* See www.advocatesforpregnantwomen.org (accessed January 30, 2009).

142—*research suggests that younger female teenagers:* These data come from A. Chandra et al., *Fertility, Family Planning, and Reproductive Health of U.S. Women: Data from the 2002 National Survey of Family Growth* (Washington, D.C.: National Center for Health Statistics, 2005), 11, 15, 32.

142—*"She was so rigid":* Carole Joffe, *Regulation of Sexuality: Experiences of Family Planning Workers* (Philadelphia: Temple University Press, 1986), 75.

143—*society's messages about gender expectations:* An eloquent case for incorporating discussions of gender into sex education programs is made by Deborah Rogow and Nicole Haberland, "Sexuality and Relationship Education: Toward a Social Studies Approach," *Sex Education* 5, no. 4 (2005): 333–44.

143—*"pleasure and danger":* Carole Vance, ed., *Pleasure and Danger: Exploring Female Sexuality* (Boston: Routledge, 1984).

143—*"over 80 percent":* U.S. House of Representatives, Committee on Government Reform, Special Investigations Division, *The Waxman Report: The Content of Federally Funded Abstinence-Only Education Programs* (Washington, D.C.: Government Printing Office, 2004), i.

144—*Women's Bill of Rights:* Ruth Rosen, *The World Split Open: How the Modern Women's Movement Changed America* (New York: Viking, 2000), 81–82.

145—*"There aren't two different kinds":* Anna Quindlen, "Beyond Doctors," *New York Times,* April 21, 1993.

145—*60 percent of abortion recipients:* Guttmacher Institute, "Facts on Induced Abortion in the United States," available at www.guttmacher.org/pubs/ fb_induced-abortion.html (accessed January 15, 2009).

145—*The main lesson:* Linda Gordon, *The Moral Property of Women: A History of Birth Control Politics in America* (Urbana: University of Illinois Press, 2002), 211–41.

146—*TANF's results:* Sharon Parrott and Arloc Sherman, "TANF at 10: Program Results Are More Mixed Than Often Understood," Center for Budget and Policy Priorities, Washington, D.C., August 2006, available at www .cbpp.org/8–17–06tanf.htm (accessed November 24, 2009).

146—*A November 2008 report:* Sharon Parrott, "Recession Could Cause Large Increases in Poverty and Push Millions into Deep Poverty," Center for Budget and Policy Priorities, Washington, D.C., November 2008, available at www.cbpp.org/11–24–08pov.htm (accessed November 24, 2008).

147—*unprecedented level of regulation of sexual and reproductive behavior:* Carole Joffe, "Welfare Reform and Reproductive Politics on a Collision Course," in Clarence Lo and Michael Schwartz, *Social Policy and the Conservative Agenda* (Malden, Mass.: Blackwell, 1998), 290–301.

147—*"Illegitimacy is the single most important"*: Charles Murray, "The Coming White Underclass," *Wall Street Journal,* October 29, 1993.

148—*"They've stepped over the line"*: Sharon Jayson, "Abstinence Message Goes Beyond Teens," *USA Today,* October 31, 2006.

148—*a group connected to the Unification Church:* Don Lattin, "Moonies Knee-Deep in Faith-Based Funding," *San Francisco Chronicle,* October 3, 2004.

149—*a recent large study of poor women:* Paula England and Kathryn Edin, "Understanding Low-Income Unmarried Couples with Children,"; briefing paper, Council on Contemporary Families, September 2007, 5, 7; available at www.contemporaryfamilies.org (accessed November 25, 2008).

149—*"Couples who hadn't married"*: Ibid., 4.

149—*newspapers announced a "first"*: Mary Ann Akers, "Rep. Linda Sanchez Is Having a Baby," *Washington Post,* November 20, 2008.

150—*about 40 percent of all births:* "U.S. Births Break Record," *USA Today,* March 18, 2009.

150—*ongoing relationships with the fathers:* England and Edin, "Understanding Low-Income Unmarried Couples with Children," 3.

150—*adoption rights of gay Americans:* In California voters approved Proposition 8, a ban on gay marriage. Arkansas voters approved a measure banning adoptions by unmarried couples, which was widely understood as a ban on gay adoptions. Robbie Brown, "Antipathy Toward Obama Seen as Helping Arkansas Limit Adoption," *New York Times,* November 8, 2008.

151—*"[Reproductive justice] offers"*: Loretta Ross, "What Is Reproductive Justice?"; available at www.sistersong.net (accessed November 24, 2009).

151—*"At times the issue of abortion"*: Carroll Smith-Rosenberg, "The Abortion Movement and the AMA, 1850–1880," in *Disorderly Conduct: Visions of Gender in Victorian America* (New York: Knopf, 1985), 217.

152—*"I'll get back to you"*: Michael Falcone, "Planned Parenthood Aims Ad at McCain," *New York Times,* July 16, 2008.

152—*"women's health"*: "Transcript: Third Presidential Debate," *New York Times,* October 15, 2008.

152—*evangelical pastor Joel Hunter:* David Van Biema, "Who Is Joel Hunter and Why Is Obama Praying with Him?" *Time,* November 6, 2008.

153—*"it is a faithful and moral one"*: Debra Hafner, "Unearthing Common Ground: Why Reducing Abortions Is Not the Goal," Huffington Post, December 3, 2008.

153—*only about 1 percent of American women:* As Cory Richards recently wrote, "In the United States, fewer than 14,000 newborns were voluntarily relinquished in 2003 (the latest year for which an estimate is available), according to the U.S. Department of Health and Human Services. That proportion—just under 1% of all the children born to never-married women—has remained constant for almost two decades. See "The Adoption vs. Abortion Myth," *Los Angeles Times,* October 29, 2007.

155—"science will have a rightful place": Transcript: "Barack Obama's Inaugural Address," *New York Times,* January 20, 2009.

155—2 million unwanted pregnancies: Patrick Worsnip, "UN Family Planning Agency Looks to New U.S. Funding," Reuters, January 27, 2009.

155—global AIDS policies: Donald McNeil, "After Departure, No Leader for U.S. AIDS Program," *New York Times,* January 31, 2009.

156—"Open hearts. Open minds. Fair-minded words." Transcript: "Obama's Commencement Address at Notre Dame," *New York Times,* May 17, 2009. An account of the protests at Notre Dame, including a plane flying overhead with a picture of an aborted fetus, can be found in Peter Baker and Susan Saulny, "At Notre Dame, Obama Calls for Civil Tone in Abortion Debate," *New York Times,* May 18, 2009.

156—automated calls to antiabortion activists: Lynda Waddington, "Huckabee Robocalls Iowans to Ask About Abortion Views," RHRealitycheck, November 25, 2008, www.rhrealitycheck.org/blog/2008/11/24/huckabee-robocalls-iowans-ask-about-abortion-views.

156—Republican leaders made clear: Jonathan Weisman and Gregg Hitt, "Partisan Rancor Seeps into Talks on Stimulus Plan," *Wall Street Journal,* January 24–25, 2009. Though many women's health advocates and other progressive groups were disappointed at President Obama's willingness to drop the family planning provision from the stimulus bill, the president quickly signaled his intention to increase such funding through different legislation.

157—A parting gift by the Bush administration: Editorial, "A Parting Shot at Women's Rights," *New York Times,* December 26, 2008. See also Scott Swenson, "Overwhelming Opposition Floods HHS Refusal Clause Proposal: 200,000+," RH Realitycheck, September 26, 2008, www.rhrealitycheck.org/blog/2008/09/26/overwhelming-opposition-floods-hhs-refusal-clause-proposal-200000.

"Abortion Is a Perfectly Proper Noun"

160—the Popline scandal: Robert Pear, "Health Database Was Set Up to Ignore 'Abortion,'" *New York Times,* April 5, 2008.

The Legacy of George Tiller

163—Tiller's accused assailant had vandalized: Ron Sylvester and Joe Rodriguez, "Tiller Suspect Scott Roeder Charged; Also Linked to Vandalism at KC Clinic," *Wichita Eagle,* June 3, 2009.

INDEX

abortion: alleged health risks of, 1, 67–70; and breast cancer, 1, 67–68, 71; destigmatization of, 136–39, 157–58; in Europe, 6, 48, 141; illegal abortions from 1870s to 1970s, 17–18, 24, 83, 88–89; and infertility, 67–68, 143–44; insurance coverage for, 3, 84, 108–9, 114; misinformation on, 1, 17, 67–72, 113–14, 143–44; and Popline scandal, 160–61; price of, 49, 64, 65, 101; psychological impact of, 68–70, 126–27, 136–39; public opinion on, 4, 140; reasons for controversy over, 4–9; religious or moral grounds for opposition to, 6, 35; safety of legal abortions, 48–49; second-trimester abortions, 2, 64–66, 77–82, 105, 129–30, 162–63; self-abortions, 17, 74–75; statistics on, 28, 48, 65, 68, 79, 101, 107, 137, 145, 148, 162; third-trimester abortions, 134, 163–64. *See also* antiabortion movement; hospital-based abortions; stigma of abortion; *and other headings beginning with abortion*
Abortion and Woman's Choice (Petchesky), 10
abortion counseling, 67–72, 127–30
abortion facilities and services: advantages and disadvantages of freestanding clinics, 48–51; anthrax threats against, 49, 51–54, 59; arsons against, 49, 54–57; ASC requirement for, 64–66; beginnings of freestanding clinics, 48;

bombings of and bomb threats against, 18, 49, 50, 54, 59, 134; butyric acid attacks against, 49, 59–61; compassionate care for abortion patients by, 119–24, 134, 135; and contraception, 130–32; and family medicine, 22, 23–25, 27, 29, 33, 39–44, 121–23; geographic distribution of, 25–26, 104; high-quality abortion care, 119–39; motivations of staff of, 61; and price of abortions, 49, 64, 65; protests at abortion clinics, 18–19, 41, 49–50, 57–59; referrals to, 86; and "rogue clinics," 119–20; and safety of legal abortions, 48–49; security for, 42, 51, 71, 141; and social circumstances of patients, 132–36; staffing difficulties of, 46–47, 72; statistics on, 25, 48; and TRAP laws, 63–66; turnaways of clients from, 65; violence and harassment at, 18–19, 47–61, 134. *See also* hospital-based abortions
abortion laws. *See* abortion regulation
abortion patients: anti-abortion beliefs of, 116, 127; and appropriate language for abortion counseling, 127–30; children of, 145; compassion for, 36, 119–24, 134, 135; and contraception, 130–32; and destigmatization of abortion, 136–39, 157–58; difficulties of poor women to obtain abortions, 5, 99–106, 145–46; financial aid for, 99–106, 145–46; and guilt, 136–39; hotlines

for, 99–106; and informed consent, 66–72; misinformation to, 1, 17, 67–72, 113–14, 143–44; outing of, by antiabortion movement, 116; "owning" abortion decision by, 124–27; and parental notification and consent, 72–77, 85, 124–25; and post-abortion counseling, 137–39; and "post-abortion syndrome" (PAS), 68–70, 81; psychological impact on, 68–70, 126–27, 136–39; sadness of, 116–17, 121, 126; shame of, 5, 114–17; social circumstances of, 132–36; spiritual care for, 135–36; and stigma of abortion, 5, 113–18, 136–39; teenagers as, 72–77, 104; and turnaways from abortion clinics, 65

abortion procedures: cervical dilators, 37–38; D&C (dilation and curettage), 48; digoxin injections, 80; intact dilation and extraction (D&E), 77–82; manual vacuum aspirator (MVA), 28, 30, 32, 36–37, 68, 80, 96; medication abortion, 27–28, 29, 30, 32, 36, 40, 80, 114, 133; vacuum suction machine, 48

abortion providers: as activists, 22, 44–45; allies for, 22–25, 33, 43–44, 55–57; and ambivalence of abortion patients, 124–27; and appropriate language for abortion counseling, 127–30; backup by other doctors for, 36–37, 40; as champions, 33–34; compassion of, 36, 119–24, 134, 135; concerns of, for self and family, 22–25, 31, 36–39; and contraception, 130–32; costs of abortion wars to, 20; and illegal abortions from 1870s to 1970s, 17–18, 24, 83, 88–89; image of "back-alley butchers," 18; inept and unethical abortion providers, 119–20; and integrating abortion into family medical practice,

39–44; legal defense of, 64; marginalization and social ostracism of, 20, 43, 46–47, 49; motivations of, 29; murders of, 18, 49, 50, 51, 134, 156, 162–64; obstacles for, 34–39; potential role of primary-care clinicians, 27–30; requests for abortions for patients from medical colleagues of, 86; residency training programs for, 30–33, 44–45, 93, 156–57; and security issues, 42, 51, 71, 141; shortage of, 21, 25; and social circumstances of patients, 132–36; statistics on, 35; training challenges for, 25–27; violence against and harassment of, 18–19, 20, 22, 26, 41–42, 47–61, 125, 134–35, 156, 162–64. *See also* physicians

abortion regulation: and abortion counseling, 67–72; and child abuse laws, 15; Church Amendment, 26; Coats Amendment, 26–27; FACE (Freedom of Access to Clinic Entrances) law, 50; and *Gonzales v. Carhart*, 2, 77–82, 125; Hyde Amendment, 11, 99, 100; and informed consent, 66–72; and "kiss and tell law" in Kansas, 15; national and international policies for, 1, 11–14, 17, 26–27, 50, 77–82, 93, 99, 155, 157; and parental notification and consent, 72–77, 85, 124–25; prohibition of public funds for abortion, 11, 99; and *Roe v. Wade*, 1, 4, 7, 10, 45, 48, 78; of second-trimester abortions, 2, 64–66; state laws and policies for, 2, 14–15, 17, 48, 62–63, 66–77, 159; and *Stenberg v. Carhart*, 125; and teenagers, 72–77, 104; TRAP (Targeted Regulation of Abortion Providers) laws, 63–66; and U.S. Supreme Court, 2, 70, 77–82, 125, 156; and waiver of parental notification and consent, 75–77 abortion rights movement: compared with reproductive justice movement, 150–51; and "ick factor," 16–17; national organizations for, 44, 117–18, 141–42, 144; and "second-wave" feminism, 117, 144–45; slogans of, 5, 9. *See also specific organizations*

abortion wars: costs of, 19–20; as distraction from appropriate sexual and reproductive agenda, 140–44, 154; and fetal politics, 1; in local communities, 1–2, 15–17; partial truce in, during Obama presidency, 14, 51, 151–59; and physicians, 3–4, 17–19; in popular culture, 2–3; reasons for, 4–9; and religious right, 9–17. *See also* abortion regulation; antiabortion movement; Bush, George W.; religious right; stigma of abortion

abstinence-only sex education, 6, 14, 112, 140, 142–44, 147, 155

Access Hotline, 104–6, 118

Accreditation Council for Graduate Medical Education (ACGME), 26–27

ACGME. *See* Accreditation Council for Graduate Medical Education (ACGME)

ACLU. *See* American Civil Liberties Union (ACLU)

ACOG. *See* American College of Obstetricians and Gynecologists (ACOG)

adolescent medicine, 27, 29

adolescents. *See* teenagers

adoption, 150, 152, 153

advanced practice clinicians (APCs), 27

AFDC, 146

African Americans, 107–8, 111–12

AIDS, 14, 155

Aid to Families with Dependent Children (AFDC), 146

Alabama, 50, 75

Alaska, 16

AMA. *See* American Medical Association (AMA)

ambulance cases, 88, 92

ambulatory surgery centers (ASCs), 64–65

American Academy of Family Physicians, 17

American Civil Liberties Union (ACLU), 64, 118

American College of Obstetricians and Gynecologists (ACOG), 17, 21, 77

American Medical Association (AMA), 39, 48–49

American Medical Women's Association (AMWA), 40, 44

American Psychiatric Association, 69

American Psychological Association, 7, 69

AMWA. *See* American Medical Women's Association (AMWA)

anthrax threats against abortion clinics, 49, 51–54, 59. *See also* violence and harassment

antiabortion movement: and abortion counseling, 67–72; and Catholic Church, 6, 10–11; and discomfort over sexuality, 6–7, 142–44; and emergency contraception (EC), 131–32; and emotional rules on abortion, 137; and image of "back-alley butchers," 18; and local politics, 1–2, 15–17, 58–59; messages of, 4–5; and misinformation on abortion, 1, 17, 67–72, 113–14, 143–44; outing of abortion patients by, 116; and Sarah Palin, 16, 152; pro-life caucus within American College of Obstetricians and Gynecologists (ACOG), 17, 21; and reasons for controversy over abortion, 4–9; and redefinition of contraception as abortion, 131–32, 153; religious or moral reasons of, 6, 35; and religious right, 9–17; on "rogue clinics," 119–20; and ultrasounds and fetal medicine, 8; violence against and harassment of abortion providers by, 18–19, 20, 22, 26, 41–42, 47–61, 125, 134–35, 156, 162–64. *See also* abortion wars; Catholic Church; religious right; stigma of abortion

APCs. *See* advanced practice clinicians (APCs)

Archer, William Reynolds "Reyn" III, 12, 13

ARHP. *See* Association of Reproductive Health Professionals (ARHP)

Army of God, 134

arson against abortion clinics, 49, 54–57

ASCs. *See* ambulatory surgery centers (ASCs)

Asian Americans, 107

assisted reproductive services, 87, 92

Association of Reproductive Health Professionals (ARHP), 160–61

Atkins, Rachel, 145

Austen, Philip, 33, 34

Baker, Aspen, 138

Bancroft, Renee, 129–30

Basoria, Erica, 74–75

Bennett, David, 119

Beresford, Terry, 70

Biden, Joe, 152

bioethical issues, 67, 90–91

birth control pills, 108–9, 111, 112, 130, 132. *See also* contraception

black women, 107–8, 111–12

Bloom, Ethel, 83, 88–89

Boehner, John, 156

bombings and bomb threats against abortion clinics, 18, 49, 50, 54, 59, 134. *See also* violence and harassment

Boston, Mass., 13, 50

breast cancer, 1, 67–68, 71

Buffalo, N.Y., 18, 50

Bugarin, Bertha and Raquel, 120

Bureau of Alcohol, Tobacco, and Firearms, 55

Bush, George H. W., 12, 131

Bush, George W.: abortion wars as distraction during presidency of, 140–44, 154; and abstinence-only sex education, 6, 148; and decrease in violence against abortion facilities and providers, 50–51; and emergency contraception (EC), 1; and global gag rule, 14; and Iraq War, 1; and Keroack as DASPA, 13; and misinformation on abortion and contraception, 1, 17, 67–68; and Popline scandal, 160–61; and redefinition of contraception as abortion, 131–32, 153; and stem cell research, 155; Supreme Court appointments by, 156; and United Nations Population Fund, 155

butyric acid attacks against abortion clinics, 49, 59–61

California, 10, 104–6, 120, 138–39, 143, 148

CARASA. *See* Committee for Abortion Rights and Against Sterilization Abuse (CARASA)

Carhart, Leroy and Mary, 125–26

Caspar, Monica, 8

Catholic Church: and abortion providers, 37; and antiabortion movement, 6, 10–11, 42; and contraception, 87; and "Ethical and Religious Directives for Catholic Health Care Services," 86–87; hospitals run by, 26, 35, 86–92; and Obama candidacy, 152–53; and programs serving the poor, 11; and undocumented immigrants, 11; and welfare reform, 147–48

Center for Reproductive Rights, 64, 118, 129

cervical dilators, 37–38
cesarean sections, 141
child abuse laws, 15
child care, 10, 144
children's allowances, 150
Childs, Ruth, 23–24
Christian Medical and Dental
 Society, 17, 21
Christian Right. *See* religious right
Church Amendment, 26
*A Clinician's Guide to Medical
 and Surgical Abortion,* 68,
 70–71
clinics providing abortions. *See*
 abortion facilities and services
Clinton, Bill, 5, 12–13, 14, 50, 146,
 154
Clinton, Hillary, 155
Coats, Dan, 27
Coats Amendment, 26–27
Coburn, Tom, 77
Colorado, 1, 15, 75–77
Committee for Abortion Rights
 and Against Sterilization Abuse
 (CARASA), 144
condoms, 1, 17, 108, 109, 112, 113, 131,
 145. *See also* contraception
Congressional Black Caucus, 107
conscience clause, 157
contraception: abortion providers'
 discussion of, 130–32; and African
 Americans, 112; and antiabortion movement, 131, 153; Catholic
 opposition to, 87; emergency contraception (EC), 1, 2, 4, 12–13, 87,
 92, 131–32; health insurance for,
 108–9; methods of, 2, 108–9; in
 Netherlands, 141; for poor women,
 12, 106–13; public funding for, 12,
 109–11, 131, 156; sabotage of, 112–13;
 and sex education, 6; statistics on,
 108, 109, 140, 153; Title X program
 on, 12, 109, 112
Cosby, Kate, 115, 116–17
counseling. *See* abortion counseling

CPCs. *See* crisis pregnancy centers
 (CPCs)
crisis pregnancy centers (CPCs), 13,
 14, 74, 110, 132

Dallas, Tex., 110
DASPA (deputy assistant secretary
 for population affairs), 12–13
D&C (dilation and curettage), 48
deep poverty, 146–47
Democratic Party, 151–59
Depo-Provera, 108
Diamond, Natalie, 29
Dickson, Debra, 160–61
Diedrich, Justin, 160–61
digoxin injections, 80
doctors. *See* physicians
domestic violence, 101, 102, 112–13

Eagle Forum, 11
EC. *See* emergency contraception
 (EC)
economic crisis (2008–2009), 145–47,
 150, 154–55, 157
ectopic pregnancies, 87, 90–91
Edin, Kathryn, 149
emergency contraception (EC), 1, 2,
 4, 12–13, 87, 92, 131–32
emotional rules, 136–37
England, Paula, 149
eugenics, 107
Europe, 6, 48, 141, 143, 144
Exhale group, 138–39

FACE (Freedom of Access to Clinic
 Entrances) law, 50
Falwell, Jerry, 11
family medicine, 22, 23–25, 27, 29, 33,
 39–44, 121–23
family planning. *See* contraception
Family Research Council, 11
fanaticism. *See* abortion wars; antiabortion movement; religious
 right
Fargo, N.D., 1

FBI, 60, 163

FDA. *See* Food and Drug Administration (FDA)

feeling rules, 136

Fellowship in Family Planning (University of California at San Francisco), 44–45

feminism, 9–10, 117, 144–45

fetus: development of, 68; and fetal medicine, 8; fetal politics and "fetal personhood" initiative, 1, 15, 74, 75; good-bye ritual for aborted fetus, 121, 135, 136; "product of conception (POC)" as term for, 128–30; talking about, by abortion providers, 127–30; ultrasonography of, 8, 40, 94–95, 122–24, 128–30

financial aid: for abortion patients, 99–106, 145–46; for contraception services, 12, 109–11, 131, 156

Flores, Geraldo, 74

Florida, 26, 50

Focus on the Family, 11

Food and Drug Administration (FDA), 1, 12, 28, 29, 40

Fox, Deborah, 36

Foyle, Iris, 93–98

framing rules, 136

Franklin, Christopher "Ace," 36

Freedman, Lori, 35, 88–90

freestanding abortion clinics. *See* abortion facilities and services

funding sources. *See* financial aid

gay rights movement, 9–10, 92, 150, 153

Gilliam, Melissa, 111–12

Ginsburg, Ruth Bader, 81

Girl Scout cookie boycott, 1–2, 4, 16

Girls on the Stand (Silverstein), 75

global gag rule, 13–14, 155

Goffman, Erving, 3–4, 5, 19

Goldberg, Michelle, 16

Golden, Susan, 39–45

Gonzales v. Carhart, 2, 77–82, 125

Gordon, Justine, 22–23

Gould, Rachel, 23, 24

Gunn, David, 26, 50

Guthrie, Woody, 62

Guttmacher Institute, 13, 25, 67, 68, 108, 109

gynecology. *See* obstetrics and gynecology

Hafner, Rev. Debra, 153

harassment. *See* violence and harassment

Health and Human Services, U.S. Department of (HHS), 12, 157

health insurance, 3, 84, 108–9, 114, 142, 154–55

health-worker refusals, 2, 14, 26, 92–97, 157

Hellman, Louis, 12

Herdt, Gilbert, 7

Hernandez, Christina, 115, 130

HHS. *See* Health and Human Services, U.S. Department of (HHS)

HIV, 14, 143

Hochschild, Arlie, 136, 137

homosexuality. *See* gay rights movement

hospital-based abortions: and anti-abortion policies of hospitals, 35, 86–87; Catholic hospitals' refusal of, 26, 35, 86–92; in Europe, 48; and health-worker refusals, 26, 33, 92–97, 157; and medical necessity for abortion, 83–92; and nurses, 33, 85, 93–98; price of, 49, 64; rule-breaking regarding, 88–92; and second-trimester abortions, 105

Hunter, Joel, 152

Hyde Amendment, 11, 99, 100

"ick factor," 16–17

illegal abortions (1870s–1970s), 17–18, 24, 83, 88–89

illegitimacy, 147, 149–50

immigrants. *See* undocumented immigrants
incest, 16, 62, 99, 103, 116, 152
infertility, 67–68, 143–44
informed consent, 66–72
injectable contraception, 108
insurance. *See* health insurance
intact dilation and extraction (D&E), 77–82
internal medicine, 27
International Women's Health Coalition, 14
Internet, 6
intrauterine devices (IUDs), 112. *See also* contraception
Iowa, 156
Iraq War, 1
Issues4Life, 107–8
IUDs. *See* intrauterine devices (IUDs)

Jacobs, Rebecca, 29
James, Jeannette, 22, 37
Johns Hopkins University, 160–61
Jones, Bonnie Scott, 64–65
Juno (movie), 2

Kansas, 15, 18, 134–35, 162–64
Kennedy, Anthony, 77–78, 81
Kenneth J. Ryan Residency Training Program in Abortion and Family Planning, 44–45
Keroack, Eric, 13
Kerry John, 153
"kiss and tell law," 15
Kline, Phill, 15, 134
Knocked Up (movie), 2
Koop, C. Everett, 69

Latinas, 105–8, 120
Lawrence, Michelle, 40, 41, 44
laws on abortion. *See* abortion regulation
Lazzarini, Zita, 72
lesbians. *See* gay rights movement
Linchez, Linda, 149

Los Angeles, Calif., 104
low-income women. *See* poor women
Lyons, Emily, 50

Majors, George, 78–79
The Making of the Unborn Patient (Caspar), 8
malpractice insurance, 38, 40
manual vacuum aspirator (MVA), 28, 30, 32, 36–37, 68, 80, 96
marriage-promotion efforts, 147, 148–50
marriage rights for gay Americans, 150
Massachusetts, 13, 50
McCain, John, 152
Medicaid, 5, 13, 99, 100, 102–4, 109–12, 156
Medi-Cal, 105
medical education, 25–27, 30–33, 44–45, 156–57
medical ethics, 67, 90–91
medical necessity for abortion, 83–92, 103
Medical Students for Choice (MSFC), 26, 44, 45, 162
Medicare, 155
medication abortion, 27–28, 29, 30, 32, 36, 40, 80, 114, 133
medicine. *See* abortion providers; family medicine; obstetrics and gynecology; physicians
mental health, 68–70
methotrexate, 27, 87
Michigan, 74
mifepristone (RU-486), 27–28, 29, 32, 36, 133
Miller, Julia, 121–23, 125–27, 136
Minnesota, 51
minority women. *See* African Americans; Asian Americans; Latinas; Native Americans; poor women
misoprostal, 133
Moiv, 63–64, 66–67
Moonies, 148

Moral Majority, 11

Moses, Annie, 103–4, 132, 134

MSFC. *See* Medical Students for Choice (MSFC)

murders of abortion providers, 18, 49, 50, 51, 134, 156, 162–64. *See also* violence and harassment

Murray, Charles, 147

MVA. *See* manual vacuum aspirator (MVA)

NAAPC. *See* National Association for the Advancement of Preborn Children (NAAPC)

NAF. *See* National Abortion Federation (NAF)

Nairn, Thomas, 91

Napoli, Bill, 62–63

NAPW. *See* National Advocates for Pregnant Women (NAPW)

NARAL Pro-Choice America, 148

National Abortion Federation (NAF), 42, 44, 49, 59, 77, 99–103, 118, 130

National Advocates for Pregnant Women (NAPW), 141–42

National Association for the Advancement of Preborn Children (NAAPC), 1

National Cancer Institute (NCI), 67–68

National Conference of Catholic Bishops, 87, 147–48

National Organization for Women (NOW), 144, 148

National Right to Life Committee, 11, 12, 147–48

National Sexuality Resource Center, 7

Native Americans, 107

NCI. *See* National Cancer Institute (NCI)

Nebraska, 51, 125

neonatology, 8

Netherlands, 140–41

New Right. *See* religious right

New York State, 18, 48, 50

Nixon, Richard, 10

North Dakota, 1, 16

NOW. *See* National Organization for Women (NOW)

nurses, 33, 85, 93–98

Oakland, Calif., 148

Obama, Barack, 14, 51, 151–59, 163

obstetrics and gynecology, 8, 26–27, 35, 44–45

Oklahoma, 77, 129

O'Neill, Tip, 56

Operation Rescue, 60, 135

oral contraception (the Pill), 108–9, 111, 112, 130, 132. *See also* contraception

Our Bodies, Ourselves, 7

Palin, Bristol, 2–3

Palin, Sarah, 16, 152

Paltrow, Lynn, 141–42

parental notification and consent, 72–77, 85, 124–25

partial birth abortion (PBA), 2, 77–82

PAS. *See* "post-abortion syndrome" (PAS)

Paul, Maureen, 39

PBA. *See* partial birth abortion (PBA)

Pennsylvania, 7, 50, 75

Pensacola, Fla., 50

PEPFAR (President's Emergency Plan for AIDS Relief), 14

Perillo, Linda, 40–43

Petchesky, Rosalind, 10

pharmacists, 2, 14, 92, 132, 140

Pharmacists for Life, 2, 132

Philadelphia, Penn., 50

physicians: antiabortion views of, 17, 21; in group medical practices, 35, 36; legal right of, to refuse to participate in abortions, 26, 93, 157–58; and normalization of abortion within health-care circles, 157–58; refusals of, to inform or refer patients for treatments they are unwilling to perform, 92–93; reluctance of patients to disclose abortions to, 114–15; and stigma of abortion, 3–4, 17–29, 21, 35, 47. *See also* abortion providers; family medicine; obstetrics and gynecology

Physicians for Reproductive Choice in Health (PRCH), 22, 44

picketing at abortion clinics. *See* protests at abortion clinics

Plan B, 12–13

Planned Parenthood: and abortion providers, 30, 38, 44; and abortions for women of color, 107–8; and antiabortion policies of group practices, 35; and ban on intact dilation and extraction (D&E), 77; and communication with abortion patients, 137; and contraception information for abortion patients, 130; funding cuts for, 110–11; and Girl Scouts, 2, 4, 16; and misinformation in state-mandated abortion counseling, 72; opposition to Planned Parenthood clinics, 52–53, 56, 107, 110; racist charges against, 107–8; referrals to, 32; and regulation of abortion, 63, 72; services provided by, 110–11

poor women: abortion statistics for, 107, 148; contraception for, 12, 106–13; and deep poverty, 146–47; difficulties of, in obtaining abortions, 5, 99–106, 145–46; financial aid for abortions for, 99–106, 145–46; and marriage-promotion efforts, 148–49; and poverty level, 146–47; social programs for, under Obama presidency, 154; Title X program for contraceptive services for, 12, 109, 112; unplanned pregnancies

of, 106–7, 111; and welfare reform, 146–48

Popline scandal, 160–61

Poppema, Suzanne, 22, 113–14

post-abortion counseling, 137–39

"post-abortion syndrome" (PAS), 68–70, 81

poverty level, 146–47. *See also* poor women

PRCH. *See* Physicians for Reproductive Choice in Health (PRCH)

pregnancy: ectopic pregnancies, 87, 90–91; and medical necessity for abortion, 83–92; poor women and unplanned pregnancies, 106–7, 111; of prisoners, 141; reasons for high rates of unplanned pregnancies, 111–13; rubella in pregnant women, 88–89; statistics on, 108, 137; teenage pregnancies, 2–3, 10, 75, 104

premature infants, 8

prenatal care, 4, 8, 52, 59–60, 99, 115, 122

President's Commission for the Study of Ethical Problems in Medicine and Biomedical and Behavioral Research, 67

price of abortions, 49, 64, 65, 101

"product of conception (POC)," 128–30

Pro-Life Action League, 131

protests at abortion clinics, 18–19, 41, 49–50, 57–59. *See also* violence and harassment

psychological impact of abortion, 68–70, 126–27, 136–39. *See also* stigma of abortion

public funding. *See* financial aid

Public Health Service Act Title X, 12, 109, 112

Ragsdale, Katharine, 137

Randall, Lynne, 140–41

rape, 16, 62–63, 87, 99, 100–103, 112, 116, 152

Reagan, Ronald, 11, 12, 13, 69, 154

regulation of abortion. *See* abortion regulation

Religious Coalition for Reproductive Choice, 135

religious right: and abortion, 9–17, 62–63; and abstinence-only sex education, 6, 14, 112, 140, 142–44, 147; beginnings of, 9–10; and child-care programs, 10; and contraception, 131–32; and emergency contraception (EC), 131–32; and health-worker refusals, 157; and local politics, 1–2, 15–17; and marriage-promotion efforts, 147, 148–50; and Reagan, 11, 12, 69; and Republican Party, 9, 11–14, 156; and state laws and policies on abortion, 14–15, 62–63. *See also* antiabortion movement; Catholic Church

reproductive health. *See* abortion; contraception; pregnancy; sexually transmitted infections (STIs)

reproductive justice movement, 150–51

reproductive rights. *See* abortion rights movement

Republican Party, 9, 11–14, 152–53, 156

Riley, Margaret, 83–86, 92, 93, 97–98

Roe v. Wade, 1, 4, 7, 10, 45, 48, 78

Ross, Loretta, 151

RU-486 (French abortion pill), 27–28. *See also* mifepristone (RU-486)

rubella, 88–89

Ryan Residency Training Program in Abortion and Family Planning, 44–45

salpingectomy, 87

San Diego, Calif., 104

San Francisco, Calif., 104, 105–6, 138–39

Sanger, Margaret, 107

Schlafly, Phyllis, 11

school counselors, 15. *See also* sex education

Scott, Liz, 46–47, 49

Seattle, Wash., 114

second-trimester abortions, 2, 64–66, 77–82, 105, 129–30, 162–63

security issues, 42, 51, 71, 141

self-abortions, 17, 74–75

sex education, 2, 6, 10, 112, 140, 142–44, 147, 148

sexual assault. *See* rape

sexuality: discomfort with, 6–7, 142–44; and "kiss and tell law" in Kansas, 15; media depictions of, 6; and sexual literacy, 7; of teenagers, 142–44

sexual literacy, 7

sexually transmitted infections (STIs), 12, 14, 15, 111, 112, 142

shame of abortion recipients, 5, 114–17

Shawn, Tim, 37–39

Shore, Sylvia ("Sylvie"), 93–97, 132–33

Silverstein, Helena, 75

Sistersong, 151

Slepian, Barnett, 18, 50, 51

Smith-Rosenberg, Carroll, 151, 154

Sorrough, Gail, 160–61

South Dakota, 2, 15, 62–63, 68, 72, 81

Spears, Jamie Lynn, 2–3

spiritual care for abortion patients, 135–36

state laws and regulations. *See* abortion regulation; *and specific states*

Steinauer, Jody, 35

stem cell research, 155

Stenberg v. Carhart, 125

sterilization, 87, 107, 144

Stewart, Felicia, 12–13

stigma: definition of, 3–4; and shame, 5. *See also* stigma of abortion

Stigma (Goffman), 3

stigma of abortion: and abortion patients, 5, 113–18, 136–39; and

Bush administration, 1; and costs of abortion wars, 19–20; and discomfort about sexuality, 6–7, 142–44; and fetal politics, 1; and guilt, 136–39; and legal developments, 2, 14; in local communities, 1–2, 15–17; and physicians, 3–4, 17–19, 21, 47; and popular culture, 2; and post-abortion counseling, 137–39; and psychological impact of abortion, 68–70, 126–27, 136–39; real-world examples of, 2–3; reasons for controversy over abortion, 4–9; reduction of, 136–39, 157–58; and shame, 5, 114–17; and teenagers, 73. *See also* abortion wars; antiabortion movement

STIs. *See* sexually transmitted infections (STIs)

Stottland, Nada, 69

Stulberg, Debra, 90–91

Supreme Court, U.S., 2, 70, 77–82, 125, 156. *See also specific cases, such as* Roe v. Wade

TANF. *See* Temporary Assistance to Needy Families (TANF)

teachers and school counselors, 15. *See also* sex education

teenagers: abortion regulation pertaining to, 72–77, 104; and birth-control sabotage, 112–13; domestic violence against, 112–13; and parental notification and consent for abortions, 72–77, 85, 124–25; parents' coercion of, for abortion, 124–25; pregnancy of, 2–3, 10, 75; sexuality of, 142–44; and waiver of parental notification and consent, 75–77

Temporary Assistance to Needy Families (TANF), 146–48

Tennessee, 75

Texas, 1–2, 65, 66–67, 74–75, 110–11, 131

Texas Fetal Protection Law, 74

third-trimester abortions, 134, 163–64

Tiller, George, 18, 51, 134–35, 156, 162–64

Title X of Public Health Service Act, 12, 109, 112

training in abortion procedures, 25–27, 30–33, 44–45, 93, 156–57

TRAP (Targeted Regulation of Abortion Providers) laws, 63–66

UCSF. *See* University of California at San Francisco (UCSF)

ultrasonography, 8, 40, 94–95, 122–24, 128–30, 157

undocumented immigrants, 11

UNFPA. *See* United Nations Population Fund (UNFPA)

Unification Church, 148

United Nations, 13–14, 155

United Nations Population Fund (UNFPA), 155

universal health care, 154–55

University of California at Berkeley, 136

University of California at San Francisco (UCSF), 35, 44–45, 105, 114–15, 157–58, 160

University of Chicago, 90, 111–12

University of Notre Dame, 156

University of Texas health center (Dallas), 110

U.S. Agency for International Development (USAID), 155, 160–61

U.S. Supreme Court. *See* Supreme Court, U.S.

vacuum suction machine, 48

vasectomies, 108

Vermont, 145

violence and harassment: against abortion providers/clinics, 18–19, 20, 22, 26, 41–42, 47–61, 125, 134–35, 156, 162–64; anthrax threats against abortion clinics, 49, 51–54, 59; arsons against abortion clinics, 49, 54–57; bombings of and bomb threats against abortion clinics, 18, 49, 50, 54, 59, 134; butyric acid attacks against abortion clinics, 49, 59–61; concerns about, 22–24, 57; murders of abortion providers, 18, 49, 50, 51, 134, 156, 162–64; protests at abortion clinics, 18–19, 41, 49–50, 57–59; and security issues, 42, 51, 71, 141; statistics on, 49, 59

Waagner, Clayton, 52
Waco, Tex., 1–2
Wagoner, James, 148
Waitress (movie), 2
waiver of parental notification and consent, 75–77
Wal-Mart, 132
Washington, D.C., 48, 70
Washington State, 114

Waxman, Henry, 6, 143
Weitz, Tracy, 64–65
welfare reform, 146–48
Wichita, Kans., 18
Willis, Ellen, 7
WOC. *See* Women's Options Center (WOC), San Francisco General Hospital
Wolff, Alex, 30–33
women of color. *See* African Americans; Asian Americans; Latinas; Native Americans; poor women
Women's Options Center (WOC), San Francisco General Hospital, 105–6
women's rights movement, 9–10, 117, 144–45
Won, Gloria, 160–61

Yanow, Susan, 137

Printed in the United States
By Bookmasters